This book may be
FO

SO-AIS-290

THE CATHOLIC COMPANION
TO THE BIBLE

By the Editor of

A TREASURY OF CATHOLIC THINKING
THE CONSOLATIONS OF CATHOLICISM
A TREASURY OF THE FAMILIAR
A SECOND TREASURY OF THE FAMILIAR
A TREASURY OF INSPIRATION

The CATHOLIC COMPANION *to the* BIBLE

Compiled and Edited by

RALPH L. WOODS

05951

Foreword by

THE MOST REVEREND

JOHN J. WRIGHT

Bishop of Worcester, Massachusetts

BS
538
.W89

BS538.W89   ST. JOSEPH'S UNIVERSITY   STX
The Catholic companion to the Bible.

3 9353 00005 2686

J. B. LIPPINCOTT COMPANY
PHILADELPHIA AND NEW YORK

β5538
W89
co,2

NIHIL OBSTAT:

Very Rev. Msgr. John J. Dougherty, S.T.L., S.S.D.

Censor Deputatu

IMPRIMATUR:

Most Reverend Thomas A. Boland, S.T.D.

Archbishop of Newar

Newark, N. J.
November 29, 1955

Copyright © 1956 by Ralph L. Woods
First Edition
Printed in the United States of America

Library of Congress Catalog Card Number 56–6416

Acknowledgments

The editor and the publisher are grateful to the following publishers, authors, copyright owners and agents for their cooperation in granting permission to use material from the works indicated below:

THE AMERICA PRESS: Rev. Francis P. LeBuffe, S.J., *What Is the Bible?*, copyright, 1946, The America Press.

BENZIGER BROTHERS, INC.: Rev. M. Devivier, S.J., *Christian Apologetics,* trans. by Ella McMahon, ed. by Rt. Rev. S. G. Messmer, copyright, 1903, 1931, Benziger Brothers, Inc.; Rev. Francis E. Gigot's *General Introduction to the Study of Holy Scripture,* copyright, 1900, 1928, Benziger Brothers, Inc.

BLACKFRIARS PUBLICATIONS, London, England: *The Life of the Spirit,* vol. viii, nos. 1-2, February-March, 1954.

THE BRUCE PUBLISHING COMPANY: Rev. Gerard Rooney, C.P.,

Preface to the Bible, copyright, 1949, The Bruce Publishing Co.; *Biblical Questions—the Old Testament,* by Rudolph G. Bandas, copyright, 1935, The Bruce Publishing Co.; *Mary and Joseph: Their Lives and Times,* by Rev. Denis O'Shea, copyright, 1949, The Bruce Publishing Co.; Msgr. Louis Baunard's *The Evening of Life,* trans. by John L. Stoddard, copyright, 1930, The Bruce Publishing Co.

BURNS OATES AND WASHBOURNE, LTD.: Msgr. Ronald A. Knox's *Trials of a Translator;* Rev. E. C. Messenger's *Evolution and Theology,* copyright U. S., 1932, The Macmillan Company; Rev. Hilarin Felder, O.F.M. Cap., *Christ and the Critics,* trans. by John L. Stoddard; *The New Testament: Papers Read at Summer School of Catholic Studies,* Cambridge, England, 1937; Rev. Joseph Rickaby, S.J., *Oxford Conferences;* Rev. Hugh Pope, O.P., *The Catholic Students' "Aids" to the Study of the Bible;* Rev. Henri de Lubac, S.J., *Catholicism,* trans. by Lancelot Sheppard; St. Thomas Aquinas' *Summa Theologica,* trans. by Fathers of the English Dominican Province; Dom Hubert Van Zeller, O.S.B., *Isaias: Man of Ideas;* Rt. Rev. John S. Vaughan's *Concerning the Holy Bible;* Rev. Fernand Prat, S.J., *The Theology of St. Paul,* trans. by John L. Stoddard; Rev. C. C. Martindale, S.J., *Prince of His People, St. John the Evangelist,* a volume in "The Household of God Series"; Rev. O.-R. Vassall-Phillips, C.SS.R., *Apostolic Christianity;* Rev. M. J. La Grange, O.P., *The Gospel of Jesus Christ,* trans. by Members of the English Dominican Province; Most Rev. Alban Goodier, S.J., *Witnesses to Christ.*

CATHOLIC TRUTH SOCIETY, London, England: Rev. Bede Jarrett, O.P., *Meditations for Layfolk;* Msgr. Ronald A. Knox's *Miracles.*

CATHOLIC WORLD: from the issue of February, 1929.

MISS D. E. COLLINS: G. K. Chesterton's *The Everlasting Man.*

J. M. DENT AND SONS, LTD.: W. F. Trotter's translation of Pascal's *Pensées.*

DODD, MEAD AND COMPANY, INC.: G. K. Chesterton's *The Everlasting Man.* Reprinted by permission of Dodd, Mead & Company, Inc. from *The Everlasting Man* by G. K. Chesterton. Copyright, 1925, Dodd, Mead & Company, Inc. Renewal Copyright, 1953, by Oliver Chesterton.

E. P. DUTTON AND CO., INC.: W. F. Trotter's translation of Pascal's *Pensées.*

EYRE AND SPOTTISWOODE (PUBLISHERS) LTD.: Daniel-Rops' *Sacred History,* trans. by K. Madge.

FATHERS OF THE CHURCH, INC.: *The Fathers of the Church,* vol. 4, St. Augustine's *De Doctrina Christiana,* trans. by Rev. John J. Gavigan, O.S.A., copyright, 1947, Ludwig Schopp.

FIDES PUBLISHERS ASSOCIATION: *Introduction to Theology,* vol. 1 of Theology Library, by a Group of Theologians under the editorship of Rev. A. M. Henry, O.P., trans. by William Storey, copyright, 1954, Fides Publishers Assn.; *St. Paul, Apostle of Nations,* by Daniel-Rops, trans. by J. Martins, copyright, 1952, Librairie Artheme Fayard, Paris, France.

MOST REV. JOSEPH M. GILMORE, BISHOP OF HELENA, MON
TANA: Msgr. Victor Day's translation of Bossuet's *Discourse on Un
versal History,* copyright, 1930.

W. HEFFER AND SONS, LTD.: *Religion of the Scripture, Papers fro
Catholic Bible Congress,* Cambridge, England, 1921.

B. HERDER BOOK COMPANY: *Religion of the Scripture, Papers fro
the Catholic Bible Congress,* Cambridge, England, 1921; Rev. L. (
Fillion, S.S.; *The Life of Christ,* trans. by Rev. Newton Thompson, cop
right, 1928, B. Herder Book Company; *Where We Got the Bible,* b
Rt. Rev. Henry G. Graham; Rt. Rev. S. G. Messmer's *Outlines of Bib
Knowledge.*

HODDER AND STOUGHTON, LTD.: G. K. Chesterton's *The Eve
lasting Man.*

P. J. KENNEDY AND SONS: *The Golden String,* by Dom Bede Griffith
O.S.B., copyright, 1954, P. J. Kennedy & Sons; Rev. Brendan Lawler, S.J
The Epistles in Focus, copyright, 1954, P. J. Kennedy & Sons; Rev. L. (
Fillion, S.S., *The Study of the Bible,* trans. by John C. Reville, copyrigh
1926, P. J. Kennedy & Sons.

MONSIGNOR RONALD A. KNOX: his *Trials of a Translator.*

THE LITURGICAL PRESS: Rev. Paul Heinisch's *Theology of the O
Testament,* trans. by Rev. Wm. G. Heidt, copyright, 1950, The Order c
St. Benedict, Inc., Collegeville, Minn.

LONGMANS, GREEN AND CO., INC.: Daniel-Rops' *Sacred History
trans. by K. Madge, copyright, 1949, Longmans, Green and Co., Inc
Margaret T. Monro's *Enjoying the New Testament,* copyright, 1945, Ma
garet T. Monro.

LONGMANS, GREEN AND CO. LTD.: Rt. Rev. William F. Barry's *Th
Tradition of Scripture;* Rev. B. W. Maturin's *Self-Knowledge and Sel
Discipline.*

THE MACMILLAN COMPANY: Rev. Hugh Pope, O.P., *The Catholi
Church and the Bible,* copyright, 1929, The Macmillan Company; Michae
Cardinal von Faulhaber's *Judaism, Christianity and Germany,* trans. b
Rev. Geo. D. Smith, copyright, 1943, The Macmillan Company.

McMULLEN BOOKS, INC.: Rev. Humphrey J. T. Johnson's *The Bib
and Early Man,* copyright, 1948, The Declan X. McMullen Co., Inc.

JACQUES MARITAIN and THE ATLANTIC MONTHLY: passage
from "The Leaven of Conscience," *The Atlantic Monthly,* April, 1944.

THOMAS NELSON AND SONS, LTD.: *A Catholic Commentary o
Holy Scripture,* under the editorial direction of Dom Bernard Orchard
et al., copyright, 1954, Thomas Nelson and Sons.

THE NEWMAN PRESS: Rev. M. J. La Grange, O.P., *The Gospel o
Jesus Christ,* trans. by Members of the English Dominican Province
Rev. Robert A. Dyson, S.J. and Rev. Alexander Jones' *The Kingdom o
Promise.*

PHILOSOPHICAL LIBRARY, INC.: Beryl Smalley's *The Study of th
Bible in the Middle Ages,* copyright, 1952, Philosophical Library, Inc.

WILLIAM H. SADLIER, INC.: *A Commentary on the New Testament,* prepared by the Catholic Biblical Association, under patronage of The Episcopal Committee of the Confraternity of Christian Doctrine, published by Catholic Biblical Assn., copyright, 1942, William H. Sadlier, Inc.

ST. ANTHONY'S GUILD: Rev. Thomas Plassmann's *The Book Called Holy,* copyright, 1933, St. Anthony's Guild, Paterson, N. J.

SANDS AND CO. (PUBLISHERS), LTD.: Rev. J. P. Arendzen's *The Gospels—Fact, Myth or Legend;* Rt. Rev. Henry G. Graham's *Where We Got the Bible.*

SHEED AND WARD, INC.: F. J. Sheed's *Theology and Sanity.* Copyright 1946, Sheed & Ward, Inc., New York; Arnold Lunn's *Now I See.* Published by Sheed & Ward, Inc., New York; Rev. Léonce de Grand-maison, S.J., *Jesus Christ,* trans. by Dom Basil Whelan, O.S.B. Published by Sheed & Ward, Inc., New York; Monsignor Ronald A. Knox's *The Trials of a Translator.* Copyright 1949 by Sheed and Ward, Inc., New York; Rev. Alexander Jones' *Unless Some Man Show Me.* Copyright 1951 by Sheed & Ward, Inc., New York; Rev. Jean Danielou, S.J., *Advent,* trans. by Rosemary Sheed. Copyright 1950 by Sheed & Ward, Inc., New York; Rev. Vincent McNabb, O.P., *Frontiers of Faith and Reason.* Published by Sheed and Ward, Inc., New York; Rev. Joseph Huby, S.J., *The Church and the Gospels,* trans. by Fenton Moran, copyright, 1931, Henry Holt and Company, Inc., published by Sheed and Ward, Inc., New York.

THE SODALITY OF OUR LADY, THE QUEEN'S WORK: Rev. Daniel A. Lord, S.J., *The Best Best Seller,* copyright, 1932, by The Queen's Work, Inc.

JOSEPH F. WAGNER, INC.: *A Companion to the New Testament,* by Rev. John E. Steinmueller and Kathryn Sullivan, copyright, 1944, Joseph F. Wagner, Inc.; Dr. Michael Seisenberger's *Practical Handbook for the Study of the Bible,* trans. by A. M. Buchanan and ed. by Rev. Thomas J. Gerrard, copyright, 1911, 1939, Joseph F. Wagner, Inc.

A. P. WATT AND SON: G. K. Chesterton's *The Everlasting Man;* Msgr. Ronald A. Knox's *Trials of a Translator.*

MOST REV. JOHN J. WRIGHT: from his *Pastoral Letter* of September 21, 1952.

I am happy to acknowledge the many excellent suggestions of sources made by Rita Keckeissen of St. Peter's Catholic Lending Library, New York, N. Y., and the courtesies extended me by Miss Dorothy Sorg of St. John's Library Forum, New York, N. Y. Tay Hohoff, the publisher's New York Editor, has given me acute critical guidance throughout.

RALPH L. WOODS

To the Right Reverend Monsignor
THOMAS RAYMOND WOODS
of the Archdiocese of St. Louis, Missouri

FOR what things soever were written were written for our learning: that, through patience and the comfort of the scriptures, we might have hope.

ST. PAUL, *Romans* 15:4

WHAT is more sublime than to scrutinize, explain, propose to the faithful and defend from unbelievers the very word of God, communicated to men under the inspiration of the Holy Ghost?

POPE PIUS XII, *Divino Afflante Spiritu* (1943)

Preface

ALTHOUGH THIS book's title and Table of Contents immediately indicate its nature, nevertheless a few brief explanatory comments may be useful to the reader.

The purpose of this volume is to provide, from the literary riches of Catholicism, authoritative, interesting and thoroughly readable writings that will encourage, guide and enlighten Catholics who read or want to read the Bible.

Although the book is addressed to the thoughtful Catholic, it deliberately avoids involved theological discussion and the ponderous scholarly intricacies of Biblical experts.

Those who are habitual readers of Scripture will, I believe, find much that is interesting and new to them in these pages. They will often be given fresh insights and a deeper appreciation of the sacred words they have been reading.

And those to whom Bible reading is a new experience will find encouragement and guidance in these notable writings from the glowing pens of the Church's Scriptural experts.

It has often and truly been said that the difficulties people encounter when reading the Bible arise more often from their lack of preparation than from the obscurity of Scripture itself.

Obviously, this volume does not pretend to explain every allusion and obscurity in the Bible. One must consult a Catholic Commentary on Scripture for that.

But it is intended that this book shall provide interesting introduction and guidance for the Bible reader by placing the Book in the full context of Catholic faith and teaching. Consequently it is expected that these writings will enrich one's reading of Scripture by making it more meaningful and by emphasizing its spiritual content.

There is, of course, no intention that this book should serve as substitute for the Bible. No amount of writing *about* Scripture can compare with the Holy Book itself.

But most of us need a guide if we are to extract from divine revelation its full measure of timeless wisdom, beauty, charm and its infinite spiritual riches. The divine Book comes to us from remote ages and reflects institutions, customs and modes of thinking and speaking which need to be understood if one is to recapture the spirit of the Biblical writings.

Since no one person can speak with equal authority on all phases and aspects of Scripture, an anthology seems a particularly appropriate way in which to give guidance to the Bible. A careful selection of writings can be more authoritative and more stimulating than any one writer could hope to be in treating with the entire Bible. Moreover, an anthology—by drawing on Catholic writings of all periods and nations—best illustrates the vitality and universality of the Church's thinking on Scripture.

I would like to think that this book will be as fascinating to read as it has been to compile and edit. I began it with scant knowledge of Scripture. I end it with certainly more understanding, appreciation and reverence for the Book of Books.

R.L.W.

Contents

One

THE NATURE, VALUE AND AUTHORITY OF THE BIBLE

Two

THE OLD TESTAMENT

Three

THE NEW TESTAMENT

Foreword

RALPH L. Woods has given the reading public many and excellent anthologies on a variety of subjects. In these latter years his anthologies have centered about the person and the teaching of Our Lord and Saviour, Jesus Christ.

In this present collection, Mr. Woods gives us an "anthology about an anthology," for the Bible is, from one point of view, an anthology of many writings, writings the central figure of which is Our Lord. Christ is present on every page of Scripture from the line in the earliest book which promises an eventual Redeemer to fallen humanity to the lines with which the New Testament closes, lines which look forward to Christ's Second Coming.

Mr. Woods has entitled his anthology *The Catholic Companion to the Bible*. The selections which he has brought together emphasize the extent to which the Bible is itself a Catholic book. Together with Tradition, in the special sense understood by the Church, the Bible is a source of the Catholic faith. The Old Testament tells in prophecy and in type the story of the coming of the Messias and His establishment of the Kingdom of God on earth, a kingdom which is identified with the Holy Catholic Church. The New Testament tells of the revelations which Christ made to those who became the infant Church, revelations which He committed to the custody and interpretation of that Church of which He was the Visible Founder and remains the Invisible Head.

History reveals that the Bible is a Catholic book in yet another sense. It is to the jealous, prudent vigilance of the Church that we owe the very survival of the Bible. For fifteen full centuries it was Catholic ecclesiastical authority, Catholic scholarship and devoted Catholic love of the Sacred Scriptures which preserved the text and

19

promoted the study of the Bible. Finally, as Mr. Woods' antholog abundantly confirms, the Bible has been a book beloved by Catholic in every age, Catholics of many and diverse backgrounds.

People generally, including many Catholics, sometimes fail to ap preciate the degree to which the Bible is a Catholic book and th measure of authentic Catholic love for the Bible. The fact that Catho lics are frequently less articulate about their love for the Bible than are other Christian peoples, has been explained in terms of a certain neglect of the Scriptures on the part of Catholics. One wonders if a more accurate explanation would not be the presence among Catho lics of an awe, reverential and profound, which makes them fee humble in the presence of this mighty compendium of divine revela tion and sacred mysteries.

Certainly the Church has done everything possible to inculcate such an awe. The legislation with which she surrounds the editing publishing, reading and study of the Bible is less the result of a nega tive attitude toward the Scriptures, the attitude of which she is some times accused by the uncomprehending, than it is the result of a positive determination to protect the least syllable of Holy Writ from distortion or disrespect.

Before she permits her priests to read even the fragment of the Bible which is the Gospel in Holy Mass, the Church requires that he pause and bow before the altar to offer a special prayer for purity that he may speak worthily the words of Scripture. In Catholic ceremonial the pages of the Bible are reverently kissed. The reading of the Bible by the people is indulgenced as are the most sacred acts of devotion. One of the Orders integrated in the Holy Orders of the priesthood is the Order of Lector, and the ordination of the lector includes impres sive reminders of the uniquely sacred place which the Bible holds in the faith and practice of Catholics.

Small wonder, then, that a reverential awe for the Bible should characterize Catholics. St. Augustine once said something which, be cause of the manner in which he compared the Sacred Scriptures to the Sacred Species of the Eucharist, has necessarily haunted the col lective memory of Catholics across the intervening centuries. He said: "Whoever negligently receives or reads the Word of God is not less guilty than he who, through his own fault, permits the Sacred Host to fall on the ground to be trampled by men." These are strong words, but they are words which we readily understand once we have the Catholic sense of the dignity of the Word of God as it is given us in the Holy Bible.

Mr. Woods has already given thousands of readers the elements of a greater love for Christ by means of one of his anthologies and a more intimate understanding of the Church by means of another. In his *Catholic Companion to the Bible* he has placed thoughtful people once again deeply in his debt. What a privilege it is to have contributed, as Mr. Woods does in this book, to the growth of understanding and appreciation of the Word of God Himself in the minds of those who strive to love God and everything that pertains to Him! "Not by bread alone doth man live, but by every word that procedeth from the mouth of God." This book will inspire many to seek their full nourishment where, in such great part, it can so easily be found.

✠ JOHN WRIGHT
Bishop of Worcester

Feast of St. Peter's Chair
1956

ONE

The Nature, Value
and Authority of the Bible

*And these things we write to you, that
you may rejoice and your joy may be full.*

1 ST. JOHN, 1:4

COUNSEL FOR BIBLE READING

THE REV. BEDE JARRETT, O.P.

THOUGH for a Catholic there is much other teaching than can be found in the Scriptures, yet these always are the written Word of God. He is their author, in the sense that He inspired the thoughts and fashioned them into language, while He adapted to His purposes the personal and contemporary circumstances of the human scribe. But it is obvious that there are many passages, indeed whole chapters, that seem to have nothing to say that is likely to be at all helpful to us. We can read through descriptions of the tabernacle, with the detailed injunctions as to how every part of it is to be constructed, and yet feel when all is finished that we have learnt nothing at all that can be said to carry warmth to our souls. So again, the long lists of warring tribes leave us cold. Yet we are bidden to search the Scriptures, for there is to be discovered the enlightenment that God wishes to shed upon His people. The trouble probably comes because we make the confused mistake of supposing the Bible to be a book. It is not a book, but a literature. Each separate portion has to be understood in the light of its own meaning, and we cannot, therefore, suppose that each chapter or each book will be equally illuminating or even illuminating at all. Though all must be treated with reverence, not all need to be read.

In fact, we may suppose that as each part of the Bible has its different human author, with his own different style and different message, so each part will also appeal differently to different souls. Merely to take the various commentaries written by various hands is to see clearly the totally different concept which each writer brings to his study of the Scriptures. We have, therefore, to single out the particular part from which we can manage to learn most. Solidly to read through the whole text would not be conducive to much profit, and since the Scriptures were written for our instruction, it would be foolish to continue what experience tells us will give us no benefit. For the majority, therefore, it will be the New Testament which will be the most frequently and hopefully used. . . . I must try to understand the purpose for which each book was written, the audience for which it was intended, the point of view which governed the selection of certain portions of the Sacred History and the mission of other portions. For this, again, there are various introductions and aids to the study of the Bible.

I must study carefully, if I really wish to make the Bible my own, not, indeed, in detail, but the main lines of the writer's intentions, what he chiefly wishes to prove or to emphasize. This must precede my meditation, if my meditation is to be intelligent. It means some trouble on my part, but once I have taken the pains to understand even a little, I shall find that the interest will grow and that there will follow constant food for my soul. I should read just enough to provide myself with a thought for the day, in no hurry to get to the end of the incident or parable, but calmly stopping at some sentence or phrase that brings with it a sudden illumination. Then I can afford to put aside all other books of meditation and prayer, and cleave to the Word of God, consulting from time to time some work of doctrinal exposition lest my own interpretation err in any way; but the staple food shall be the New Testament, for there is none that can be better for my soul. No better advice, no more healing comfort, no more piercing devotion can be found than in the Life of the Master. . . .

For our purposes it is necessary only to realize that the Bible is intended as a literature of moral and doctrinal teaching. It is a literature and not a single book: that is to say, it is made up of parts which, to be understood, must be interpreted in the sense in which they were written. It would be foolish to take poetry as literally as prose, nor should I be surprised if, in a professed abridgement, statements should occur seemingly contradictory, since the space was not sufficiently ample to allow of a full explanation. Therefore it is of first importance I should find the purpose that lay behind the author's mind and his object in composing, or the circumstances which inclined him to insert this and omit that. Secondly, not only have I to realize the intention of the human author, but I have also to bear in mind that the Divine Author had His own vaster designs in the composition of the work. He saw before Him all those people and occaions whence comfort, or help, or perplexity were to arise; and for them, for me, the whole was issued. Just as I can say that God died for me, so as truly can I say that for me, too, for my instruction, were the whole Scriptures composed; for my moral and doctrinal enlightenment were these several books inspired; in them am I to find the teaching my soul needs. Particularly is this true of the New Testament, wherein I can see the record of that Perfect Life which is to be the model of my own. In language simple and full of force, that has formed the meditation and consolation of numberless souls, this life has made men and women devoted to their fellows. Above all, it should lift me up to a union with Himself where I can be buried in His love.   (1915)

THE MESSAGE OF THE BIBLE

THE REV. THOMAS PLASSMANN, O.F.M.

WHAT is the message of the Holy Bible? The human mind cannot conceive it, nor human language find words to express it. "For," exclaims the Doctor of the Gentiles, "who hath known the mind of the Lord, or who hath been His counselor?" (Romans, xi, 34). And the great mediaeval Schoolmen who spent themselves in the study of this holy Book called it "a great and spacious ocean" upon which human genius may indeed launch its frail raft, but whose rising billows will soon enforce a retreat. If schools and scholars have spent ages upon the study of Homer, of Dante, of Shakespeare, without exhausting the subject, without even succeeding in putting out commentaries that will satisfy the public, how can we expect or dare to expound the full message and meaning of Sacred Scripture? Nor should we flatter ourselves with the thought that the Infinite God has revealed Himself fully on the pages of Holy Writ. If Saint John confesses that, were all things written that our Savior Jesus Christ said and did while He lived here among us, the world could not contain the books, how may we expect to find in one little book the full account of the infinite mercy, power, goodness and love of the Triune God?

A great theologian has said that, with all this unfathomable wealth of revealed truth before us, we have only touched the fringe of the flowing garment of the Almighty. But those who hold to that fringe will some day realize how truly Isaias declared: "The eye hath not seen, O God, besides Thee, what things thou hast prepared for them that wait for Thee" (LXIV, 4).

It is hard to find a more comprehensive or penetrating analysis of the contents of Sacred Scripture than the one given by Master Alexander of Hales, who was the first of the thirteenth-century Scholastics, and the first Doctor of Theology in the Franciscan Order. In the introduction to his great *Summa* of four large tomes he writes: "Theology [and by this he means Sacred Scripture] is the science which comes from God; which treats of God; which is directed by God, and which leads to God." This is the entire body of Sacred Scripture, with all its lessons and mysteries, in a nut shell.

Aside from the spiritual revelation and the human information that the Holy Bible imparts, there are three characteristics which mark every line of the inspired Book, as they mark every touch of God's finger. These characteristics are unity, holiness and truth.

When an engineer studies the details of a landscape, his eye may view with misgivings the roughness and unevenness of the valleys, the steepness of the cliffs and promontories, the depths of ravines and river beds—for these create perhaps insurmountable obstacles to the construction of a driveway or railroad. Not so the artist! He views the scene with wonder and amazement. He perceives order in disorder, and unity in confusion. He exclaims: "There is the finger of God." Such is the Bible to him who regards it from a loftier point of view, in the light of divine Providence. To him this collection of ancient Hebraic and Hellenic literature reveals a unity of plan and purpose that must have originated in the mind of the Ruler of Nations, Whose voice resounds through the ages: "My thoughts are not your thoughts; nor your ways my ways" (Isaias, LV, 8).

There is a marvelous harmony and unity among those wonderful biblical events that rise like rocky mountains in the wilderness: among those rushing streams and torrents of Hebrew prophecy: those quiet and tranquil groves of the Sapiential Writings, and withal, in that wide expanse of the serene sky, shedding the light of divine Revelation upon the enchanting scene.

From the first sentence of Genesis, "God created heaven and earth," to the last words of the Apocalypse "The grace of our Lord be with you, Amen," the finger of God is discernible to the trained eye, that finger which reacheth "from end to end mightily, and ordereth all things sweetly" (Wisdom, VIII, 1). . . .

26

How strikingly this oneness of plan and purpose contrasts with the variety of the different biblical writings. There are the quaint and irregular verses of the ancient folk-songs, such as the patriarchal benedictions; the measured stanzas of artistic poetry, as in the Psalms of David and the book of Job; the elaborate orations of the sixteen prophets; the brief and pithy sayings of the wise men; the practical and pointed remarks of the catechist, as in the Epistles of Peter and James; the plain and ofttimes circumstantial narrative of the Oriental historian. Some of the writers are original; others narrate what they have heard and seen; still others collect and compile or transcribe verbally portions from other books. Some write with ease and facility; some with painstaking care and labor. Compare, for example, the grace of Saint Luke, that refined and cultured physician, with the author of the second book of the Machabees, who confesses his work has caused him much watching and sweating, (II, 24).

The unity of the Bible is strikingly manifest in the ideas of Divinity which it presents. Monotheism, the belief in one God, as revealed in the Old Testament, is a standing miracle among all the religions of old. It is complemented in the mystery of the Blessed Trinity, as revealed in the New Testament. The God of Abraham is the God of Peter, and Peter confesses that Christ is the Son of the Living God. No more solemn statement occurs in Holy Writ than that terse, fundamental self-expression of Christ: "I and the Father are one." In those few words He lifted, as it were, the veil which hangs before the throne of the Triune God. . . .

Christ is the Alpha and the Omega of the Holy Bible, the beginning and the end as well as the central Figure. The Holy Book is Christocentric. As the electric current is generated from a central point, so is the leading thought of the Bible message generated from Him Who was the Hope of the Nations, the Savior of the World: from Him Who, though endowed with Divinity, spoke to the children of men the simplest speech, the most human tongue, because He knew human nature best, and He loved it best. Aptly did the ministers of the temple characterize the message of the Bible as well as the commanding position of this Master Pedagogue when they confessed: "No man ever spoke as this man spake" (John, vii, 46).

Again, in a thousand variations and synonyms the Holy Bible teaches us holiness, and shows us the way to salvation. The history of the Bible is not primarily the history of the world or the universe, but the history of our Fall and Redemption. The wisdom it inculcates is not the wisdom of Athens or ancient Egypt, but the wisdom of

leading a life pleasing to God. It is primarily meant to impart no
secular knowledge but the knowledge of virtue and the science of
sanctity.

The third characteristic of the Bible is that of truth. . . . The
Bible teaches the truth and nothing but the truth—even though truth,
let us remember, may be told in different ways. Holy Writ is a bulwark of truth. God is the Builder, and the sacred writers were the
workingmen, and because they were the workingmen, and because
this magnificent structure bears the marks of human workmanship
critical mortals have found fault with many of the details—even at
times with the entire structure.   (1933)

The utterances of Holy Scripture are a great deep. As on the lips
of childhood, in a language of metaphors, by lowly symbol stooping
to the world's rudest desert-folk, they reveal mysteries; but they
mingle with high thought, as life itself does, things of every day, and
by the story of a household or a tribe bring home to us how real is
God's Providence. Inspiration enlarges the ripples that float upon
the surface of time until they become a flood bearing Humanity onwards. From such beginnings has the universal religion sprung. When
we view its amazing fortunes, well may we cry out to Him who has
guided it and watched over its chronicle, "Thy way is in the sea, and
Thy path in the great waters, and Thy footsteps are not known."

THE RT. REV. WILLIAM BARRY (1906)

As in Paradise, God walks in the Holy Scriptures, seeking man.
When a sinner reads these Scriptures, he hears God's voice saying,
"Adam, where art thou?"

ST. AMBROSE (ca. 390)

GOD'S METHOD OF PERSUASION

ST. GREGORY OF NAZIANZEN

IN THE history of religion there have been two revolutions, called the two Testaments or, by St. Paul, "tremors of the earth." In the first man passed from idolatry to the Law, and in the second from the Law to the Gospel. And now we proclaim a third cataclysm, the transference from the present order to that beyond, where there can be no further change or disturbance.

One element the two Testaments have in common. They were established without any abrupt or instantaneous transformation.

It is well to realize the reason for this. God did not wish us to be coerced, but persuaded. For that which is not voluntary is not enduring, as we may see by comparison with the forceful repression of a stream or a plant. On the other hand, a transformation undertaken voluntarily is more lasting, more surely grounded. Coercion is the work of an external and tyrannical power, but choice is our own and is consonant with the goodness of God.

God, then, did not desire us to conform to the good under compulsion, but to choose the good. Hence, in the manner of one instructing children or tending the sick, he withdrew some of our traditional practices while condoning others, yielding to us on some small point to keep us happy. . . . For it is not easy to abandon customs which long usage has invested with dignity and veneration. . . .

The Old Testament unambiguously proclaimed the Father, the Son more obscurely; the New Testament gave full revelation of the Son, but put forward more tentatively the divinity of the Holy Ghost. But today the Holy Spirit is resident and active in our midst, giving us a clearer manifestation of his nature.

For it would have been misleading to proclaim decisively the divinity of the Son at a time when that of the Father was not openly admitted, or to add that of the Holy Ghost before the Son had been fully recognized, as an additional burden to our intellects, if I may use so bold an expression. We might, as children given food beyond their power of assimilation, or as men of weak sight turning their gaze upon the sun, have imperiled what here and now lay within our grasp. It was more fitting that by piecemeal additions and, in the words of David, by gradual advance from splendor to splendor, the full radiance of the Trinity should come to shine upon us. (ca. 380)

OF THE READING OF
HOLY SCRIPTURE

THOMAS À KEMPIS

CHARITY is to be sought in Holy Scripture and not eloquence. And it should be read with the same spirit that it was first made. We ought also to seek in Holy Scripture ghostly profit rather than curiosity of style, and as gladly shall we read simple and devout books as books of high learning and cunning. Let not the authority of thine author mislike thee, whether he were of great cunning or little: but let the love of the very pure truth stir thee to read. Ask not who said this, but take heed what is said. Men pass lightly away, but the truth of the Lord endureth for ever.

Almighty God speaketh to us in His Scripture in divers manners without accepting of persons: but our curiosity oft hindereth us in reading of Scripture, when we will reason and argue things that we should meekly and simply pass over. If thou wilt profit by reading of Scripture, read meekly, simply, and faithfully, and never desire to have thereby the name of cunning. Ask gladly and hear meekly to sayings of the Saints, and mislike not the parables of ancient Fathers, for they were not spoken without great cause.   (ca. 1450)

For as the Virgin Mary conceived the work of the Holy Spirit and brought forth THE WORD OF GOD clothed with human flesh, so also these sacred writers, inspired by the Holy Spirit, conceived and brought forth the WRITTEN WORD OF GOD. And just as divinity lay concealed in human nature, carrying therein all the hidden treasures of wisdom and knowledge, wherefore his human nature was luminous with the splendor of divinity; so also beneath the literary garments of the sacred scriptures there lies hidden divine truth, shining through with divine wisdom.

THE REV. J. V. BAINVEL, S.J. (1895)

SPIRITUAL AND HISTORICAL REALITY OF SCRIPTURE

THE REV. HENRI DE LUBAC, S.J.

GOD acts in history and reveals himself through history. Or rather, God inserts himself in history and so bestows on it a "religious consecration" which compels us to treat it with due respect. As a consequence historical realities possess a profound sense and are to be understood in a spiritual manner: conversely, spiritual realities appear in a constant state of flux and are to be understood historically. The Bible, which contains the revelation of salvation, contains, too, in its own way, the history of the world. In order to understand it, it is not enough to take note of the factual details it recounts, but there must also be an awareness of its concern for universality, in spite of its partial, schematic and sometimes paradoxical mode of expression. It was in this way that the Bible was read by the Fathers of the Church. From Irenaeus to Augustine, by way of Clement of Alexandria and Eusebius, they all found in it a treatise on the history of the world. Had they known all the facts now in our possession doubtless the treatise would have been of far greater complexity, but the essential form would have been the same. For they would have been faithful, as we ought to be, to that fundamental principle they learnt from scripture: that if salvation is social in its essence it follows that history is the necessary interpreter between God and man.

This principle governs the whole of their exegesis; it divides off their method of interpretation very sharply from that of the allegorical philosophers, whose works they may have known, or even from Philo. There are two features in the allegorism of the philosophers that appear constantly whatever the text on which their work is based or the system that they deduce from it; whatever purpose guides them or the precise nature of the method they use. For on the one hand they reject as myth what appears as an historical account, and deny to its literal sense what they claim to reveal in its meaning as a mystery. "It does not mean that these things ever happened," they all exclaim with Sallust, Julian the Apostate's friend. On the other hand, if they "spiritualize" in this way whatever purports to be historical, it is not for the purpose of a deeper understanding of

31

history. They do not see mythical events as symbols of spiritual happenings; but they perceive beneath the historical veil scientific, moral or metaphysical ideas: "It is not that these things ever happened—for they are thus from all eternity." The idea of a spiritual Reality becoming incarnate in the realm of sense, needing time for its accomplishment, that without prejudice to its spiritual significance should be prepared, come to pass, and mature socially in history—such a notion is entirely alien to these philosophers. Confronted with it, they find it a stumbling-block and foolishness.

Philo's exegesis, too, is very far removed, even in its form, from what Christian exegesis was to be. Of course this orthodox Jew was very far from denying altogether the literal meaning of the Bible story. He believes in the past greatness of his people; he believes in its future and the coming of the Messias. He is uncompromising, too, toward those of his fellow countrymen who excuse themselves from observing the laws of Moses by pretending that they "are symbols of intelligible realities." Yet even Philo in trying to derive a spiritual teaching from the Bible denudes it somewhat of its historical significance. . . .

It is quite otherwise with the Fathers. Far from diminishing the historical and social character of Jewish religion, their mysticism strengthens it by discovering its depths. . . . They all mean "to understand the spirit of history without impairing historical reality." For "there is a spiritual force in history" (it is a Greek, one of those least interested in a purely "historical" approach, who tells us this); by reason of their finality the very facts have an inner signifiance; although in time, they are yet pregnant with an eternal value. On the other hand, the reality which is typified in the Old—and even the New—Testament is not merely spiritual, it is incarnate; it is not merely spiritual but historical as well. For the Word was made flesh and set up his tabernacle among us. The spiritual meaning, then, is to be found on all sides, not only or more especially in a book but first and foremost *in reality itself*. Indeed what we call nowadays the Old and New Testaments is not primarily a book. It is a twofold event, a twofold "covenant"; a twofold dispensation which unfolds its development through the ages, and which is fixed, one might suppose, by no written account. When the Fathers said that God was its author—the one and only author of the Old and New Testaments—they did not liken him merely, nor indeed primarily, to a writer, but saw in him the founder, the lawgiver, the institutor of these two "instruments" of salvation, these two economies, two dispensations

32

which are described in the scriptures and which divide between them the history of the world. "There is only one God of both," they said, "one same Father." And did not St. Paul mention the two covenants or testaments before our New Testament was written? Convinced that all therein was full of deep and mysterious meaning, the Fathers bent over the inspired pages in which they could trace through its successive stages the covenant of God with the human race; they felt that, rather than giving a commentary on a text or solving a verbal puzzle, they were interpreting a history. History, just like nature, or to an even greater degree, was a language to them. It was the word of God. Now throughout this history they encountered a mystery which was to be fulfilled, to be *accomplished* historically, and socially, though always in a spiritual manner: the mystery of Christ and his Church.

As this mystery is in process of fulfillment and will not be completed until the very end of time, the New Testament does not contain, any more than the Old, a complete meaning in its literal sense. Both contain, then, a spiritual meaning, and equally in both this spiritual meaning is prophetic. Yet from the expositors' point of view their position is very different. For truth itself is present in the New Testament, though it can be perceived only as a reflection, and to such effect that if the Christian Passover is a transition, yet this necessary and continual transition from the Gospel in time to the Gospel in eternity never goes beyond the Gospel. If Christ is beyond all figures of him, the Spirit of Christ cannot lead further than Christ. The New Testament will never date; it is of its very nature the "Testament that never grows old," the last Testament—*novissimum Testamentum*. It should therefore be interpreted—as far as is possible while we are still in this world—in accordance with those principles that are laid down in it; whereas the Old Testament, beyond the facts and events which the literal meaning of the text teaches us, designates also "something else" the very reality of which (not merely the manifestation of it) is to come. In consequence it is true to say that its symbols are prophetic ones: a declaration, a foreshadowing, as well as a preparation. "The Law," says the Epistle to the Hebrews, repeating an expression which occurs, with differences of meaning negligible for present purposes, in the Epistle to the Romans and the Epistle to the Colossians, "The Law" was a "shadow of the good things to come."

Do we realize how daring such an expression is? And do we understand how it involves the complete reversal of the accepted notions of the old exemplarism and of common thought? For see how the body follows its shadow, the exemplar its "type." The rough sketch is the preparation for the archtype, the imitation comes before the model. The figure is what comes first, and the dawn is a reflection of the day that it heralds. This is the truth that is to come and will arise one day on earth. Unheard of paradox! Was not Truth before all ages? Is it not that divine Logos which Philo said was the eldest of God's sons? "Never does the shadow exist before the body," says Tertullian, "nor does the copy come before the original." Yet that is the disconcerting reality of the Christian fact; it is both the substance and the model, the truth that is foreshadowed and reflected in the Jewish history that went before it. The whole Christian fact is summed up in Christ—as the Messias who was to come, who had to be prepared for in history, just as a masterpiece is preceded by a series of rough sketches; but as the "image of the Invisible God" and the "first born of all creation" he is the universal Exemplar. The Son of David, he who is desired of all nations, is at the same time that mysterious mountain on which Moses beheld the ideal forms of all he was to establish for the formation of God's people. Christ, in so far as transcendent and existing before all things, is anterior to his figures, yet as a historical being, coming in the flesh, he appears after them. . . .

It is tempting to say that it was the peculiar genius of the first Christians thus to graft the new religion on to the old, establishing the unique cohesion of the two interwoven parts which we call the two Testaments. "What conception of God and the world enabled men not only to place the Old and New Testaments side by side, but even to understand one in the light of the other?" But the question of genius does not arise here, and in this conception of the world we are confronted with a consequence and not a cause. We have not to do with some wonderful creation, some scheme invented by an intellectual, the vision of some contemplative. Rather was it the consequence of the fact of the Incarnation on the conscience of some few Jews. In the end what was originally known by intuition was developed into a skillfully constructed theory capable of withstanding Jewish attacks on the one hand and those of the Gnostics on the other, at the same time providing the means for preserving the scriptures and using them as a basis, while yet freeing itself from Judaism. . . . Very early, of course, separate traditions in the interpretation of scripture were established, different schools arose, some restrained, others exuberant; differing habits of mind came into conflict. But the same fundamental principle compelled the recognition of all. From the beginning "the harmonious agreement of the Law and the Prophets with the Testament delivered by the Lord" was the "rule of the Church." In the conjunction of the two Testaments was woven a single vesture for the Word; together they formed one body, and to rend this body by rejecting the Jewish books was no less a sacrilege than to rend the body of the Church by schism. If indeed the coming of Christ determined the "end of the Law," the Law itself bore witness that its end was Christ. History and the Holy Ghost had met at last, and with the abandonment of an outworn literalism scripture was made new in the everlasting newness of the Spirit.

If the Old Testament was to be understood in its "true," "absolute" meaning, it was imperative that the time should be accomplished, and that Christ should come. For he alone could "break the mysterious silence, provide the clue to the riddles of the prophets"; he alone could open the book sealed with seven seals. He alone, the one corner-stone, could join the two arms of the arch of history, as he was, too, the junction of the two peoples. For a Christian to understand the Bible means to understand it in the light of the Gospel. "No one can understand the Old Testament without the teaching of the New, since the spiritual meaning of the Old Testament is nothing else than the New. If in scripture we perceive, so to say, a body and a soul, we can assert—and it amounts to the same thing—that this body and this soul are the literal meaning and the spiritual meaning, or that they are the Old and New Testaments. The former requires the latter, else it is no more than a vain shadow, the "letter which kills." Or, as Origen remarks, "We who belong to the Catholic Church do not despise the Law of Moses, but accept it, so long as it is Jesus who interprets it for us. Only thus shall we understand it aright." But it should be added that this interpretation is not a mere commentary. For there is no comparison of Jesus's relation to scripture with that of Chrysippus or Proclus to Homer or the Orphic myths. He comes not to explain it intellectually but to fulfill it in deed. (1950)

Holy Scripture is so fashioned and so composed by the Holy Ghost as to be accommodated to all plans, times, persons, difficulties, dangers, diseases, the expulsion of evil, the obtaining of good, the stifling of errors, the establishment of doctrines, the ingrafting of virtues, the averting of vices. Hence it is deservedly compared by St. Basil to a dispensary which supplies various medicines against every complaint. From it did the Church in the age of Martyrs draw her firmness and fortitude; in the age of Doctors, her wisdom and light of knowledge; in the time of heretics, the overthrow of error; in time of prosperity, humility and moderation; fervor and diligence, in a lukewarm time; and in times of depravity and growing abuse, reformation from corrupt living and return to the first estate.

THE REV. ALFONSO SALMERON, S.J.   (ca. 1865)

THE SYMBOLISM OF THE BIBLE

DOM BEDE GRIFFITHS, O.S.B.

THE symbols of the Bible have a very special character. They are essentially historical symbols. The original revelation to mankind, which is typified by the Covenant with Noe and has for its sign the Rainbow, was a revelation of the natural order; God revealed himself through the signs of nature, the movement of the stars, the rhythm of the seasons. But the revelation which was made to Abraham was the beginning of a historical revelation; the divine mystery was manifested in a series of historical events culminating in the life and death and resurrection of Christ. Thus the symbols under which this revelation was made have always a definite historical character. We may see this best if we take one of the original and most fundamental of all the symbols of the Old Testament: that of the Promised Land. "Get thee out of thy country and from thy kindred and from thy father's house, unto the Land which I will show thee," it was said to Abraham (Gen. 12, 1). This is a definite historical event, the beginning of the history of a particular people, which can be related to contemporary history. It is moreover the promise of a definite land. It is not only historical, it is geographical. The land is the land of Canaan, and from this time the fortunes of the people will be bound up with the fate of the land. We can trace the development of the promise step by step from Abraham to Isaac, to Jacob, and to Moses, until finally Josue enters into the land and the people are settled

36

in it. Then comes the establishment of the kingdom under David, the building of the Temple by Solomon. The Land and the People, the Kingdom and the Temple, each is a definite historical reality. But now there occurs an astonishing change. No sooner has the promise been fulfilled in the temporal sphere than the whole thing collapses, the Temple is destroyed, the Kingdom comes to an end, the people is led away captive, the land is left desolate. It seems that the promise has failed.

But it is now that the real significance of these things begins to be revealed. Amid the desolation of the temporal and material world the prophets begin to look forward to a return of the people to the land. Once again one can trace the long course of the development of the idea of the land through the prophets, beginning with the first of the prophets Amos and continuing through to the last prophet Malachi. Here it will be sufficient to point out the main lines of its development. We find that the idea of the land undergoes, like all the other symbols which we have mentioned, a profound transformation. The return to the land begins to be seen as man's return to the land of Paradise from which he had been driven forth. The Messianic age is seen as the restoration of man to the state of original justice, in which the Spirit is poured out upon him and there is no more conflict, "They shall beat their swords into ploughshares and their spears into pruning hooks" and nature is once more at peace with herself; "The wolf shall dwell with the lamb and the leopard shall lie down with the kid, and the calf and the young lion and the fatling together" (Isaias 11, 6). Gradually it appears that the whole earth is to be transformed; "The wilderness and the solitary place shall be glad, and the desert shall rejoice and blossom as the rose . . . they shall see the glory of the Lord and the excellency of our God" (Isaias 35, 1-12). Until finally the prophet's vision sees beyond the Land of Promise, beyond the earthly Paradise to the creation of the world and he looks forward to a new creation: "For behold I create new heavens and a new earth; and the former things shall not be remembered nor come into the mind" (Isaias 65, 17). Could anything be more marvellous than this transformation under the light of divine revelation of the humble return of a group of Jewish captives to their land into the vision of a new creation?

The Land like all the other signs of the Old Testament has now become a symbol of a new order of being which is about to be revealed. In order to see the final evolution of these symbols we have to turn to the New Testament. It is impossible now to do more than indicate how the whole revelation of the New Testament is given in terms of this historical symbolism. The two fundamental ideas of the gospel teaching, that of the Messias and his Kingdom, are clearly in the direct line of development from the Old Testament. . . . For us now it will be sufficient to indicate just two references to the land in the gospels which may easily be overlooked. There is first the reference in the Beatitudes, which is unfortunately obscured by the usual translation. "Blessed are the meek, it is said, for they shall inherit (not the earth, but) the *land*" (Matt. 5, 4). How much significance this gains when it is related to the original promise of the land! Then there are the words of our Lord to the thief on the cross: "I promise thee this day thou shalt be with me in Paradise (Luke 23, 43). Is any more evidence needed that our Lord Himself habitually thought and spoke in terms of this ancient symbolism?

But the authentic interpretation of the symbol of the Land is, of course, to be found in the Epistle to the Hebrews. There we are told of the patriarchs of the Old Testament: "It was faith they lived by, all of them, and in faith they died; for them the promises were not fulfilled, but they looked forward to them and welcomed them from a distance, owning themselves no better than strangers and exiles on earth. Those who talk so make it clear that they have not found their home. Did they regret the country they had left behind? If that were all they could have found opportunities for going back to it. No, the country of their desires is a better country, a heavenly country. God does not disdain to take his title from such names as these; he has a city ready for them to dwell in" (Heb. 11, 13-6). Here then we have the mystery of the Land finally revealed: it is a "heavenly country," the place into which the people of God is to enter at the end of time. It is one with the new creation, the city of God, the kingdom which has been prepared from the foundation of the world. Thus as we trace them to their conclusion all these symbols are found to coalesce; they are all but aspects in human terms of that unfathomable mystery which is the object of our faith.

But when we have traced them to their conclusion, have they no further function to perform? . . . If our study of the Bible remains a thing apart, it will bear no fruit: all this symbolism will simply be reduced like everything else to an abstract scheme. It is only when our meditation on the Bible is brought into vital relation with our life of prayer that it begins deeply to affect our lives. For these mysteries of faith are not shut up in a book; they are continuously operative in our lives. The mysteries which were prepared in the

Old Testament and fulfilled in the New continue to energize in the life of the Church. The mighty acts of God in the Old Testament and the New are continued in the present time, as Père Danielou has said, in the sacraments of the Church. Under the same symbols as they were originally presented, they continue to operate among us. At our baptism we begin to enter into the Promised Land; we go beneath the waters of the Flood, and rise again as members of a new creation. We are restored to Paradise and clothed again in the garments of Justice; we are given the Holy Spirit, the "pledge of our inheritance." In the Eucharist we are fed with the bread of the Land, the fruit of the tree of Life; we drink the new wine which our Lord promised us when he said: "I shall not drink of this fruit of the vine, until I drink it with you, new wine, in the kingdom of God." But unfortunately all this symbolism tends to be lost on us. The sacraments are said to "effect what they signify," but our theology, as Père Danielou has again said, tends to consider almost exclusively the causal efficacy of the sacraments and to neglect altogether the mode of their signification. It is here that our study of the symbolism of the Bible can assist us: for the symbolism of the sacraments is based, as we have seen and as Père Danielou has shown at length in his book, *Bible et Liturgie,* on the symbolism of the Bible.

But if these symbols are to have their proper effect on us we must learn to experience their power as creative energies and not allow them to become mental abstractions. For all these symbols have their roots not in the conscious but in the unconscious mind. The earth and the water, the bread and the wine, the Land and the people, the kingdom and the Temple, all these are symbols derived from the archetypes of the unconscious, going back in their origins to the collective experience of mankind and forming the basis of all religion. If we are to experience their power we have to recover for ourselves that primeval habit of thought from which they spring. This means that we have to undergo nothing less than a conversion. We have ourselves to go under the waters of the unconscious; we have to return to the land of our origin and renew our contact with mother earth. For we are all exiles from this lost Paradise, we have become separated from our Mother, we are wandering in a far country, away from our Father's home. We have, then, to find the Land within ourselves; it is a psychological change of a depth which we hardly suspect. It involves an Exodus from this world, from Egypt and Babylon; it leads to a long and difficult journey in the wilderness, in which the pillar of cloud is our only light. But only through this experience can we come to understand the mystery of our faith.

This experience of a return to the Land is something which we have each to discover for ourselves, but at the same time we shall find it leads to a profound and new sense of community. For these symbols of the unconscious are communal symbols; they are derived from the collective memory of mankind. Thus as we begin to discover the mystery of the land we shall discover also the mystery of the People. We shall recover our sense of community with all mankind; we shall become aware of our membership of a common body. The *res,* the thing signified by the sacrament of the Eucharist, is the "unity of the Body of Christ." By sharing a meal together, by partaking of the fruits of the Land, we are incorporated into the "people of God"; we become members of that new humanity, which is being created out of the peoples of this world, in which there is "no more Jew or Gentile, no more slave nor freeman, no more male and female, but all are one in Christ." This is the mystery of the new Adam, the whole and perfect man, for which all mankind is created. In it there are no distinctions of race or of class, or even of sex. It is a return to the original unity of man, before there was any division of tongues, before the rib of the woman was taken from the body of man. For just as the return to the Land is a return to the Mother which must take place within, so the restoration of the people is a return to unity, a marriage of the male and the female, which must also take place within. (1953)

One stream flows out from the throne of God, and that is the Grace of the Holy Spirit, and that Grace of the Holy Spirit is in the Holy Scriptures, that is in the stream of the Scriptures. Yet has that stream twin banks, the Old Testament and the New, and the Tree planted on either side is Christ. . . .

When I read the Gospel and find there testimonies from the Law and from the Prophets, I see only Christ; I so see Moses and the Prophets that I understand them of Christ. Then when I come to the splendor of Christ Himself, and when I gaze at that glorious sunlight, I care not to look at the lamplight. For what light can a lamp give when it is lit in the daytime? If the sun shines out, the lamplight does not show. So, too, when Christ is present the Law and Prophets do not show. Not that I would detract from the Law and the Prophets; rather do I praise them in that they show forth Christ. But I so read the Law and the Prophets as not to abide in them but from them to pass to Christ.

ST. JEROME (ca. 408)

HIGH TRUTHS CONCEALED IN SCRIPTURE

JOHN HENRY CARDINAL NEWMAN

Now there are two attributes of the Bible throughout, which, taken together, seem to meet this difficulty [i.e., why a doctrine is not introduced in the Bible when there is an actual call for it, and why when a doctrine is introduced, it is mentioned obscurely]—attributes which, while at first sight in contrast, have a sort of necessary connection, and set off each other—simplicity and depth. Simplicity leads a writer to say things without display; and depth obliges him to use inadequate words. Scripture then, treating of invisible things, at best must use words less than those things; and, as if from a feeling that no words can be worthy of them, it does not condescend to use even the strongest that exist, but often takes the plainest. The deeper the thought, the plainer the word; the word and thought diverge from each other. Again, it is a property of depth to lead a writer into verbal contradictions; and it is a property of simplicity not to care to avoid them. Again, when a writer is deep, his half sentences, parentheses, clauses, nay his words, have a meaning in them independent of the context, and admit of exposition. There is nothing put in for ornament's sake, or for rhetoric; nothing put in for the mere sake of anything else, but all for its own sake; all as the expressions and shadows of great things, as seeds of thought, and with corresponding realities. Moreover, when a writer is deep, or again when he is simple, he does not set about exhausting his subject in his remarks upon it; he says so much as is in point, no more; he does not go out of his way to complete a view or to catch at collateral thoughts; he has something before him which he aims at, and, while he cannot help including much in his meaning which he does not aim at, he does aim at one thing, not at another. Now to illustrate these remarks, and to apply them.

41

One of the most remarkable characteristics of Scripture narrative, which I suppose all readers must have noticed, is the absence of expressions by which the reader can judge whether the events recorded are presented for praise or blame. A plain bare series of facts is drawn out; and whether for imitation or warning, often cannot be decided except by the context, or by the events or by our general notions of propriety—often not at all. The bearing and drift of the narrative are not given. . . .

Thus the style of Scripture is plain and colorless, as regards the relation of facts; so that we are continually perplexed what to think about them and about the parties concerned in them. They need a comment—they are evidently but a text *for* a comment—they have no comment; and as they stand, may be turned this way or that way, according to the accidental tone of mind in the reader. And often the true comment, when given us in other parts of Scripture, is startling. I think it startling at first sight that Lot, being such as he is represented to be on the whole in the Old Testament, should be called by St. Peter "a just man." I think Ehud's assassination of Eglon a startling act—the praise given to Jael for killing Sisera, startling. It is evident that the letter of the sacred history conveys to the ordinary reader a very inadequate idea of the facts recorded in it, considered as bodily, substantial and (as it were) living and breathing transactions.

Equal simplicity is observed in the relation of great and awful events. For instance, consider the words in which is described the vision of God vouchsafed to the elders of Israel. "Then went up Moses and Aaron and Nadab and Abihu, and seventy of the elders of Israel; and they saw the God of Israel; and there was under His feet as it were a paved work of a sapphire stone, and as it were the body of heaven in his clearness. And upon the nobles of the children of Israel He laid not His hand: also they saw God, and did eat and did drink." (Exodus xxiv. 9-11) Or consider the account of Jacob's wrestling with the Angel. Or the plain, unadorned way in which the conversations, if I may dare use the word, between Almighty God and Moses are recorded. . . .

Such is the plain and (as it were) unconscious way in which great things are recorded in Scripture. However, it may be objected that there is no allusion to Catholic doctrines, even where one would think there must have been, had they been in the inspired writer's mind; that is, supposing them part of the Divine Revelation. For instance, if Baptism is so indispensable for the evangelical blessings,

42

why do we hear nothing of the baptism of the Apostles? If Ordinances are so imperative now, why does not our Lord say so, when He says "Neither in this mountain, nor yet at Jerusalem, shall ye worship the Father"? That is, the tone of the New Testament is unsacramental; and the impression it leaves on the mind is not that of a Priesthood and its attendant system. This may be objected: yet I conceive that a series of Scripture parallels to this, as regards other matters, might easily be drawn out, all depending on this principle, and illustrating it in the case before us; viz., that when the sacred writers were aiming at one thing, they did not go out of their way ever so little to introduce another. The fashion of this day, indeed, is ever to speak about all religious things at once, and never to introduce one, but to introduce all, and never to maintain reserve about any; and those who are imbued with the spirit which this implies, doubtless will find it difficult to understand how the sacred writers could help speaking of what was very near their subject, when it was not their subject. Still we must admit to facts, which abundantly evidence that they could. This omission of the Sacraments in St. Paul and St. John, so far as distinct mention is omitted (for in fact they are frequently mentioned), as little proves that those Apostles were not aware and thinking of them, as St. James' Epistle is an evidence that he did not hold the doctrine of the Atonement, which is not there mentioned. . . .

Now let us review cases in which matters of doctrine, or the doctrinal tone of the composition, is in question. Is the tone of Scripture more unfavorable to the doctrine of A Priesthood than it is to the idea of Christianity, such as we have been brought up to regard it—I mean of an established, endowed, dignified Church; and, if its establishment is not inconsistent (as it is not) with the New Testament, why should its mysticalness be? Certainly, if anything is plain, it is that Scripture represents the very portion of Christians, one and all, to be tribulation, want, contempt, persecution. I do not—of course not, far from it—I do not say that the actual present state of the Church Catholic and the text of the New Testament, are not reconcilable; but is it not a fact, that the first impression from Scripture of what the Church should be, is not fulfilled in what we see around us?

Again: I suppose another impression which would be left on an unbiased reader by the New Testament would be, that the world was soon to come to an end. Yet it has not. As, then, we submit to facts in one case, and do not exercise our so-called right of private judgment to quarrel with our own consciousness that we do live, and that the world does still go on, why should we not submit to facts in the other instance? And if there be good proof that what the Church teaches is true, and is conformable to given texts of Scripture, in spite of this vague impression from its surface to the contrary, why should we not reconcile ourselves to the conclusion that that impression of its being opposed to a Sacramental or Priestly system is a false impression, is private and personal, or peculiar to a particular age, untrustworthy, in fact false, just as the impression of its teaching that the world was soon to come to an end is false, because it has not been fulfilled? . . .

It is objected that the Church system, the great Episcopal, Priestly, Sacramental system, was an after-thought, a corruption coming upon the simplicity of the primitive and Apostolic religion. The primitive religion, it is said, was more simple. More simple! Did objectors never hear that there have been unbelievers who have written to prove that Christ's religion was more simple than St. Paul's—that St. Paul's Epistles are a second system coming upon the three Gospels and changing their doctrine? Have we never heard that some have considered the doctrine of our Lord's Divinity to be an addition upon the "simplicity" of the Gospels? Yes: this has been the belief not only of heretics, as the Socinians, but of infidels, such as the historian Gibbon, who looked at things with less of prejudice than heretics, as having no point to maintain. . . .

Is there any reason that we, who have not heard Christ speak, should have a clearer apprehension of the meaning of His recorded discourses on a given point, than the Apostles who did? and if it be said that we have now the gift of the Holy Spirit, which the Apostles had not during our Lord's earthly ministry, then I ask again, where is there any promise that we, as individuals, should be brought by His gracious influences into the perfect truth by merely employing ourselves on the text of Scripture by ourselves? However, so far is plain, that a doctrine which we see to be plainly contained, nay necessarily presupposed, in our Lord's teaching, did not so impress itself on the Apostles. . . .

These remarks surely suffice in this subject, viz., to show that the impression we gain from Scripture need not be any criterion of any measure of its true and full sense; that solemn and important truths may be silently taken for granted, or alluded to in a half sentence, or spoken of indeed, yet in such unadorned language that we may fancy we see through it, and see nothing;—peculiarities of Scripture which

44

result from what is the peculiar character of its teaching, simplicity and depth. Yet even without taking into account these peculiarities, it is obvious, from what meets us daily in the course of life, how insufficient a test is the surface of any one composition, conversation, or transaction, of the full circle of opinions of its author. How different persons are, when we know them, from what they appeared to us in their writings! how many opinions do they hold, which we did not expect in them! how many practices and ways have they, how many peculiarities, how many tastes, which we did not imagine! . . .

I have been arguing that Scripture is a deep book, and that the peculiar doctrines concerning the Church . . . are in its depths. Now let it be remarked in corroboration, first, that the early Church always did consider Scripture to be what I have been arguing that it is from its structure,—viz., a book with very recondite meanings; this they considered, not merely with reference to its teaching the particular class of doctrines in question, but as regards its entire teaching. They considered that it was full of mysteries. Therefore, saying that Scripture has deep meanings, is not an hypothesis invented to meet this particular difficulty, that the Church doctrines are not on its surface, but is an acknowledged principle of interpretation independent of it.

Secondly, it is also certain that the early Church did herself conceal these same Church doctrines. I am not determining whether or not all her writers did so, or all her teachers, or at all times, but merely that, viewing that early period as a whole, there is on the whole a great secrecy observed in it concerning such doctrines (for instance) as the Trinity and the Eucharist; that is, the early Church did the very thing which I have been supposing Scripture does—conceal high truths. To suppose that Scripture conceals them, is not an hypothesis invented to meet the difficulty arising from the fact that they are not on the surface; for the early Church, independent of that alleged difficulty, did herself in her own teaching conceal them. This is a second very curious coincidence. If the early Church had reasons for concealment, it may be that Scripture has the same; especially if we suppose, —what at the very least is no very improbable idea,—that the system of the early Church is a continuation of the system of those inspired men who wrote the New Testament. (1838)

If the Scripture comprehends mysteries capable of perplexing the most enlightened understandings, it also contains simple truths fit for the nourishment of the humble and illiterate; it carries externally wherewith to suckle infants, and in its most secret recesses wherewith to fill the most sublime geniuses with admiration; like a river whose current is so shallow in certain parts that a lamb may cross it, and deep enough in others for an elephant to swim there.

POPE ST. GREGORY THE GREAT (ca. 590)

BENEFITS OF SCRIPTURE

LEO XIII

AMONG the reasons for which the Holy Scripture is so worthy of commendation—in addition to its own excellence and to the homage which we owe to God's Word—the chief of all is, the innumerable benefits of which it is the source; according to the infallible testimony of the Holy Ghost Himself, who says: *All Scripture inspired of God is profitable to teach, to reprove, to correct, to instruct in justice: that the man of God may be perfect, furnished to every good work.* That such was the purpose of God in giving the Scripture to men is shown by the example of Christ our Lord and of His Apostles. For He Himself who "obtained authority by miracles, merited belief by authority, and by belief drew to himself the multitude" was accustomed, in the exercise of His divine mission, to appeal to the Scriptures. He uses them at times to prove that He is sent by God, and is God Himself. From them He cites instructions for His disciples and confirmation of His doctrine. He vindicates them from the calumnies of objectors; He quotes them against Sadducees and Pharisees and retorts from them upon Satan himself when he dares to tempt Him. At the close of His life His utterances are from the Holy Scripture, and it is the Scripture that He expounds to His disciples after His resurrection, until He ascends to the glory of His Father. Faithful to His precepts, the apostles, although He Himself *granted signs and wonders to be done by their hands,* nevertheless used with the greatest effect the sacred writings, in order to persuade the nations everywhere of the wisdom of Christianity, to conquer the obstinacy of the Jews, and to suppress the outbreak of heresy. This is plainly seen in their discourses, especially those of St. Peter; these were often little less than a series of citations from the Old Testament making in the strongest manner for the new dispensation. We find the same things in the Gospels of St. Matthew and St. John and in the Catholic Epistles; and, most remarkable of all, in the words of him who "boasts that he learned the law at the feet of Gamaliel, in order that, being armed with spiritual weapons, he might afterwards say with confidence, 'the arms of our warfare are not carnal but mighty unto God'." Let all, therefore, especially the novices of the ecclesiastical army, understand how deeply the sacred books should be esteemed, and with what eagerness and reverence they should approach this great arsenal of heavenly arms. For those whose duty it is to handle Catholic doctrine before the learned or the unlearned will nowhere find more ample matter of more abundant exhortation, whether on the subject of God, the supreme Good and the all-perfect Being, or the works which display His glory and His love. Nowhere is there anything more full or more express on the subject of the Saviour of the world than is to be found in the whole range of the Bible. As St. Jerome says, *To be ignorant of the Scripture is not to know Christ.* In its pages His Image stands out, living and breathing; diffusing everywhere around consolation in trouble, encouragement to virtue, and attraction to the love of God. And as to the Church, her institutions, her nature, her office and her gifts, we find in Holy Scripture so many references and so many ready and convincing arguments that, as St. Jerome again most truly says, "A man who is well grounded in the testimonies of the Scriptures is the bulwark of the Church." And if we come to morality and discipline, an apostolic man finds in the sacred writings abundant and excellent assistance; most holy precepts, gentle and strong exhortation, splendid examples of every virtue, and finally the promise of eternal reward and the threat of eternal punishment, uttered in terms of solemn import, in God's name and in God's own words.   (1893)

It is Our desire that all the children of the Church should be inspired and strengthened by the charm of Holy Scripture, and so attain to the excelling knowledge of Jesus Christ.

BENEDICT XV (1920)

The Word of God is the "two-edged sword." Whence "two-edged"? It speaketh of things temporal, it speaketh of things eternal. In each it establisheth what it saith, and whom it striketh, it separateth from the world. Whatever is promised us in time, belongeth to one part of the sword; whatever to eternity, belongeth to the other part of the sword. Our Lord came then, bearing a two-edged sword, promising things eternal, fulfilling those of time. For therefore also they are called the two Testaments.—Do the two Testaments belong to the "two-edged sword"? The Old Testament promiseth things earthly, the New eternal. In both the Word of God is found true as a two-edged sword.

ST. AUGUSTINE (415)

"A BOOK TO BE MEDITATED"

THE REV. JOSEPH RICKABY, S.J.

THE Bible is a collection of books that vary greatly in style and matter. The Epistles of St. Paul are not like the Canticle of Canticles; there is much difference between St. Luke and the Apocalypse. For the ordinary Christian, some books are much more profitable reading than others. The first thing is to know well the four Gospels, to be well acquainted with the story of all that our Lord did, suffered, and said. This concerns us much more than the vicissitudes of Israel under the Judges, or the succession of the Kings of Juda. In the Old Testament, the "Sapiential Books," Proverbs, Wisdom, and Ecclesiasticus, form good ground for a beginner. It is well to know the Messianic prophecies. The latter half of Isaias will commonly do the reader more good than Leviticus. St. Paul needs a commentator.

The Bible forms the theme of Christian meditation, Christian preaching, and Christian art: it is also the staple of the liturgy of the Church. It is a book to be meditated, and not gabbled over. It is the meditation-book of those who practice mental prayer. An hour's meditation on twenty verses will often teach us more of the inner mind of the Bible than many hours spent in Biblical criticism. It is possible to be a great Biblical critic, and have scarce any inward knowledge of the Bible at all: just as a foreigner in a continental city may write an erudite work on Oxford, with less real understanding of the University than an undergraduate who has kept two terms.   (1897)

48

QUOTING AND UNDERSTANDING SCRIPTURE

ST. AUGUSTINE

A MAN speaks more or less wisely in proportion as he has made more or less progress in the Holy Scriptures. I do not mean in the extensive reading and memorizing of them but in a thorough understanding and careful searching into their meanings. Some men there are who read them, but pay no attention to them; they read in order to remember, but they are indifferent about understanding. Undoubtedly, we must greatly prefer to these men those who have less grasp of the words, but see with the eyes of their heart the soul of Scripture. But, better than either of these is the man, who, when he wishes, both cites Scripture and understands it as he should.

Therefore, it is particularly essential for the man who would say with wisdom even what he cannot say eloquently to remember the words of the Scriptures. For, the poorer he sees himself to be in his own speech, the more he should enrich himself with that of the Scriptures, so that he may prove from them what he says in his own words and, although inferior in his own words, he may rise in distinction, as it were, by the testimony of the great. His proofs give pleasure where his manner of speaking does not. (397)

I prefer to say nothing of men, who, like myself, have passed from profane literature, to Biblical study, but who, if they happen once to have caught men's ears by their ornate sermons, straightway begin to fancy that whatsoever they say is God's law. Apparently they do not think it worthwhile to discover what the Prophets and Apostles really meant; they are content to string together texts made to fit the meaning they want. One would almost fancy that instead of being a degraded species of oratory, it must be a fine thing to pervert the meaning of the text and compel that reluctant Scripture to yield the meaning one wants!

ST. JEROME (ca. 400)

49

THE POWER OF GOD'S WORD

LEO XIII

THOSE who infuse into their efforts the spirit and strength of the Word of God speak *not in word only, but in power also, and in the Holy Ghost, and in much fulness* (I Thess. i, 5). Hence, those preachers are foolish and improvident who, in speaking of religion and proclaiming the things of God, use no words but those of human science and human prudence, trusting to their own reasonings rather than to those of God. Their discourses may be brilliant and fine, but they must be feeble and they must be cold, for they are without the fire of the utterance of God and they must fall far short of that mighty power which the speech of God possesses: *for the Word of God is living and effectual, and more piercing than any two-edged sword; and reaching unto the division of the soul and the spirit* (Hebr. iv. 12). But, indeed, those who have a right to speak are agreed that there is in the Holy Scripture an eloquence that is wonderfully varied and rich and worthy of great themes.   (1893)

Vainly does the preacher utter the Word of God exteriorly unless he listens to it interiorly.

ST. AUGUSTINE (ca. 419)

ERROR CANNOT CO-EXIST WITH INSPIRATION

LEO XIII

IT IS true, no doubt, that copyists have made mistakes in the text of the Bible; this question, when it arises, should be carefully considered on its merits, and the fact not too easily admitted, but only in those passages where the proof is clear. It may also happen that the sense of a passage remains ambiguous, and in this case good hermeneutical

50

methods will greatly assist in clearing up the obscurity. But it is absolutely wrong and forbidden either to narrow inspiration to certain parts only of Holy Scripture or to admit that the sacred writer has erred. For the system of those who, in order to rid themselves of these difficulties, do not hesitate to concede that divine inspiration regards the things of faith and morals, and nothing beyond, because (as they wrongly think) in a question of the truth or falsehood of a passage we should consider not so much what God has said as the reason and purpose which He had in mind when saying it—this system cannot be tolerated. For all the books which the Church receives as sacred and canonical are written wholly and entirely, with all their parts, at the dictation of the Holy Ghost; and so far is it from being possible that any error can co-exist with inspiration, that inspiration not only is essentially incompatible with error, but excludes and rejects it as absolutely and necessarily as it is impossible that God Himself, the Supreme Truth, can utter that which is not true. This is the ancient and unchanging faith of the Church. . . .

Because the Holy Ghost employed men as His instruments, we cannot, therefore, say that it was these inspired instruments who, perchance, have fallen into error, and not the primary author. For, by supernatural power, He so moved and impelled them to write—He was so present to them—that the things which He ordered, and those only, they, first, rightly understood, then willed faithfully to write down, and finally expressed in apt words and with infallible truth. Otherwise, it could not be said that He was the Author of the entire Scripture. Such has always been the persuasion of the Fathers. . . .

It follows that those who maintain that an error is possible in any genuine passage of the sacred writings either pervert the Catholic notion of inspiration or make God the author of such error.

(1893)

REVELATION AND INSPIRATION

THE RT. REV. WILLIAM BARRY

PROPHECY has kinds and degrees, but need not imply agitation of the human subject or frenzy; and it tends towards a permanent record of its message in writing. The man is first filled with the Holy Spirit; a portion of his charge is sometimes to set down for future remembrance the things he has uttered. No small part of the Bible is due to the Prophets themselves, who first preached and then wrote their preaching. But besides these we have another class to keep in view, the recorders who were not prophets. And it deserves observation that a large part of the difficulties raised by modern critics bear on this class,—the chroniclers and historians in Scripture. No one maintains that in Joshua, Judges, Kings, Paralipomena, there is revelation strictly so termed, *i.e.*, a disclosure of supernatural secrets or divine counsels. Yet they are a necessary framework. Coming to the New Testament, St. Mark or St. Luke has no message of his own; their task is compilation from sources oral and written. But, as we said on occasion of it, 2 Maccabees declared itself not to be an original in any sense; it is the inspired compendium of a book which was probably not inspired.

Clearly, then, Revelation is one thing, the impulse to write a book of Scripture is something else, distinct and independent of it; the inspired writer need not be a prophet. For by Revelation, as our theologians determine it, is meant the divine gift of new ideas, *"species sensibiles aut intellectuales,"* which makes known things hitherto dark, mysteries of Heaven or facts and truths of earth not before in the prophet's possession. But to be inspired for writing is to have one's knowledge so governed and one's powers so moved that the result shall be a document free from approved error, conveying that information (and neither more nor less) which the Holy Spirit willed to have put on record. The chief purpose is not to teach but to preserve revealed truth, of course in such a way that we can apprehend, so far as necessary, the circumstances, historical and ethical, under which the deposit of faith has been left to us. New matter belongs, in some sort, to the essence of Revelation; it is not a condition without which inspiration ceases to exist.   (1906)

The men of God, borne along by the Holy Spirit, and gifted with prophecy, having inspiration and wisdom from God, were taught of Him and became holy and just. Wherefore, also, they were deemed worthy to be made the instruments of God and receive the wisdom which cometh from Him, by which wisdom they spoke of the creation of the world and all other things.

ST. THEOPHILUS OF ANTIOCH (ca. 181)

"THE INSPIRED RECORD
OF REVELATION"

THE RT. REV. WILLIAM BARRY

HOLY WRIT, in make and purpose, stands alone among books. It is
not a secular history; nor a treatise on morals from the pen of a philosopher; it teaches no physical science; it does not proceed by metaphysical reasoning. Perhaps the simplest way of describing it would
be to call its pages the inspired record of Revelation. Whatever we
meet in them falls under this account of it. Much of Scripture came
to its writers through the channels of ordinary knowledge, and did
not ask to be revealed. But nothing was admitted into the Bible except
as it furnished occasion, matter, scope, whereby the object of revealed
truth found its fulfilment. Hence, from this point of view, we cannot
look upon the Scriptures as we do on any other product of human
literature; for the efficient and final causes to which we owe them
are supernatural. There is a divine element, the very essence of the
Bible, in all its parts; its primary author is the Holy Ghost.

But every distinct portion of Scripture does not tell us that it
was writen under such an influence; rarely do its sections affirm that
they are Scripture at all. We learn the extent and limit of the Canon
(which is coterminous with inspired documents binding on Christians) not merely by our judgment regarding its spiritual value, but
from the witness appointed, *viz.,* the Church. St. Paul lays down or
implies a principle which affects "all Scripture"; but he does not say
where we shall find the catalogue. St. Peter again says, "No prophecy
is made by private interpretation." and "the holy men of God spake,
inspired [literally in the Greek 'Borne upward'] by the Holy Ghost."
Yet neither has he given us the books which were thus composed.
Moreover, an internal criterion will not avail to decide: (1) for in
fact, it has never done so, all Churches setting up their Bible on testimony; (2) because it would be hopeless to look for unanimity of
impression among different ages and civilizations; (3) inasmuch as
the Bible is an organic whole, and its parts, if severed by analysis,
would often lose their vital meaning. A book such as Esther or Canticles, out of its Scriptural frame, would surely not be accepted as
having a greater religious importance than the Epistle of Clement,

or Barnabas, or the Pastor of Hermas, all at one time read in some Churches under the notion that they were inspired. When Catholic tradition puts these aside, but never hesitates over the Books of Kings, Chronicles, Eccles. and other writings in which the prophetic strain—"the heavenliness of matter"—is disputed by modern critics, clearly it appeals to "the law and the testimony," it goes upon the facts, and refuses *a priori* grounds of argument. We do not first imagine a theory of inspiration and then apply it; we open the volumes known to be of divine authorship to discover in them what the statement signifies. . . .

The spirit in both Testaments comes upon man, being symbolized in the storm-wind, in thunder and lightning, in fire; but also in the still small voice on hearing which Elijah wrapped his face in his mantle. The afflatus or breath, seizing on the human instrument, of a sudden, may produce ecstacy, wherein the prophet, "falling into a trance but having his eyes open," speaks words of import unknown to his ordinary self, perceives the distant or the future, and reveals God's purpose.

(1906)

Neither by nature, nor by human thought can men recognize such great and divine truths, but the gift which came down from above upon the holy men, who needed neither art of words, nor skill in captious and contentious speaking, but only to offer themselves in purity to the energy of the Divine Spirit, in order that the divine power of itself might reveal to us the knowledge of divine and heavenly things, acting on just men as a plectrum on a harp or lyre.

ST. JUSTIN MARTYR (ca. 150)

THE PROCESS OF INSPIRATION

THE REV. VINCENT MCNABB, O.P.

INSPIRATION is not necessarily self-conscious. It is a subjective light. Consciousness reveals interior acts. The existence of faculties, habits, dispositions, is made known by reflection. We are not conscious of

54

our intellect, of our good disposition, of meekness, of our virtues of faith, hope and charity. We can conclude that they exist from the evidence of their effects. But this is to reason, not to intuit immediately. St. Thomas lays it down most emphatically that an inspired author need not be conscious that the Holy Ghost is moving him.

Add to this that inspiration may be afforded in order to certify purely natural knowledge. St. Thomas explained this with a skill and completeness which is the more remarkable as his age was not one of critical Biblical study. He distinguishes between the hagiographer who has been granted inspiration and the prophet who has received a revelation. The prophet, being a partaker of a divine truth through revelation, *i.e.,* an infusion of supernatural species representing a supernatural object, speaks in God's name. "Thus saith the Lord," is the prophetic formula. The inspired writers, on the other hand, speak most frequently of knowledge acquired by human industry, though with the aid of divine light, of which they may, however, be unconscious. Hence they speak not in the person of God, but in their own person. . . .

Take the case of Genesis. The question is not whether the first chapter is to be taken as a whole, literally or metaphorically. Commentators seem agreed that some phrases or words are to be taken metaphorically; but here, as elsewhere, a wide liberty has always been allowed in the Church. The real question is, what does the inspired writer mean to put forward? Père Lagrange would think it possible, perhaps even probable, that the Biblical Hexaemeron is not put forward as more than a record of the Hebrew tradition, which, through the course of ages, has been modified accidentally by popular use. We may make this clear by calling attention to another species of Biblical literature. When a parable, such as Dives and Lazarus, is transmitted to us by an inspired author, it is clearly not put forward as historically true. Whoever would deny inspiration, because neither Dives nor Lazarus could be verified in history, would have missed the whole purpose and essence of Holy Writ. So, too, Père Lagrange would urge, may it not be that the Hexaemeron is put forward as the current Hebrew tradition, which stands out in contrast with neighboring traditions by its unmistakable insistence on the fundamental truths of Natural Religion and those supernatural truths which could only come from revelation, viz., the existence of a personal God, the inherent goodness of matter and human nature, the spirituality and creation of the human soul, the mysterious lapse into sin, the need and promise of a Redeemer, and lastly, the doctrine, so much needed in the East, of the natural equality of the two sexes of the human race.

To say that Holy Writ is not inspired, because there is nothing in modern science to countenance the existence, say, of such a serpent as spoke to Eve, is to miss the whole point of the inspired narrative.

Or to take the later historical books. No doubt would seem to exist that their compilers freely consulted the archives, in which were preserved the public records of national events and the geneological trees of the various clans of the Hebrew people. . . . To quote the words of a contemporary author, the Rev. R. Clarke, D.D. (The Weekly Register, October 28, 1899), ". . . the writer said just what God would have him say, and said it because God moved him to do so. He might then, if they were in place on his lips, make use of current representations of matters of science or current accounts of past events, saying, or leaving it to be understood from the circumstances, that he gave them for what they were worth; or he might make extracts or quotations without thereby in the slightest degree intending to pledge himself to the literal exactitude of what they would convey if taken *au pied de la lettre*." . . .

Inspiration presupposes revelation. Inspiration may be called the guardian of revelation. Its most kindred divine gift is infallibility, by which the divine and supernatural deposit of faith is safeguarded to all time. We may, thus, go on to conclude that in a certain sense *ens revelatum,* or divine revelation, is the formal object of inspiration. The inspired writer is thus moved by God to apprehend the presence of a revelation and to intend to transmit the revelation by writing.

To make this clearer we have only to reflect that in point of fact prophesy is hardly ever recognized until after its fulfilment. This need call for no surprise. For what is the aim of prophesy except to bring conviction to others on the forecast taking effect? In such an event it may well be recognized that other mysterious words are prophetic utterances which the course of time will decipher. But on the whole, and speaking formally, prophesy is clear on its fulfilment, seeing that its aim was to carry conviction by being fulfilled. It was one of the trials of the prophets that they enounced a doom which was long in coming. How loudly they complain to God that their warning falls on unheeding ears! . . .

If it is evident that prophesy was not generally recognized until after its fulfilment, we can account for the authentic re-editing of the prophetic discourses long after the prophet's death. The prophesies of Isaias, for example, were disbelieved in his day. Again and again he threatened the Jews with captivity, but they thanked him with jeers. However, his words came true at last. In the day of exile we might well conceive that they recognized the truth of the holy man's warnings. To make amends for their past foolishness, as well as to keep his wise counsels ever before their thoughts, they brought their record of his sayings and sermons into one. Whoever, then, enlightened and moved by God, *judged* these discourses to contain a revelation, and *intended* to transmit this revelation by writing, was inspired. We must not be taken to mean that any writer is inspired who recognizes a revelation and intends to transmit it; otherwise, we should find it difficult to deny inspiration to all subsequent editors of the sacred books. But inspiration, when granted, would run in these grooves. The inspired author would necessarily judge something to be a revelation, and would intend to transmit it. The Biblical Commission has decided that "there is no solid argument . . . that the Book of Isaias is not to be attributed solely to Isaias."   (1936)

It makes no difference at all that the Holy Ghost should have taken men to be as it were his tools in writing, as if forsooth the men who were inspired, but not the divine author, might let fall some error. Not so, for he himself so stirred and roused them by his supernatural power to write, and was so present to them in their writing that they conceived correctly, and were minded to write faithfully, and expressed fittingly with unfailing truth, all those things and those only which he bade them write.

BENEDICT XV (1920)

THE CANON OF SCRIPTURE

THE REV. A. M. DUBARLE, O.P.

THE collection that the Church recognizes as canonical, that is to say, as regulative of her faith and practice (canon means rule in Greek), was slowly established during the course of fourteen centuries, from the legislation given by Moses to Israel departing from Egypt during the thirteenth century before our era, down to the end of the first century of the Christian era. All the books do not date from the same period, and all have not enjoyed from the beginning the authority that is now accorded them.

This collection of books is divided into two great parts: the old Testament and the New. The word testament comes to us from a Latin translation of a Greek word which can mean covenant as well as testament. The old covenant includes a whole series of divine initiatives from the patriarchs to Moses and the prophets; the new covenant is that inaugurated by Our Lord Jesus Christ.

The Old Testament

In the Jewish canon the Old Testament includes three smaller collections corresponding, at least partially, to a logical arrangement and to their more or less recent dates of reception as inspired Scripture.

1. The *Law* (in Hebrew *Torah,* or according to a Greek word meaning five recipients, five books, Pentateuch) is a collection at once historical as well as properly legislative; it goes from the beginning of the world to the death of Moses. It includes *Genesis, Exodus, Leviticus, Numbers, Deuteronomy.* Its official recognition as the normative book for the Jewish religious community dates from the reform of Josias (622) which was occasioned by the discovery of a book of the Law, Deuteronomy surely, and must have become a definitely accomplished fact by the time of Esdras' mission (around 457).

2. The *Prophets* include a subdivision: the earlier prophets are in reality historical books going from the entry into the Promised land (about 1200) until the taking of Jerusalem by Nabuchodonosor (587); they include *Josue, Judges, Samuel and Kings.* The later prophets are truly the echo of prophetic preaching: *Isaias, Jeremias, Ezechiel* and the Twelve lesser prophets: *Daniel* is not included among them.

3. The *Historical and Sapiential Books* form a class of books which are a great deal less unified in composition and accepted at a later date. We can distinguish: the poetical and sapiential books— *Job, Psalms, Proverbs, Qoheleth (or Ecclesiastes), Lamentations, Canticle of Canticles;* the narrative books—*Ruth, Esther, Esdras, Nehemias, Chronicles;* and a prophetic book—*Daniel.*

The copies of the Greek translation, called the Septuagint, have kept other books and have not followed exactly the order of the Hebrew. They added, besides some apochrypha, the following canonical books: narrative—*Tobias, Judith, I* and *II Machabees;* prophetic— Baruch, added in an appendix to *Jeremias;* sapiential—*Ecclesiasticus* (or *Ben-Sirah* according to the Hebrew original), *Wisdom,* and some additions to *Daniel* and *Esther.*

The New Testament

The properly Christian Scriptures are divided in this way:

1. The historical-legislative books: The Gospels of Matthew, Mark, Luke, and John, the first three being called synoptic because their close resemblance generally permits a synoptical arrangement. That of John is of a later date (end of the first century), and is more independent of the oral catechesis.

2. An historical book: the *Acts of the Apostles* goes from the Resurrection of the Saviour to the captivity of St. Paul at Rome (towards 60-62).

3. The apostolic epistles: thirteen epistles in which St. Paul is named in the introduction, the epistle to the *Hebrews,* derived indirectly from the teachings of the same St. Paul, and seven epistles called *Catholic,* although some of them are addressed to particular communities: *James,* I and II *Peter,* and III *John, Jude.*

4. A prophetic book: The *Apocalypse* of St. John.

The Formation of the Canon of Scripture

An essential part of this double collection has always been regarded as sacred and canonical by the Christian communities. Nevertheless, certain books were for some time the subject of doubts and discussion in the early Church. Such books are called *deutero-canonical* as opposed to the *proto-canonical* ones which were always unanimously admitted. There were not two successive lists, the one long, the other short, officially promulgated by authority. From the beginning, the essential core of Scripture was accepted by universal consent without any solemn judgment of the Church. Then, after a period of hesitation, certain apochrypha which had enjoyed favor in certain limited circles were definitely eliminated, and some contested books were received beside those which had never been doubted. These deutero-canonical books are, for the Old Testament, those that the Septuagint Bible added to the Hebrew collection of the Jewish rabbis; for the New Testament, the epistle to the Hebrews, the epistle of James, the second epistle of Peter, the second and third of John, and the Apocalypse.

A complete list of the scriptural canon is already to be found in the acts of African provincial councils in 393 and 397, then in a private letter of Pope Innocent I in 405. This list was taken up and solemnly sanctioned at the councils of Trent (1546) and of the Vatican (1870).   (1954)

THE COUNCIL OF TRENT

THE most holy, ecumenical and general Council of Trent, legitimately assembled in the Holy Spirit, under the presidency of the three legatees of the Apostolic See, keeping constantly in mind the proposal to set aside errors and to conserve in the Church the purity of the Gospel promised *formerly* by the prophets in the Sacred Scriptures, *first* promulgated by the Son of God, Our Lord Jesus Christ Himself, who *then* ordered that it be preached by His Apostles to all men as being the source of every salutary truth and of all moral discipline; considering, moreover, that this truth and this discipline are found contained in the written books and in the unwritten traditions which, having been received by the Apostles from Jesus Christ Himself, or transmitted as though from hand to hand by the Apostles themselves at the dictation of the Holy Spirit, have come down to us; following the example of the Orthodox Fathers receives and venerates with equal piety and reverence, both all the *Books* of the Old and New Testament since both have for Author the one and the same God, and also the *traditions* themselves whether having to do with faith or morals, and in so far as they have been dictated orally by Christ, or by the Holy Spirit, and conserved in the Catholic Church with uninterrupted continuity.

*   *   *   *

The same Holy Synod, feeling that it would be no small gain to the Church of God if it were clearly stated which, *of all the Latin editions* of the Scriptures which are in circulation, is to be held authentic, hereby declares and enacts that the well-known old Vulgate edition, which has been proved by its long-continued uses throughout so many centures in the Church, is, in public conferences, disputations, preachings and expositions, to be held as authentic, and that no one is, upon any pretext, to dare or presume to repudiate it.

(1546)

THE VATICAN COUNCIL

THIS supernatural Revelation is, according to the faith of the Universal Church as declared by the Holy Synod of Trent, contained in written Books and in unwritten traditions which, received from the mouth of Christ by the Apostles, or, at the dictation of the Holy Spirit, as it were delivered by hand by the same Apostles, have come down to us. Now the entire Books of the Old and New Testament, with all their parts, as they are enumerated in the Decree of the said Council, and as they are contained in the old Vulgate Latin edition, are to be received as Sacred and Canonical. Nor does the Church regard them as Sacred and Canonical simply because, fashioned by human industry, she has subsequently given them her authoritative approval, nor again because they contain Revelation with no admixture of error, but because being written by the inspiration of the Holy Spirit they have God for their Author, and as such have been handed down to the Church.

Since however the Decrees drawn up by the Holy Synod of Trent touching the interpretation of Holy Scripture—Decrees wisely framed with a view to curbing men's impatient minds—have been distorted by certain people, we hereby renew the Decrees and declare that the meaning of the Council was that in things of faith and morals, things that is, touching the building up of Christian doctrine, that is to be held as the true meaning of Holy Scripture which Holy Mother Church has held and holds; for it is hers to decide on the true meaning and interpretation of the Bible. Consequently no one is allowed to interpret Holy Scripture contrary to that meaning nor against the unanimous consent of the Fathers.   (1870)

THE PROBLEM OF AUTHORSHIP

THE RT. REV. WILLIAM BARRY

NO DEFINITION, fixing the authorship of a sacred volume, has ever been issued by the Church. Titles in the Canon are not inspired. Like those of Papal documents they serve as rubrics to the matter, not as

61

subscriptions guaranteeing the writer's name. . . . Even should we meet them in the work itself, they need not be more than pseudepigraphs, as is clear from the Wisdom of Solomon, which no authority binds us to trace back to the son of David. Every title, therefore, stands or falls by its own merit. This does not imply that all questions regarding the author may be treated as indifferent. If St. Paul, for example, be denied his Epistles undoubtedly the faith is concerned to refute such hypotheses; but in many books of Scripture it is otherwise; we do not know and are not called on to find out, who wrote Kings, Chronicles, Job, Macabees, to mention no others. Hence it is patent that inspiration, though admitted, does not tell us anything about the author except the bare fact that he was inspired. He may be unknown, or even pseudonymous, a compiler and editor as well as an original historian, poet or legislator. In itself, the problem of authorship belongs to criticism; it touches the faith only in certain cases, and which these are has never been defined.

"It does not much signify," says Melchior Canus, Tridentine theologian, writing in 1503, "to the Catholic faith that any book was written by this or that author, so long as the Holy Spirit is believed to be the author of it." St. Thomas remarks, "It seems in a way superstitious that one should be very careful to inquire touching the instrumental causes (i.e. human writers) of the Sacred Scripture."

(1906)

GUIDANCE IN RENDERING A BOOK CANONICAL

ST. FRANCIS DE SALES

IF THESE Books were not of indubitable authority in the Church from the very beginning, how can the mere passage of time confer any authority on them? Truly the Church cannot render a book canonical if it were not from the beginning, but the Church can declare that a certain book, which was not regarded as canonical by everyone, is in fact so; in doing this she in no way changes the substance of the book, which was always canonical, but she does change the minds of Christians who formerly doubted what they can now hold with full assurance. But as regards the Church herself, how can she

decide that a book is canonical? She is no longer guided by new revelations but by the primitive apostolic ones of which she is the infallible interpreter; but if the Apostles had no revelation about the
authority of a particular book, how can she know it? She considers
the witness of antiquity, the conformity of this book with others
already received, and the general feeling of the Christian people towards it. . . . thus when the Church sees that the Christian people
generally regard a book as canonical and draw profit from it, she
can regard it as fitting and sound food for Christian minds: . . . thus
when the Church has judged a book to have the flavor, the fragrance,
and the color, the holiness of style of her doctrine and mysteries,
similar to several good and incontestable witnesses from antiquity,
she can declare the book under consideration to be blood brother to
the other canonical ones. And it must not be doubted that the Holy
Spirit assists the Church in this judgment, because your ministers
confess that God has committed the Sacred Scriptures to her care,
which is why St. Paul calls her the pillar and mainstay of the truth
(I Tim. 3:15); and how could she have them in her care if she did
not know how to separate them from the mixture of other books? . . .

Now it must not be thought that the primitive Church and these
primitive Doctors would have had the temerity to include these books
in the canonical collection if she had not had some counsel to that
effect by the Tradition of the Apostles and their disciples, who
were in a position to know to what degree the Master Himself
esteemed them.   (ca. 1595)

THE REJECTED BOOKS

THE REV. FRANCIS E. GIGOT

BESIDES the books of the Old and New Testament which the Church
of God regards as sacred and inspired, there is a whole literature
made up of works which are commonly called *Apocryphal* [i.e. hid-
den]. As might naturally be expected, this name has been understood
differently in different ages; but in the present day, as indeed for several centuries, it is usually applied to books whose claims to canonicity are not recognized by the Church. It is in this sense that Protes-

tants call "apocryphal" our deutero-canonical books of the Old Testament. . . .

Of course, the importance attached to this *Apocryphal* or *Uncanonical* literature has greatly varied through centuries. By most of the early writers of the Church, because of its containing things "contrary to faith or otherwise objectionable" it was considered as dangerous and worthy only of anathema. Others, however, whilst not approving of its indiscriminate use, thought that real advantages might be derived from a careful perusal of its contents, and this is unquestionably the prevalent view of scholars in our century. In the present day the apocryphal books are studied attentively by the biblical interpreter, who hopes to find in them facts or expressions which throw light on obscure passages of the canonical writings; by the student of history, who seeks to discover in them the impress of the ideas and anticipations of the period in which they appeared or which they describe; by the apologetic writer, who compares their contents with those of the canonical books, and is thereby enabled to show the incomparable superiority of the latter, etc. . . .

Among the apocryphal books of the Old Testament it is usual to reckon works which ecclesiastical writers tell us are quoted as authorities in the inspired books of the New Testament. Of course it is not easy in the present day to determine whether such books—and which, if any—are thus cited by the New Testament writers. Almost all the apocryphal compositions to which early ecclesiastical writers refer in this connection are known to us only by name. . . .

It was but a short time after our canonical Gospels had begun to be widely circulated in the early churches, and had been fully approved for public use in Christian services, when pious believers in Christ, struck with the incompleteness of these authentic *Memoirs*, earnestly desired whatever additional information might be secured. Moreover, at that time, there were still disconnected stories and more or less local traditions put forth under the names of such Apostles as James, Thomas, etc. or intimately connected with the facts of personages barely mentioned in the canonical Gospels, so that it was only natural that some, at least, of the current stories or traditions should be written down and freely circulated with such title as the Gospels of James, of Thomas, of the Infancy, etc. To these were soon added pure fictions, which were given also sacred names as a passport; and in this way a large apocryphal literature having some manner of connection with our Gospels was formed within the Church itself: it has received the general name of the

Apocryphal Gospels

It cannot be denied that most of the uncanonical productions have left but few traces in the writings of the Fathers of the Church, and that even the least fanciful among them are regarded by all as apocryphal and add little real information to the data supplied by our canonical sources. Yet, . . . the legends which they relate have exercised a very great influence upon the popular notions of the Middle Ages, . . . they are at times the only ground for certain popular beliefs about Our Lord, His Blessed Mother, His Apostles, etc., which survive down to the present day, and . . . the scenes which they describe have been often utilized in art and literature. . . .

It would be a long and useless task to reproduce here the list of all the apocryphal Gospels which are known to us only by their title, or by a few passages still found in some one or other of the great ecclesiastical writers of the third and fourth centuries. Issuing from heretical pens, and written for the purpose of spreading or supporting heterodox doctrines, these productions were naturally looked upon with suspicion by Catholic writers at their first appearance, and soon afterward put under the public ban of the Church, so that being practically confined within the narrow limits of a sect, they gradually ceased to be circulated, and ultimately disappeared. . . .

As might naturally be expected, apocryphal writings connected with the other books of the New Testament besides the Gospels, appeared during the early ages of Christianity. Most of these productions under the different names of Acts, Circuits, Miracles, Martyrdom, profess to record the apostolic labors of the first preachers of the Gospel, and are on that account usualy designated under the general name of the *Apocryphal Acts of the Apostles*. The principal among them are in the second century the Acts of Paul and Thecla, the Acts of St. John, those of St. Peter and St. Paul and of St. Andrew; and in the third century, the Acts ascribed to St. Thomas, the Teaching of Addai (Thaddaeus), and the Clementine Recognitions.

If we except the last of these apocryphal writings, they all seem to have taken their origin in heretical circles, and despite their alterations and recastings by orthodox hands, bear still traces of the tenets of the sects for the use of which they were originally composed. In the early Christian ages Ebionites, Gnostics, Encratites, etc. were busily engaged writing tales of wonders wrought by the Apostles, which would have a lively interest for heretics and orthodox alike, and by means of which doctrinal errors would be easily propagated. . . .

65

These apocryphal books easily fell into the hands of Catholics, and were circulated freely among them under the form of expurgated copies which, whilst containing the events whose substance was supposed to be faithfully recorded, had been rendered inoffensive to orthodox readers by the correction or removal of whatever was deemed objectionable. It is clear, therefore, that beside the fact that these apocryphal writings presuppose the existence of our canonical book of the Acts, and prove its incomparable superiority by way of contrast, all such compositions add very little, if anything, to our knowledge of the manner in which our New Testament writings were composed and finally gathered up into one authoritative collection. It cannot be denied, however, that a careful study of their contents may at times light up the path of the Catholic interpreter.   (1900)

SOURCE OF THE CHURCH'S
AUTHORITY CONCERNING SCRIPTURE

THE REV. HUGH POPE, O.P.

Now it is one thing to think that God did speak to certain men, quite another to believe their written record of what God said to them. Why should we believe it? I may believe that a particular General won such-and-such a battle, but that will not make me believe his account of that battle. Indeed, the very fact that he is narrating his own doings would incline me to skepticism. It would be ridiculous to say that we believe the Biblical records because God spoke to the writers. What He said to them is one thing; their account of it is another. Moreover, is it true that God did speak to all Biblical writers? Did He reveal Himself to Luke, for instance, or to the writer of Esther?

As a matter of fact we only believe God's revelation to men when we have proof of the fact that He did so speak. Proof we must have if our acceptance of such revelation is to be reasonable, and therefore a "human" act. The proof for those who listened to the claims put forward by such men as Isaias and Jeremias—the claim that God had actually spoken to them—lay in the miracles they worked in support of their claims, in the prophecies they uttered and which men saw fulfilled—at least in part; and this proof found confirmation in the personal lives of the Prophets themselves. But on what grounds do we at this day believe that such men as Isaias ever lived? Why believe that God spoke to him or the others? Why believe that the account of such revelations was really written by them? Still more: granting that they actually did commit these records to writing, what guarantee have we at this date of the accuracy of the record? . . .

The real position is an exceedingly simple one. There exists in the world a Book, or rather a collection of books, which claims to contain God's revelations. We are not, be it noted, concerned with the truth or falsity of this claim but simply with the fact it is made, and that it constitutes a challenge to the human race. Men can, if they choose, leave the claim alone, or pass it by with a shrug. But the thinkers of the world have never allowed it to go by default; they have assailed it from every possible point of view. This claim might be formulated some- what as follows:

The earlier portion of the Bible, the Old Testament, tells us that a Redeemer of the world is to come. In the New Testament we are faced with the figure of One who calmly asserts that He is that Redeemer, and adds that He is not simply man, but God-made-man, for our sakes; in support of this claim he proceeds to work a series of stupendous miracles culminating in His Resurrection from the tomb.

Those for whom this claim proves incontestable are Christian, people who cannot rest content with a bare acceptance of the claim, but argue: this man has proved that He is God-made-man, consequently every act of His is the act of God, and therefore perfect. But among His many acts we find the foundation of a Church to which He gave au- thority to teach men the way of His salvation, and to do so unerringly. Now that Church teaches among other things that the Bible which brought men to knowledge of Christ is not merely an existing historical fact, a literary phenomenon taking rank with other literary products of the world, but that—though written by ordinary mortals—these latter were the instruments of God who was thus the Principal Author of their work, which is therefore said to be inspired.

Briefly, then, we prove the infallibility of the Church from the Bible as an historical fact in the world's history; we accept the inspiration of the Bible on the authority of that infallible Church. There is no so- called "vicious circle" here, nor any but the most irrefragable logic.

This enables us to understand the expression we have used so often— the Bible is the Church's charter. For if you question the Church's claims, she refers you to the Bible as an historical fact—not as histori- cally true, for that is a wholly different matter. If you tell the Church that you find it hard to accept the Bible as historically true, she will tell you to settle the question for yourself. But, she will add, once you accept the Bible—at any rate in its main features—once you accept the "fact" of Prophecy and its culmination in Jesus, the carpenter of Nazareth, who claimed to be, and proved Himself to be, the Son of God, made man for our salvation, then you must also accept me as His Divinely appointed means for preserving and interpreting His teaching for the world to the end of time, as being "the body of Christ," "the pillar and the ground of truth."

Similarly, if you quarrel with the Church's teaching, she will refer you to the Bible as its guarantee. But if you protest that you cannot discover there all the doctrines which she sets forth, the Church will not send you to the Bible for these doctrines—though for some of them she could do so if she liked; she will send you indeed to the Bible, not to discover there the particular doctrines in question, but the fundamental doctrine of the Church's authority to teach at all. And if you prove obstinate and urge that you, or competent scholars, have as much right as any theologians of the Church to discover what really are the teachings of the Bible, the Church will gently remind you that her theologians are not the Church but the Church's children; that when they, for example, teach the doctrine of Christ's Resurrection in the very same flesh in which He "walked on earth," they do not do so simply because they think it is true or in accordance with the Scripture, but because they are the children of that Church which was actually present at and witnessed those scenes, and has handed them down through the subsequent ages. (1929)

ST. JEROME: "THE GREAT INTERPRETER"

THE RT. REV. WILLIAM BARRY

St. Jerome, whose work was undertaken at command of Pope Damasus (died 384), we may sum up his immense achievements on the Bible-text as follows: Between 382 and 391 he revised the Latin versions of the Gospels and St. Paul's Epistles; of the Psalms and Job according to the Seventy; and made a second revision of the Psalter in accordance with Origen's "Hexapla." Whether he translated the whole of the Septuagint is disputed, and it remains improbable. . . . From about 390 until 404–5 he was mainly absorbed in rendering the Hebrew Old Testament directly into Latin, not omitting the Psalms; but he also revised what had been previously left untouched by him of the New Testament. . . .

St. Jerome's colossal undertaking was at once creative and organic; it gave to Western Christendom the permanent reading of that Revelation in which those nations believed, and it guided them on by moulding their religious language towards the type of civilized order thus delineated. When Jerome began his task, by order of the Holy See, what he found was confusion, "as many manuscripts, so many texts"; infinite variations and a barbarous Latin, unworthy of the sublime original. By the time of St. Gregory the Great his better version had won its place and was the acknowledged standard; then it became the Vulgate (first so called, perhaps, by Roger Bacon), the common text, and the old Latin shrank into a curiosity of literature except where preserved by Church usage as in the books of Wisdom and Ecclesiasticus. For about a thousand years the Bible to Western Christians signified the Latin of a Dalmatian scholar and monk who, partly while serving the Pope in Rome, but chiefly as a recluse in his monastery at Bethlehem, and working almost alone, had translated much of the Scriptures again and again, mastered the whole, discovered a style of language beautifully fitting it, and bestowed on us the supreme literary production of the Roman Church. I hail St. Jerome, therefore, as the Great Interpreter. . . . Latin itself was baptized by a miracle of conversion, and at the same time this old and new idiom was in such a manner to be handled that it would easily survive when the Imperial speech of Rome broke up into the Romance dialects to which it gave place. From Hebrew and Hellenistic Greek to Latin; but this Latin again, not the rhetorical involutions of Cicero, not Livy's pictured page, neither Horatian nor Virgilian, but simple, elevated, moving like the primitive style which it sought to reproduce; and, yet once more, capable of being domestic, familiar in their mouths as household words, among tribes that were not of Italian, still less of Jewish pedigree—such was the amazing problem in fact offered to St. Jerome for solution by Pope Damasus. . . .

It is certain that St. Jerome's version of Holy Scripture did become the religious code of the West; setting it free in this respect from dependence on Greek authorities. It contributed powerfully to make Latin the language of the Church and to keep it so. It inspired the boundless medieval literature, from the sacred offices contained in Pontifical,

Sacramentary, and Breviary, to the innumerable volumes of devotions and private prayers, while the philosophy and theology which together form what is known as the scholastic system borrowed terms and quotations from it without ceasing. Thus it served to express the visible rites, the active intelligence, and the union of the spirit to which Rome gave a living center. One faith, one Church, one Bible—a triple cord which was not easily broken.

Well, then, might the English translators of 1611 acknowledge of St. Jerome how he had executed his task, "with that evidence of great learning, judgment, industry, and faithfulness, that he hath for ever bound the Church unto him in a debt of special remembrance and thankfulness." More, however, must be added to this commendation. In presenting future ages with an authentic Bible, the Saint was obeying the Pope, and keeping the injunction before him, "No Scripture is of any private interpretation." . . .

Providence has chosen to shape the future by guiding the Holy See when it established the Canon of Scripture on lines of tradition against the pseudo-Bible of the Gnostics; even as in the second century, the Episcopate became the bulwark of dogma threatened on all sides by the same ubiquitous Illuminism. What happy gift, we may enquire, was bestowed on St. Jerome, so that in the moment of danger and decision his enthusiastic long-continued study in every line of literature should have qualified him for this particular task. His reading, as St. Augustine knew, was universal, his memory a portent, his faculty of working without a break incredible, and his temper only whetted by opposition. These were notable advantages. But another was probably one which he shared with men like the Senecas, or Martial, or Prudentius, namely, that he was not strictly speaking a Roman. Born at Stridon, a place where Dalmatia bordered on Pannonia, he manifested the sort of provincial independence which has been remarked in the Spaniards, and in African writers such as Tertullian, Cyprian, Augustine. He studied under the memorable Donatus, and dreamt that he was a Ciceronian; but happily the accusation was a dream. St. Jerome's own Latin is admittedly pure, idiomatic, and correct in grammar as copious in vocabulary. He was an accomplished man of letters, a somewhat florid rhetorician, but no philosopher, little given to poetry, and in disputation highly impetuous. He loved facts and details, geographical, historical, personal. Not being a metaphysician, he moved among the subtle Eastern dialecticians rather at random, but kept his eye on Rome. . . . Hence, St. Jerome has been reckoned with St. John Chrysostom and the School of Antioch, which dwelt much on the letter of the Bible. . . . We may define him as a late Latin "grammarian," a Bible scholar and critic of the literal type, and a translator on definite though more or less unrecognized principles. . . .

His general aim in translating was to give the meaning as well as he knew how, "non verbum e verbo, sed sensum exprimere de sensu." Careful scrutiny of the most authentic Vulgate readings, made in comparison with what we may suppose to have been the Hebrew text before him, tends to confirm this opinion. . . .

He differs from Cicero when turning his original into Latin; and this he does by permitting the Hebrew, so far as possible, to control the structure of his composition, whereas the Roman orator keeps to the native period, or at least subdues to it the Greek authors whom he was importing. More clearly still, the vocabulary—the *lexis*, of Jerome is Latin undefiled; the syntactical order and construction are simplified to the utmost, that they may match or reproduce the Hebrew. This was a miraculous stroke, with infinite happy consequences. The classic style no more; but one which had a wealth of Christian associations; which the Church could claim as her own; which would dominate and inspire the new-springing languages of the West; which, finally, would consecrate on our altar old Roman terms, purged of their Pagan memories, or, as I have said, baptized in the sacred stream of the Jordan. That many such terms had been already adopted is, of course, true; but in the Bible now they were stereotyped, made indelible, and so full of strength to recover, that when cast out of the English Bible by Tyndale they came back under Coverdale and keep their place in it to this day. It is impossible to exaggerate the spiritual and literary importance of a standard thus created, set up for a thousand years in sight of the nations, and ruling their heart, their fancy, their conduct as on an identical pattern. They would have been exceedingly slow to assimilate the artificial verse and prose of Rome's Augustan age; but the Hebrew stories, songs, and prophecies, given to them in a simple moving rhythm, could not fail to become their dearest treasure. The Middle Ages are like a vast Museum, picture-gallery, and sounding-board of the Bible— St. Jerome's Bible, from which it might seem all their art and wide realms of their poetry and romance were derived. Yet, a curious observation must not be passed over. If by his version of the Scriptures holding a supreme rank among books, this rude Istrian from the Danube had, as it were, dethroned the literary Senate of Rome, he provided a shelter in which they might take refuge, thanks to the monastery with its scriptorium where his own work was unceasingly copied. Hallam has observed, and a recent author echoes the statement, that "unless the Church [the Roman] had thrown a halo of sanctity over the Latin tongue by retaining it as the language of her Bible and her worship, as well as the channel of her diplomatic intercourse, her ecclesiastical education, and her religious study, the fate of classical learning must inevitably have been sealed." (*Middle Ages,* III, 335 seq.; Hoare, *Our English Bible,* 15.) . . .

In the second half of the thirteenth century a small group of scholars, among them Roger Bacon the Franciscan, projected a translation from the Hebrew. By that time undoubtedly St. Jerome's text had been spread in countless manuscripts, and was liable to extensive corruption. Then came the printing-press, and among its very first books was the Latin Bible in 1456, which we call the Mazarin; no fewer than ninety-eight complete editions were published before the year 1500. The first German Bible, founded on St. Jerome, came out in print not later than 1466. Fourteen translations of the Vulgate into German, five into Low Dutch, are known to have existed before Luther undertook his self-appointed task. From a collation of these with his Bible it is evident that he consulted previous recensions, and that his work was not entirely original. (*Cambridge Modern Hist.,* I, 639.)

Luther's Bible opens a fresh era, no less decidedly than did St. Jerome's eleven hundred years before. Two roads divide, the Catholic leading up to the Council of Trent and onward to the Sixtine and Clementine recensions, approved by their respective Pontiffs; and the Protestant, which has developed into a number of Bible Societies, scattering millions of copies in hundreds of languages all over the world. On this consummation I have only the briefest concluding remarks to offer. Although non-Catholic translations profess to come direct from the original tongues, the influence of the Vulgate may still be traced in them. Especially may we follow it through the long and complicated series of English versions down even to the last Revision. Wycliffe, as is well known, had recourse only to the Latin; if it be held that his choice of a particular dialect determined the subsequent translators to imitate him, consider how much this implies. When I say Wycliffe, I am using the name impersonally for a national movement, since we do not find evidence of the man's own share in translation. Tyndale certainly wished to make an absolute beginning; but Coverdale's version was derived from "the Dutch and Latin," *i.e.,* the Vulgate, as he frankly admitted. And Coverdale's happy renderings have been largely preserved in subsequent Bibles, as in that of Rogers, called by him the "Matthew" Bible, in the Prayer-Book Psalms, and above all in the Authorized Version of 1611. This latter work, which has grown to be the standard text for the whole English-speaking world outside Catholicism, owed corrections and emendations of importance to the Rheims New Testament, which was as literal a version of the Latin Vulgate as its very learned authors could achieve. It follows, then, that St. Jerome, by virtue of his piety, genius, industry, and approval from the Holy See of Rome, enjoys a kind of Biblical ubiquity. No English translation is there upon which he has not left his mark. To the future as to the past he will be known as "Doctor Maximus." And if ever the Authorized Version, its errors purged away, should be reconciled to the Catholic Church, not a little of St. Jerome's work on the Bible, direct or indirect, would be discerned by exploring eyes within its pages.

(1921)

THE BIBLE IN THE MIDDLE AGES

THE RT. REV. HENRY G. GRAHAM

JUST as the Catholic Church at the very beginning wrote and collected together the sacred books of the New Testament, so by her monks and friars and clergy generally she preserved them from destruction during the Middle Ages and made the people familiar with them. . . .

Monasteries were centers of learning in those times even more than they are today, because education was not so widely spread. An indispensable part of the outfit of every monastery was a library. "A monastery without a library," writes a monk of the twelfth century to another monk, "is like a castle without an armory." And he goes on to declare that the great defense in the monastic armory should be the Bible. Sometimes the libraries were very large, and we read of Emperors and other great people borrowing from them. The monks were the most learned men of those days, and were by profession scholars, men who had renounced worldly pursuits and pleasures, and dedicated themselves to a retired life of prayer and study; and one of the principal parts of their scholastic activity was the copying and transcribing of the Sacred Scriptures. For this purpose there was a large room called the Scriptorium in which a dozen or more monks could be engaged at one time, but there were also many monks employed, each in his own cell, which contained all the necessary apparatus for literary work. These cells were so arranged around the central heating chamber that in winter their hands would not get benumbed with so much writing. Day by day, year after year, the monks would persevere in their holy labors, copying with loving care every letter of the sacred text from some old manuscript of the Bible, adorning and illuminating the pages of vellum with pictures and illustrations in purple and gold and silver coloring, and so producing real works of art that excite the envy and admiration of modern generations. Some Bishops and Abbots wrote out with their own hands the whole of both the Old and New Testaments for the use of their churches and monasteries. Even nuns—and this point I would bring under special notice—nuns took their share in this pious and highly skilled labor. We read of one who copied with her own hands two whole Bibles, and besides made six copies of several large portions of the Gospels and Epistles. Every monastery and church possessed at least one, and some possessed many copies of the Bible and the Gospels. In those ages it was a common thing to copy out particular parts of the Bible (as well as the whole Bible); for example, the Gospels, or the Psalms, or Epistles, so that many who could not afford to purchase a complete Bible, were able to possess themselves of at least some part which was specially interesting or popular. This custom is truly Catholic, as it flourishes amongst us today. At the end of our prayer books, for instance, we have Gospels and Epistles for the Sundays, and various publishers, too, have issued the four Gospels separately, each by itself, and the practice seems to harmonize entirely with the very idea and structure of the Bible, which was originally composed of separate and independent portions, in use in different Churches throughout Christendom. And so we find that the monks and clergy often confined their work to copying out certain special portions of Sacred Scripture, and naturally our Gospels were the favorite part.

The work, we must remember, was very slow and expensive as well. Dr. Maitland reckons that it would require ten months for a scribe of those days to copy out a Bible; and that £60 or £70 would have been required if he had been paid at the rate that law-stationers pay their writers. Of course, with the monks it was a labor of love, and not for money; but this calculation of Dr. Maitland only refers to the work of copying; it leaves out of account the materials that had to be used, pen and ink and parchment. Another authority (Buckingham) has made a more detailed calculation, and assuming that 427 skins of parchment would have been needed for the 35,000 verses, running into 127,000 folios, he reckons that a complete copy of Old and New Testaments would not have been purchased for less than £218.   (1911)

74

GUTENBERG'S BIBLE

THE MOST REV. JOHN J. WRIGHT

IT WAS a happy omen that the first book to be printed by the invention of movable type should have been the Bible. This is not surprising when we reflect upon the mentality of the man who produced this book and upon the spirit of the age which produced him.

John Gutenberg was a devout Catholic craftsman. Even as Columbus was motivated in his work of exploration by the desire to extend the Holy Catholic Faith, so Gutenberg made of his printing an apostolate for the spread of the Faith. . . .

The times in which he lived were avid for the preaching and exposition of the Word of God. The widespread passion to read the Scriptures had prompted the Church to make ever more broad provisions for bringing the Bible, open and complete, within reach of the multitudes. Prior to the invention of printing this was an exceedingly costly and difficult task. The many books of the Scriptures had to be copied diligently by hand and manuscript Bibles, thus lovingly but laboriously produced, immediately became priceless possessions beyond the reach of almost any but princes. Each Bible was a separate work involving months of patient, persistent toil by devoted monks whose reverence for the sacred text impelled them to illuminate and embellish their manuscripts with those exquisite decorations which make even single pages of the Medieval Bibles museum pieces and coveted objects of art. . . .

There is no book which has been more studied than the Bible. No Bible has been more studied than John Gutenberg's. Every copy, every page, column, line and letter has been the object of careful and critical scrutiny. Its historical significance could not be greater. The Gutenberg Bible, as has been remarked, is not a unique book; there are forty-five known copies. It is by no means the rarest of books, though a complete copy is so costly to acquire that only an exceedingly wealthy person or an endowed corporation would consider its purchase. Neither is it the finest book in existence either from the point of view of printing or from that of other artistic considerations; it has hundreds of rivals in beauty and in technical perfection. But it holds an incomparable place in the world of science and of learning because it is the first of all books to be printed and particularly because it is the first complete printing of the Book of Books, the Bible.   (1952)

THE FALLACY THAT LUTHER FOUND THE BIBLE AND GAVE IT TO THE PEOPLE FOR THE FIRST TIME IN THEIR OWN LANGUAGE

MARTIN LUTHER was born November 10, 1483. Up to December 31, 1500, the time when Luther was seventeen years and two months old, there were printed in Europe one hundred and thirty-four Latin editions of the whole Bible, fifteen German editions, thirteen Italian editions, eleven French editions, two Bohemian editions, one Dutch and one Spanish edition, a total of one hundred and seventy-seven editions of the whole Bible.

THE REV. J. M. LENHART, O.F.M. CAP. (1919)

There are still preserved seventy-five handwritten Bibles and portions of the Bible in German dating from the fourteenth century and one hundred and twenty-eight written before 1500. The first printed edition of the Scriptures in the vernacular was issued at Strassburg in 1466, a Bible in High German. From 1466 till 1520 were printed forty-seven editions of the vernacular Bible; seventeen in German, thirteen Italian, twelve French, two Bohemian, one Dutch, one Spanish, and one Russian for the Catholic Ukranians and Ruthenians. These numbers do not include the edition of the Bible in Bohemian for the Hussites, printed at Venice in 1506. These forty-seven editions comprised no less than 25,000 single copies of the Bible. The number of portions of the Bible in the vernacular printed from 1462 to 1520 may run up to one hundred thousand single copies; they were never properly estimated. *Catholic World* (February, 1929).

Several successive popes, Innocent III (1198–1216), Pius IV (1559–1565) and Clement VIII (1592–1605) regarded it as a duty to take some precautions, not, indeed, to forbid the reading of Scripture—remember this and proclaim it aloud—but to limit it among the faithful. Later, when the danger had to a large extent disappeared, and Protestantism, judged by its works and results, had lost its influence, the papal restrictions were removed, and with the approbation of bishops and popes, and under their direction, the Bible was translated and published in almost every known tongue.

THE REV. L. C. FILLION, S.S. (1926)

THE DOUAY VERSION AND ITS TRANSLATORS

THE REV. HUGH POPE, O.P.

THE Catholic version of the Bible is commonly known as "the Douay," but as a matter of fact the New Testament was translated at Rheims and published in 1582, while the Old Testament, though translated before the New at Rheims, was only published at Douay in 1609.

Four great names are inseparably connected with this translation—those of William Allen, Gregory Martin, Richard Bristow and Thomas Worthington. Allen was principal of St. Mary's Hall, Oxford, when he was obliged to fly from the country owing to his staunchness in the Catholic faith. After a stay at Louvain and a brief spell in England he settled at Douay where he rendered historic service to the Catholic cause by founding Douay Seminary. He was summoned to Rome by Sixtus V who made him a Cardinal. Gregory XIV placed him on the commission for the revision of the Sixtine Vulgate, and his name occurs in the famous inscription at Zagorola commemorating the work of this commission. Gregory Martin was one of the Foundation scholars of St. John's, Oxford, and then tutor in the family of the Duke of Norfolk. His reputation for learning was very great, but he gave up all the opportunities offered by the University "for conscience's sake"; before leaving he wrote to Campion, the future martyr: "If we two can live together we can live on nothing; and if this is too little, I have money; but if this also fails, one thing remains: they that sow in tears shall reap in joy."

From Oxford Martin went to Douay where he was ordained in 1573; in 1576 he was summoned to Rome by Gregory XIII to assist in the formation of the English College. Two years later he went to Rheims whither the Douay College had been removed, and there he began the work of translating the Bible into English. His hard work and laborious days as professor undermined a constitution already delicate, and he died at Rheims, October 28, 1582, shortly after the publication of the New Testament.

Richard Bristow entered Oxford in 1555; he became a Fellow of Exeter College, and he and Campion were accounted the greatest lights of the University in their day. . . . Like the others, however, Bristow was compelled to flee the country, and in 1569 he joined Allen at Douay and became his chief support. To him we owe the very polemical notes which appeared in the early editions of the New Testament. The work at Douay, combined with his labors on the New Testament, destroyed Bristow's health, and he died on October 15, 1581, at Harrow, at the early age of forty-three.

Thomas Worthington passed from Oxford to Douay in 1572. He then went on the English mission and suffered the terrible torment of remaining in the "pit" for over two months. When released he returned to Douay where he became President of the Seminary. To him we owe the notes appended to the Old Testament. He died in 1626.

To these four men, then, we owe the Douay Bible. Martin appears to have been responsible for the whole translation, though there are reasons for thinking that the other professors also contributed their share. To Allen fell the onerous task of providing the funds for the undertaking and of correcting his companions' work.

To appreciate rightly the translation these men produced we must bear in mind the following points: These exiles were the pick of the University which had driven them out; they were most learned men. Further, they were apostles in the truest sense of the term, for their whole lives were devoted to the cause of the Catholic faith. We have seen how both Martin and Bristow died at a very early date as the result of their strenuous labors, and we can very well term them "martyrs." Again, they all lived in an atmosphere of controversy such as even in these days we can hardly understand. The heretics had their translations and, in Allen's own words, "have at their finger-tips every text of Scripture which appears to make for them, and that, too, in some heretical version; moreover, by stringing passages together and changing the sacred text, they make it seem as though they were saying nothing but what was in the Bible." Consequently there was a feeling of unrest abroad among Catholics; men began to fear lest perhaps the true Scriptures were really being withheld from them. These considerations compelled the Douay professors to present a translation direct from the original as literal as possible, and replete with notes to illustrate the controverted points. . . .

They translated directly from the Latin Vulgate and not from the Greek—we are speaking here of the New Testament only. The reasons they allege for so doing are interesting. We present them in an abbreviated form:

"We translate the old vulgar Latin text, not the common Greek text, for these causes:

1. Its antiquity; it has been in use 1,300 years.
2. It is that corrected by St. Jerome.
3. It is therefore that commended by St. Augustine in a letter to St. Jerome.
4. It has always been used in Church services, in commentaries, sermons, etc.
5. The Council of Trent declared it "authentic."
6. It is the most majestic, most brave, and most impartial of all translations.
7. It adheres so closely to the Greek as almost to merit the censure of being slavish. In this respect it compares favorably with the Protestant translations.
8. Even such opponents to Catholicism as Theodore Beza prefer it to any other.
9. Even Luther was forced to acknowledge that if everybody continued to translate at his own pleasure men would have to reinstate the old Councils in order to preserve the unity of faith.
10. It is not only better than all other Latin translations, but than the Greek itself in those places where they disagree."

At the same time the translators paid attention to the Greek text, as the original notes, now removed, fully prove, and as the translators themselves announce on their title-page.

The appearance of this translation was the signal for a storm of anger in England and on the Continent. The polemical notes especially roused indignation, for they were couched in words of emphatic condemnation of the various English translations and of the wiles of the heretics. The term "mealy-mouthed" had not then been coined; but certainly no controversialist of the period was guilty of whatever the term may mean. . . .

Still, the evident learning of the Rhemish editors, their skillful use of the Fathers and of their patent honesty—despite their invective—threw the Protestants into a panic. For Martin was not content merely to

79

publish a translation of the New Testament; in the same year that it appeared (1582) he brought out his *Discovery of the Manifold Corruptions of the Holie Scriptures by the Heretikes of our Daies, especially the English Sectaries*. This, with the polemical *Preface* to the Rheims version, roused such feeling that Elizabeth appealed to Beza to answer Martin. He declined, and suggested instead that the Puritan, Cartwright, should undertake the task; but Archbishop Whitgift, who disliked him, stopped the work when it was well begun. Fulke, the Master of Pembroke, Cambridge, took up the task, and brought out in the following year *A Defence of the Sincere and True Translation of the Holy Scriptures into the English Tongue against the Manifold Cavils, Frivolous Quarrels, and Impudent Slanders of Gregorie Martin*. Fulke followed this up six years later with a huge volume, in which he printed in parallel columns the Rheims version and "the Translation out of the Original Greek, commonly used in the Church of England." This work was republished at least three times, the fourth edition appearing in 1633, with a dedicatory letter to King Charles by Hester Ogden, daughter of Fulke. She tells the king that her father's work was the best defense against "the inrode and invasion of a Troupe of Romish and Rhemish Jesuites who endeavour . . . to build up the walls of Rome in England." Fulke himself was, as the list of his publications shows, a mighty controversialist. As we read his laborious onslaught on every sentence of the Rheims version, *Preface* and *Notes* included, we can see the genesis of most of the anti-Catholic diatribes which even now pass muster with some people.

But Fulke was determined further to destroy the credit of the Rheims version. By 1589 he had completed a *Confutation of the Rhemist Testament,* but no license for its publication could be obtained till 1618, when it appeared. This is a veritable arsenal of weapons against every peculiarly Catholic doctrine, and as such was republished in 1834, on the occasion of the publication by an American firm of the original Rheims version. . . .

In the year 1688 appeared Ward's *Errata of the Protestant Bible*. Ward was a Protestant who became a Catholic, and who was led to examine the current Protestant versions. How corrupt these were is evident from the concurrent testimonies of Protestants and Catholics alike. In this treatise Ward maintains that many of these corruptions were deliberate; he quotes the Reformers themselves as admitting they excluded the Deuterocanonical books from their canon because of the doctrine they contained. Thus *Tobias* was repudiated "for that Raphael mentioned in Tobit, neither acknowledge we these seven Angels whereof he makes mention"; similarly *Ecclesiasticus*, "neither will I believe Free Will, although the book of Ecclesiasticus confirms it an hundred times." Ward took the principal doctrinal points denied by the Reformers, and showed how in the editions of 1562, 1577, and 1579 the translation had been adapted so as to exclude such doctrines; he further showed how the Authorized Version in the edition of 1683 had only partly corrected such errors. . . .

Much capital has been made of the excessively "Latin" tone of the Rheims version; and certainly there are in the original Rheims many expressions which nowadays are laughable. . . . But these things are the exception, and no one can read a chapter of the original Rheims without feeling how forceful is the English, and how carefully the translators have done their work. . . .

Martin was profoundly versed in the various English translations of the period. If anyone will take the *English Hexapla* and compare the Rheims version with the other translations, he will be surprised at the extent to which Martin has made use of his predecessors, notably Tyndale. Men are apt to think of the Rheims version as an excrescence, as having no place in the series of translations which culminated in the Authorized English Bible, save as a vitriolic protest against them. Yet this is a grave mistake. It was a polemical age, and the various Biblical translators must rank amongst the most polemical writers of the period. They read and—in more senses than one—"devoured" one another's translations. In the "instructions" given to the framers of the Authorized Version they are told to base their version on the Bishop's Bible, and where it is defective to use "Tyndale's, Matthew's, Coverdale's, Whitchurch's, Geneva." The Rheims version would—to the uninitiated reader—appear unknown or deliberately ignored, unless it were that the pre-eminent assistance it afforded in the formation of the Authorized Version was studiously concealed; a revolting alternative, yet the truth, and the *Preface* to the Revised Version of 1885 has a tardy and quite insufficient acknowledgement of this indebtedness:

"Their work shows evident traces of the influence of a version not specified in the rules, the Rhemish, made from the Latin Vulgate, but by scholars conversant with the Greek original."

As a matter of fact, the framers of the Authorized Version must have been familiar with Fulke's edition of the New Testament according to the Bishop's Bible and the Rheims in parallel columns; hence they must have known the particular features of Rheims. To what extent they were influenced by this translation has been the subject of a very minute study by Carleton, whose conclusions may be briefly summarized as follows: . . .

"If one were to assess the degree of obligation due from the former [the Authorized] to the latter [Rheims], it might, I think, fairly be said, that while the translation of 1611, in its general framework and language is essentially the daughter of the Bishop's Bible, which in its turn had inherited the nature and lineaments of the whole line of English versions issuing from the parent stock of Tyndale, yet, with respect to the distinctive touches which the Authorized New Testament has derived from the earliest translations, her debt to Roman Catholic Rheims is hardly inferior to her debt to Puritan Geneva. . . . It is remarkable how often some familiar phrase, some well-known term in our English New Testament, proves on examination to have beeen suggested by the version of Rheims." (*The Part of Rheims in the Making of the English Bible,* J. G. Carleton, D.D., Clarendon Press, 1902). . . .

The excessive literalness of the translation and the very Latin expressions which disfigured the Rheims and Douay versions urged Dr. Challoner to revise the work. He himself published six editions between 1749 and 1777. But Challoner's revision was very drastic; and while he rendered good and indeed necessary service, he undoubtedly weakened the nervous and forcible English of the original Elizabethan translators. Subsequent editors and revisers have made matters worse, so that there is now no such thing as the Rheims *version* left.   (1926)

When I take up my English Douai Bible and say: "Here I have the very word of God, the very truths that God Himself has revealed," all I mean is that the English words and sentences before me accurately report and express the doctrine and teaching of the original text, which is itself directly inspired. Hence, though the English *words* of the Douai Bible are not inspired, the *truths* that these words contain are inspired, since they are the very self-same truths which are contained in the original. It is only because the doctrines of the vernacular and of the original correspond that we can say with perfect truth: "This English Testament is the word of God."

THE RT. REV. JOHN S. VAUGHAN (1904)

SOME PROBLEMS OF BIBLE
TRANSLATION

THE RT. REV. RONALD A. KNOX

"Transmute boldly: render the sense by the corresponding sense without troubling over the verbal difficulties in your way. Where such rendering of sense by corresponding sense involves considerable amplification, do not hesitate to amplify for fear of being verbose. . . . Sometimes, even, a whole passage must be thus transmuted, a whole paragraph thrown into a new form, if we would justly render the sense of the original; and the rule should stand that, after having grasped as exactly as possible all that the original stands for, with the proportion between its various parts, the distinction between what is emphasized and what is left on a lower plane, we should say to ourselves, not 'How shall I make this foreigner talk English?' but 'What would an Englishman have said to express the same?' That is translation. That is the very essence of the art! the resurrection of an alien thing in a native body; not the dressing of it up in native clothes, but the giving to it of native flesh and blood."

So Mr. Belloc told us in a lecture he gave at the Taylorian in 1931. Is it any use to remember these principles, or ought they be expunged ruthlessly from the mind, when you sit down to translate inspired documents for the benefit of a conservative public bred chiefly on texts, under the eye of a censor who has never reflected that the word *concordat* is derived from the word *cor*? Certainly there is no official translation of the Bible known to me which does not abandon, from the start, the dream of preserving its native idiom, which does not resign itself, from the start, to being a word-for-word translation. It is no use objecting that the Authorized Version is good English. The Authorized Version is good English only because English writers, for centuries, have treated it as the standard of good English. In itself, it is no better English than the Douay; Professor Phillimore used to maintain that the Douay was better. Only the Douay was written in the language of exiles, which became, with time, an exiled language. Lately, a generation which has revolted against the domination of the Old Masters has shown signs of revolting against Authorized Version English; Mr. Somerset Maugham, I think, led the attack.

But whatever comes of that, it remains true that the Authorized Version is essentially a word-for-word translation, no less than the Septuagint, no less than the Vulgate. "For the Pharisees, and all the Jews, except they wash their hands, eat not, holding the tradition of the elders"; is that English idiom? "For the Nazis, and all the Germans, except they say *Heil Hitler!* meet not in the street, holding their lives valuable"; is that English idiom?

Let me commit to paper some of the hesitations which make themselves felt when you sit down, trying to forget that you have ever read the Bible before, to contemplate a verse of the Vulgate, with the Greek printed on the opposite side of the page, and ask yourself, What is the English for this?

To begin with, every language has its obscurities, has words which do duty for two different meanings. The word "blood," for example, has two quite different meanings in the two sentences, "Blood will tell," and "He is out for blood." In the same way, neither Hebrew nor Greek nor Latin has two separate words for "earth," in the sense of the terrestrial globe, and "land" in the sense of a particular region of it. When we are told that there was darkness over all the *terra* at the time of our Lord's Crucifixion, how are we to know whether the darkness was world-wide, or was only noticeable in Palestine? The Greek does not help us; it would not help us if we had access to the original Aramaic of St. Matthew. In translating such a verse you must accept the responsibility for creating this or that impression in the minds of (you hope) innumerable readers, of whom only one in ten ever looks at a footnote. It is the same with *gratia;* like *charis,* it may mean "grace" or it may mean "favour." The Douay plays for safety; but is there really any sense in saying that our Lord grew in grace with men? And a similar difficulty arises over the printing of "spirit" with or without a capital S, in a verse like Matthew iv. 1 ("led by the spirit into the wilderness"); the old Douay had the courage to print "Word" with a capital W in the second verse of St. Luke. You cannot be a translator without being, to some extent, an interpreter; and the ways of the Catholic interpreter are not always plain or easy.

What obligation is there, again, of following St. Jerome's rendering of the Greek, when his meaning appears to differ from that of the Greek? I say "appears"; in some cases the appearance is quite illusory. For example, why did the Wise Men receive an "answer" in sleep? Why did Simeon receive an "answer" from the Holy Ghost that he should see the Christ? There is no suggestion, in either case,

84

that a question had been asked; and the use of the word is one of those multitudinous touches which afflict the reader of our English Bible with distractions. The solution is very simple; St. Jerome's *responsum* does not mean an answer. It means an oracle; it is a technical word for an oracle. The Greek had used *chrematizomai,* and St. Jerome, in his strict preference for verbal equivalents, did the best he could to give the oracular atmosphere without using the pagan word *oraculum.* The Douay, therefore, is translating a shade of meaning which is not there. The nearest you can get to the sense is, "a revelation."

The same sort of confusion arises in a much more serious context. One of the leading differences between the Catholic and Protestant Bibles is that the former gives "do penance" (from *poenitentiam agere*) where the latter gives "repent" (from *metanoein*). Rivers of ink flowed over the controversy; Catholic expositors were determined not to let it be supposed that sins were forgiven in return for a mere attitude of the mind, as opposed to a genuine alteration of the will. Perhaps, too, they were anxious to assert the principle of reparation, though here they had less support from the Greek. Challoner has kept to the old rendering; Lingard, in the new conditions of a Victorian world, not only adopts "repent," but sets store by the change. His admirable footnote says, "Though there can be no true repentance which produces not reformation, there is often a reformation which is not produced by repentance." Protestant thought has boxed the compass, as usual; today, what it needs to be told is, that "turning over a new leaf" does not, unless it involves regret, avail to obliterate the past. And meanwhile, what was the linguistic background of the whole dispute? Simply that St. Jerome had used *poenitentiam agere,* and St. Jerome must know. But, in point of fact, St. Jerome had to use *poenitentiam agere;* there is no other way of saying "Repent," since *poenitet* has to be impersonal, except in the participle.

There are two instances, however, in which the Greek admits of two rival interpretations, whereas the Latin only allows of one. The word *pais* can mean "son" or "servant"; which does it mean in Acts iii. 13? Westcott and Hort mark the end of the verse as a quotation from Isaias liii. 13, in which case we ought certainly to render "servant." But St. Jerome has "servus" in Isaias, and "filius" in Acts. If the translator is convinced (which I am not) that the passage in Acts is a quotation, is he bound to follow St. Jerome blindfold in an inconsistency? More annoying, because it is much more common, is the hesitation whether he can be allowed to translate *verbum* "a

85

thing." Here the ambiguity goes back behind the Greek; it is *dabhar*, not *rhema,* that does double duty and so creates a confusion. The Douay imitates, of course, Latin and Greek in their literalness. But could the shepherds really have said, "Let us go to Bethlehem and see this word which has happened?" Does it mean anything?

It is easy to say that the Vulgate must always be followed, because it enshrines Catholic tradition. But this is not always true. Almost any Catholic, if asked whether Our Lady stayed with Elizabeth until after St. John was born, would reply, "Of course she did." But if he will look in the Vulgate, or in the Douay, he will find that she did not. In the Greek, you can read it either way, since the aorists in Luke i. 37 can legitimately be taken as pluperfect. But St. Jerome represents them as perfects; can the translator go behind St. Jerome here, in order to follow a tradition? Or must he, at best, "do a straddle"—invent some formula which would fit either interpretation? And can he do that, without ceasing to be literal?

So much for ambiguities. But even where the sense is indisputable, the translator will be conscious that there is a right way and a wrong way of putting things; and the chances are that the literal way will be the wrong way. When Horace writes *Da, puer, auguris Maecenae,* we expect the phrase to be rendered, "Fill a bumper, slave, to Maecenas' augurship!"; we conceive that the translator has not done his duty if he is content with "Give, boy, of the augur Maecenas." Yet that is what we should, almost certainly, have got if the words stood in the Bible. We have all grown accustomed to "they shall not leave in thee a stone upon a stone"; but it is not English. The Jews lacked the useful phrase "one another"; they had to talk about man-stone being left on his friend. Must we really imitate their poverty of speech, under pain of discordance with the original? There is the same objection to "feared with a great fear," and "desiring I have desired"; both locutions are intelligible, but, being quite unnatural English, they make the narrative seem remote, not part of ourselves; some people call it "dignified."

Moreover, some idioms when translated into a different language lose all their meaning, and serve to darken interpretation. *Tu dixisti,* for example; evidently the Aramaic form of speech which underlies this was as definite as the modern American, "You said it." If you were translating an American novel into French you would not translate, "You said it" by "Vous l'avez dit." Are we bound, then, to translate *Tu dixisti* by "Thou hast said it"? ("Thou hast said" by itself is not even grammar.) To be sure, the faithful mostly know what is meant; they have been told about it in sermons. But why must the Catholic clergy spend so much of their time in explaining that the Bible doesn't mean what it says? . . . In one passage a Hebrew idiom has been obscured by Challoner, who does not even allude to it in his footnote on the passage. When our Lady says, at Cana of Galilee, "They have no wine," there is no reasonable doubt that our Lord replied, "Let me alone"; the Jewish idiom for which is, "What have I to do with thee?" The Protestant Bible, in translating the idiom literally, makes it sound much too harsh. But Challoner has not dared even to be literal; he adopts without comment the far less probable interpretation, "What is that (the absence of wine) to me and to thee?"

The old Douay, in the same passage, is very illuminating. It gives the translation, "What is to me and thee, woman?" without pretending that it is English. And the footnote says, "Because this speech is subject to diverse senses, we keep the words of our text, lest by turning it into any English phrase we might straiten the Holy Ghost's intention to some certain sense either not intended, or not only not intended, and so take away the choice and indifferency from the reader, whereof (in holy Scripture specially) all translators must beware." The principle is one of capital importance; where interpreters disagree, the reader must be given his choice and indifferency as much as possible, though Challoner does not seem to have thought so. But does that justify the translator in printing gibberish? Ought he not rather, in these rare cases, to resort to a paraphrase which will be vague enough to cover both interpretations? "Do not trouble me, woman"—something of that kind.

Metaphors, no less than idioms, have their difficulty for the translator. Sometimes their meaning is transparent enough; the scribes and Pharisees, for example, "sitting in Moses' seat," although the picture which the imagination conjures up is one of extreme discomfort. But is any picture conjured up at all, to the ordinary English mind, by "a horn of salvation"? And, if we must preserve all other metaphors in their exact form, out of faithfulness to the original, surely it is time we got rid of "bowels"? Cruden's concordance gives some thirty instances of the word's use, only seven of which have a literal acceptation; our own version is still more fond of the idea, which disfigures our translations of the *Miserere* and of the *Benedictus*. Surely, as a general principle, we do better justice to the author's meaning when we translate *viscera* by "heart" (and *cor* by "mind").

There are, besides, certain words of very frequent occurrence which always strike the wrong note when you translate them literally from the Latin, because they are not familiar in the sense intended. "Just," for example. Even when the connotations of the word are merely moral, it is not the word we want; the man who does not steal your umbrella is not "just," he is "honest." Far more frequently, *justus* in the Vulgate has a strictly theological sense; under the Old Dispensation the *justus* is a man who is right with God, because he is careful to keep the law, moral and ceremonial; under the New Dispensation he is simply a "justified" person (e.g. Romans v. 19). The Protestant translators preferred the word "righteous," and the word "just" has therefore passed out of English usage in that sense. . . . Take, again, the word "flesh." It suggests to the modern Catholic ear associations of bodily self-indulgence; but in the New Testament it means, nearly always, the natural as opposed to the supernatural man, and especially where his mind is concerned. Or take the word "scandal." To Protestants it means uncharitable conversation; to Catholics it means setting a bad example. But in the New Testament it means anything which "puts you off," creates misgivings in you about the religious creed which you follow, or tends to do so.

You cannot, without sacrificing clear thought, treat words like these as mere counters, internationally available; each language gives its own twist to the more intimate ideas it tries to express. Nor can you even, without sacrificing clearness of thought, use the same equivalent for the same word in every passage where it occurs. "Thou art a scandal unto me," "whosoever shall scandalize one of these little ones," "All you shall be scandalized because of me this night" —you cannot find a single English word which will fit all those three passages; except "scandal," which is not, in any of the three passages, recognizable English.

And then there is the coupling of sentences. . . . There are nearly a hundred "ands" in the first chapter of Genesis, about fifty in the first chapter of St. Luke. The unbiquitous *waw* leaves its trail, not only of monotony but of obscurity. "And thinking that he was in the company, they came a day's journey and sought him among their kinfolk"—no; that is wrong; translate "they had come a day's journey before they looked (really, before it occurred to them to look) for him among their kinfolk." "Thinkest thou that I cannot ask my Father, and he will give me . . ."—no, that is wrong; anybody can *ask* for anything; translate, "Thinkest thou that my Father will not give me, if I ask him. . . ." And so on. Has not the translator a right

88

to recondition the whole system of sentence-coupling in the Bible? What makes the matter more urgent is that the conjunction in English is tending to die out, and we are concerned to budget for two hundred years hence. We say "I must find my coat, I've left my handkerchief in it," omitting the "for." We say, "Don't touch the wire, or you will get a shock," not "lest you should get a shock." We never say, "I didn't ask for lamb, but ham"; we say, "I asked for ham not lamb," or, "I didn't ask for lamb, I asked for ham." Consequently, sentences like, "Surely thou art one of them. For even thy speech doth discover thee," or "Cast not your pearls before swine, lest they turn again," or "I have not come to bring peace, but a sword" are out of date, and will come to wear more and more of an antique look as the years go by.

And, talking of that, what is the translator to regard as pure English? Is "to abide in a place" over-antique; is "to stay in a place" over-modern? And so on. It is not till you sit down to translate the Bible that words begin to haunt you with the sense of their evasiveness, and their caducity. *Mortalia facta peribunt, nedum sermonum stet honos et gratia vivax.* Here is a salient instance. For centuries people have laughed at the old Douay version, because in Galatians v. 4 it gave the rendering, "You are evacuated from Christ." In 1940 what metaphor could be more familiar, or more significant?

(1949)

A REVELATION IMPLIES AN INFALLIBLE GUIDE

JOHN HENRY CARDINAL NEWMAN

GREAT questions exist in the subject-matter of which Scripture treats, which Scripture does not solve; questions, too, so real, so practical, that they must be answered, and, unless we suppose a new revelation, answered by means of the revelation which we have, that is, by development. Such is the question of the Canon of Scripture and its inspiration: that is, whether Christianity depends upon a written document as Judaism;—if so, on what writings and how many;—and whether the document is self-interpreting, or requires a comment, and whether any authoritative comment or commentator is provided;—whether the revelation and the document are commensurate, or the one outruns the other;—all these questions surely find no solution on the surface of Scripture, nor indeed under the surface in the case of most men, however long and diligent might be their study of it. Nor were these difficulties settled by authority, as far as we know, at the commencement of the religion; yet surely it is quite conceivable that an Apostle might have dissipated them all in a few words, had Divine Wisdom thought fit. But in matter of fact the decision has been left to time, to the slow process of thought, to the influence of mind upon mind, the issues of controversy, and the growth of opinion. . . . Notice also the structure and style of Scripture, a structure so unsystematic and various, and a style so figurative and indirect, that no one would presume at first sight to say what is in it and what is not. It cannot, as it were, be mapped, or its contents catalogued; but after all our diligence, to the end of our lives and to the end of the Church, it must be an unexplored and unsubdued land, with heights and valleys, forests and streams, on the right and left of our path and close about us, full of concealed wonders and choice treasures. Of no doctrine whatever, which does not actually contradict what has been delivered, can it be peremptorily asserted that it is not in Scripture; of no reader, whatever be his study of it, can it be said that he has mastered every doctrine which it contains. . . .

As the essence of all religion is authority and obedience, so the distinction between natural and revealed lies in this, that the one has a subjective authority, and the other an objective. Revelation consists in the manifestation of the Invisible Divine Power, or in the substitution of the voice of a Lawgiver for the voice of conscience. . . .

The very idea of revelation implies a present informant and guide, and that an infallible one; not a mere abstract declaration of Truths unknown before to man, or a record of history, or the result of an antiquarian research, but a message and a lesson speaking to this man and that. . . .

We are told that God has spoken, Where? In a book? We have tried it and it disappoints; it disappoints us, that most holy and blessed gift, not from fault of its own, but because it is used for a purpose for which it was not given. The Ethiopian's reply, when St. Philip asked him if he understood what he was reading, is the voice of nature: "How can I, unless some man shall guide me?" The Church undertakes that office; she does what none else can do, and this is the

90

secret of her power. . . . The most obvious answer, then, to the question, why we yield to the authority of the Church in the questions and developments of faith, is, that some authority there must be if there is a revelation given, and other authority there is none but she. A revelation is not given, if there be no authority to decide what it is that is given. In the words of St. Peter to her Divine Master and Lord, "To whom shall we go?" Nor must it be forgotten in confirmation, that Scripture expressly calls the Church "the pillar and ground of Truth," and promises her as by covenant that "the Spirit of the Lord that is upon her, and His words which He has put in her mouth shall not depart out of her mouth, nor out of the mouth of her seed, nor out of the mouth of her seed's seed, from henceforth and for ever." (I Tim. iii. 16; Isa. lix. 21).   (1878)

COUNSEL FOR BIBLICAL
INTERPRETERS

PIUS XII

Being thoroughly prepared by the knowledge of the ancient languages and by the aids afforded by the art of criticism, let the Catholic exegete undertake the task, of all those imposed on him the greatest, that namely of discovering and expounding the genuine meaning of the Sacred Books. In the performance of this task let the interpreters bear in mind that their foremost and greatest endeavor should be to discern and define clearly that sense of the biblical words which is called literal. Aided by the context and by comparison with similar passages, let them therefore by means of their knowledge of languages search out with all diligence the literal meaning of the words. . . .

The commentators of the Sacred Letters, mindful of the fact that here there is question of a divinely inspired text, the care and interpretation of which have been confided to the Church by God Himself, should no less diligently take into account the explanations and declarations of the teaching authority of the Church, as likewise the interpretation given by the Holy Fathers, and even "the analogy of faith". . . . With special zeal they should apply themselves, not only to expounding exclusively these matters which belong to the historical, archeological, philological and other auxiliary sciences—as, to Our regret, is done in certain commentaries,—but having duly referred to these, in so far as they may aid the exegesis, they should set forth in particular the theological doctrine in faith and morals of the individual books or texts. . . .

Let Catholic exegetes then disclose and expound this spiritual significance, intended and ordained by God, with that care which the dignity of the divine word demands; but let them scrupulously refrain from proposing as the genuine meaning of Sacred Scripture other figurative senses. It may indeed be useful, especially in preaching, to illustrate and present the matters of faith and morals by a broader use of the Sacred Text in the figurative sense, provided this is done with moderation and restraint; it should, however, never be forgotten that this use of the Sacred Scripture is, as it were, extrinsic to it and accidental, and that, especially in these days, it is not free from danger, since the faithful, in particular those who are well-informed in the sciences sacred and profane, wish to know what God has told us in the Sacred Letters rather than what an ingenious orator or writer may suggest by a clever use of the words of Scripture. . . .

In the accomplishment of this task the Catholic exegete will find invaluable help in an assiduous study of those works, in which the Holy Fathers, the Doctors of the Church and the renowned interpreters of past ages have explained the Sacred Books. For, although sometimes less instructed in profane learning and in the knowledge of languages than the scriptural scholars of our time, nevertheless by reason of the office assigned to them by God in the Church, they are distinguished by a certain subtle insight into heavenly things and by a marvellous keenness of intellect, which enables them to penetrate to the very innermost meaning of the divine word and bring to light all that can help to elucidate the teaching of Christ and promote the holiness of life. . . .

Moreover, we may rightly and deservedly hope that our times also can contribute something towards the deeper and more accurate interpretation of Sacred Scripture. For not a few things, especially in matters pertaining to history, were scarcely at all or not fully explained by the commentators of past ages, since they lacked almost all the information, which was needed for their clearer exposition. How difficult for the Fathers themselves, and indeed well nigh unintelligible, were certain passages is shown, among other things, by the oft-repeated efforts of many of them to explain the first chapters of Genesis; likewise by the reiterated attempts of St. Jerome so to translate the Psalms that the literal sense, that, namely, which is expressed by the words themselves, might be clearly revealed.

There are, in fine, other books or texts, which contain difficulties brought to light only in quite recent times, since a more profound knowledge of antiquity has given rise to new questions, on the basis of which the point at issue may be more appropriately examined. Quite wrongly therefore do some pretend, not rightly understanding the conditions of biblical study, that nothing remains to be added by the Catholic exegete of our time to what Christian antiquity has produced; since, on the contrary, these our times have brought to light so many things, which call for a fresh investigation and a new examination, and which stimulate not a little the practical zeal of the present-day interpreter. . . . What is the literal sense of a passage is not always as obvious in the speeches and writings of the ancient authors of the East, as it is in the works of the writers of our own time. For what they wished to express is not to be determined by the rules of grammar and philology alone, nor solely by the context; the interpreter must, as it were, go back wholly in spirit to those remote centuries of the East and with the aid of history, archaeology, ethnology and other sciences, accurately determine what modes of writing, so to speak, the authors of that ancient period would be likely to use, and in fact did use.

For the ancient peoples of the East, in order to express their ideas, did not always employ those forms or kinds of speech, which we use today; but rather those used by the men of their times and countries. What those exactly were the commentator cannot determine as it were in advance, but only after a careful examination of the ancient literature of the East. The investigation, carried out, on this point, during the past forty or fifty years with greater care and diligence than ever before, has more clearly shown what forms of expression were used in those far off times, whether in poetic description or in the formulation of laws and the rules of life or in recording the facts and events of history. . . .

No one, who has a correct idea of biblical inspiration, will be surprised to find, even in the Sacred Writers, as in other ancient authors, certain fixed ways of expounding and narrating, certain definite idioms, especially of a kind peculiar to the Semitic tongues, so-called approximations, and certain hyperbolical modes of expression, nay, at times, even paradoxical, which help to impress the ideas more deeply on the mind. For of the modes of expression which, among ancient peoples, and especially those of the East, human language used to express its thought, none is excluded from the Sacred Books, provided the way of speaking adopted in no wise contradicts the holiness and truth of God. . . .

Hence the Catholic commentator, in order to comply with the present needs of biblical studies, in explaining the Sacred Scripture and in demonstrating and proving its immunity from all error, should also make a prudent use of this means, determine, that is, to what extent the manner of expression or the literary mode adopted by the sacred writer may lead to a correct and genuine interpretation; and let him be convinced that this part of his office cannot be neglected without serious detriment to Catholic exegesis. Not infrequently—to mention only one instance—when some persons reproachfully charge the Sacred Writers with some historical error or inaccuracy in the recording of facts, on closer examination it turns out to be nothing else than those customary modes of expression and narration peculiar to the ancients, which used to be employed in the mutual dealings of social life and which in fact were sanctioned by common usage.

When such modes of expression are met with in the sacred text, which, being meant for men, is couched in human language, justice demands that they be no more taxed with error than when they occur in the ordinary intercourse of daily life. By this knowledge and exact appreciation of the modes of speaking and writing in use among the ancients can be solved many difficulties, which are raised against the veracity and historical value of the Divine Scriptures, and no less efficaciously does this study contribute to a fuller and more luminous understanding of the mind of the Sacred Writer.

Let those who cultivate biblical studies turn their attention with all due diligence tawards this point and let them neglect none of those discoveries, whether in the domain of archaeology or in ancient history or literature, which serve to make better known the mentality of the ancient writers, as well as their manner and art of reasoning, narrating and writing. . . .

Let all the other sons of the Church bear in mind that the efforts of these resolute laborers in the vineyard of the Lord should be judged not only with equity and justice, but also with the greatest charity; all moreover should abhor that intemperate zeal which imagines that whatever is new should for that very reason be opposed and suspected. Let them bear in mind above all that in the rules and laws promulgated by the Church there is question of doctrine regarding faith and morals; and that in the immense matter contained in the Sacred Books—legislative, historical, sapiential and prophetical—there are but few texts whose sense has been defined by the authority of the Church, nor are those more numerous about which the teachings of the Holy Fathers is unanimous. There remain therefore many things, and of the greatest importance, in the discussion and exposition of which the skill and genius of Catholic commentators may and ought to be freely exercised, so that each may contribute his part to the advantage of all, to the continued progress of the sacred doctrine and to the defense and honor of the Church.   (1943)

If there is no branch of teaching, however humble and easy to learn, which does not require a master, what can be a greater sign of rashness and pride than to refuse to study the books of the divine mysteries by the help of those who have interpreted them?

ST. AUGUSTINE (ca. 400)

The interpreter should not be a lover of contention, but possess meekness in his piety. He should be furnished beforehand with a knowledge of the original languages, lest he be at a loss in unknown words and expressions. He should possess a knowledge of certain necessary things [biblical archaeology] lest he be ignorant of the efficacy and nature of objects used in the way of similitude. He should likewise be aided by the truth of manuscripts which a skilful and diligent emendation has effected. Thus equipped, let him come to discuss and solve the difficult passages of the Scriptures.

ST. AUGUSTINE (397)

"DO NOT DESPISE WHAT IS LOWLY IN GOD'S WORD"

HUGH OF ST. VICTOR

THE mystical sense [of Holy Scripture] is only gathered from what the letter says, in the first place. I wonder how people have the face to boast themselves teachers of allegory, when they do not know the primary meaning of the letter. "We read the Scriptures," they say, "but we don't read the letter. The letter does not interest us. We teach allegory." How do you read Scripture then, if you don't read the letter? Subtract the letter and what is left? "We *read* the letter," they say, "but not according to the letter. We read allegory, and we expound the letter not literally but allegorically . . . as *lion,* according to the historical sense means a beast, but allegorically it means Christ. Therefore the word *lion* means Christ. . . ."

If, as they say, we ought to leap straight from the letter to its spiritual meaning, then the metaphors and similes, which educate us spiritually, would have been included in the Scriptures by the Holy Spirit in vain. As the Apostle says: "That was first which is fleshly, afterwards that which is spiritual" (I Cor. xv. 46). Do not despise what is lowly in God's word, for by lowliness you will be enlightened to divinity. The outward form of God's word seems to you, perhaps, like dirt, so you trample it underfoot, and despise what the letter tells you was done physically and visibly. But hear! that dirt, which you trample, opened the eyes of the blind. Read Scripture then, and first learn carefully what it tells you was done in the flesh. . . .

When we read the holy books, let us rather choose, from the great multitude of patristic explanations, which are drawn from few words [of the text], and corroborated by the Catholic faith, that which appears to have been certainly intended by the author. If this is uncertain, let us choose at least that explanation which is admissible in the context, and is consonant with the faith. If the context does not help us, then we must choose only that prescribed by the faith. It is one thing not to discern what the writer intended, another to err against piety. *If both are avoided, the fruit of reading is perfect.*

(ca. 1125)

96

Do not be fastidious about the simple and homely speech of Holy Scripture; sometimes this may be due to copyists, but it is also done deliberately, so as to provide ready instruction for rustic assemblies, also that learned and unlearned alike may gather different fruit from one and the same passage.

ST. JEROME (ca. 400)

There have been objections without number perseveringly directed against the Scripture for many a long year, which have been proved to be futile and are now never heard of; and not infrequently interpretations have been placed on certain passages of Scripture (not belonging to the rule of faith or morals) which have been rectified by more careful investigations. As time goes on, mistaken views die and disappear; but *truth remaineth and groweth stronger forever and ever* (3 Esdr. iv. 38). Wherefore, as no one should be so presumptuous as to think that he understands the whole of Scripture, in which St. Augustine himself confessed that there was more that he did not know than that he knew, so, if he should come on anything that seems incapable of solution, he must take to heart the cautious rule of the same holy doctor: "It is better even to be oppressed by unknown but useful signs than to interpret them uselessly, and thus to throw off the yoke only to be caught in the trap of error."

LEO XIII (1893)

SCRIPTURE SUPPORTS SCRIPTURE

ST. AUGUSTINE

A MAN who thoroughly examines the Holy Scriptures in an endeavor to find the purpose of the author (through whom the Holy Ghost brought Holy Scripture into being), whether he attains this goal or whether he elicits from the words another meaning which is not opposed to the true faith, is free from blame, if he has proof from some other passage of the Holy Scriptures. In fact, the author perhaps saw that very meaning, too, in the same words which we are anxious

97

to interpret. And, certainly, the Spirit of God who produced these words through him also foresaw that this very meaning would occur to the reader or listener; further, He took care that it should occur to him because it also is based upon truth. For, what could God have provided more generously and more abundantly than that the same words might be understood in several ways, which other supporting testimonies no less divine endorse?

When such a meaning is elicited that its uncertainty cannot be explained by the unerring testimonies of the Holy Scriptures, however, it remains for us to explain it by the proof of reason, even if the man whose words we are seeking to understand were perhaps unaware of that meaning. This, however, is a dangerous practice. It is much safer to walk by means of the Holy Scriptures. When we are trying to search out those passages that are obscured by figurative words, we may either start out from a passage which is not subject to dispute, or, if it is disputed, we may settle the question by employing the testimonies that have been discovered everywhere in the same Scripture. (397)

It is one of the glories of the Bible that it can enshrine many meanings in a single passage. It thus meets the needs of different minds, and each man marvels to find in the divine Scriptures truths which he has himself thought out. This is helpful, too, in defending the Bible against unbelievers, since if some meaning which a person wants to read in Scripture seems to him false, you can always appeal to some other meaning that it may have. Hence it is not absurd to suppose that there was divinely granted to Moses and the other Biblical authors a knowledge of various truths which men could know, and that they enshrined these in a single literal form of expression, with the result that each of these meanings was the sense intended by the author. Further still, if interpreters of Scripture read true meanings into the letter of the text which the author did not mean, there can be no doubt but that the Holy Spirit, who is the principal author of Holy Scripture, so understood it. Consequently, every truth which can—with due regard to the context—be read into Scripture is its meaning.

ST. THOMAS AQUINAS (1272)

FAITH IN THE AUTHORITY
OF SCRIPTURE

ST. AUGUSTINE

THE entire treatment of the Scriptures is based upon two factors: the method of discovering what we are to understand and the method of teaching what has been understood. . . .

Whoever appears in his own opinion to have comprehended the Sacred Scriptures, or even some part of them, yet does not build up with that knowledge the two-fold love of God and his neighbor, "has not yet known as he ought to know" (Rom. 13; 10; I Tim. 1. 5). . . .

Whoever understands in the Sacred Scriptures something other than the writer had in mind is deceived, although they do not lie. If he is deceived in an interpretation by which, however, he builds up charity (which is the end of the precept) (I Tim. 1. 5), he is deceived in the same way as is someone who leaves the road through error, but makes his way through the field to the place where the road also leads. Nevertheless, he must be corrected and must be shown how it is more advantageous not to leave the road, lest by a habit of deviating he may be drawn into a crossroad or even go the wrong way.

By rashly asserting something which the author did not intend, he frequently runs into other passages which he cannot reconcile to that interpretation. If he agrees that these latter are true and definite, then the opinion that he had formed concerning the former cannot be true, and it happens in some way or other, that by loving his own opinion he begins to be more vexed at Scripture than at himself. If he allows this error to creep in, he will be utterly destroyed by it. "For we walk by faith and not by sight" (Cor. 5. 7). Faith will totter if the authority of Sacred Scriptures wavers. . . .

Therefore, when anyone recognizes that "the end of the precept is charity from a pure heart and a good conscience and faith unfeigned" (I Tim. 1.5), and proposes to refer his whole comprehension of Sacred Scriptures to these three virtues, he may approach the interpretation of those books fearlessly. . . .

Those who read indiscreetly are deceived by numerous and varied instances of obscurity and vagueness, supposing one meaning instead

99

of another. In some passages they do not find anything to surmise even erroneously, so thoroughly do certain texts draw around them the most impenetrable obscurity. I am convinced this whole situation was ordained by God in order to overcome pride by work and restrain from haughtiness our minds which usually disdain anything they have learned easily. . . .

The Holy Ghost, therefore, has generously and advantageously planned Holy Scripture in such a way that in the easier passages He relieves our hunger; in the ones that are harder to understand He drives away our pride. Practically nothing is dug out from those unintelligible texts which is not discovered to be said very plainly in another place. . . .

We ought not to protest against Holy Scripture, either when we understand it and it is attacking some of our faults, or when we do not understand it and think that we ourselves could be wiser and give better advice. In this latter case we must rather reflect and believe that what is written there is more beneficial and more reasonable even if hidden, than what we could know of ourselves. . . .

It is inevitable, then, that at first, each one should discover in the Scriptures that he has been enmeshed by the love of this world, that is, of temporal things, and has been far separated from such a great love of God and of his neighbor as Scripture itself prescribes. Then, truly, that fear with which he meditates upon the judgment of God and that piety through which he must needs believe and yield to the authority of the Holy Books should force him to mourn over himself.   (397)

No error is to be admitted in the Bible, not even concerning things of but little importance. . . . If any statements should *seem* contrary to truth, we must not accuse the Author of the Book of falsehood: we should rather conclude, either than (a) the text is defective; or (b) that the interpreter has mistaken the meaning; or (c) that we have misunderstood.

ST. AUGUSTINE (ca. 400)

It is evident that the chief law of interpretation is that which enables us to discover and determine what the writer meant to say, as

St. Athanasius tells us: "Here, as in all other passages of the divine Scripture, we must observe the occasion of the Apostle's utterance, and note accurately and carefully the person and the subject which were the cause of his writing, lest ignorance or error concerning these points lead us to misconceive the meaning of the author. . . . Just as the substantial Word of God became like to men in all things, without sin, so the words of God, expressed in human language, became in all things like to human speech, except error. . . . Under the influence of the divine motion he (the sacred writer) uses his own faculties and powers in such a way that from the book which is the fruit of his labor all may easily learn the distinctive genius and the individual characteristics and features of each author."

PIUS XII (1943)

THE MATURED JUDGMENTS
OF THE CHURCH

THE REV. WILLIAM LEONARD
AND DOM BERNARD ORCHARD, O.S.B.

SOME non-Catholic works convey the idea that Catholic biblical scholars are entirely ruled by a teaching authority which is conceived as a sort of governmental machinery for giving ready decisions and imposing them under threat of censure. The teaching authority—namely the Pope and Bishops—is represented as holding the sense of every passage of the Bible ready, as it were, *in scrinio pectoris,* so that ecclesiastical interpretation is comparable to a ready-reckoner. According to this absurd view, in order to discover the meaning of a text all one need do is to find out how the local Ordinary, or the Bishops of a province, or the Pope or his representative understand it; and there can be no departure from the fixed formulae.

Now it is quite true that the Church has occasionally forbidden all further controversy for a time on a disputed point, *e.g.,* on the nature of efficacious grace in the 17th century, when so much dust was raised and heat generated that the Church thought it necessary to allow the air to clear before permitting the resumption of the discussion. Similarly at the time of the Modernist Movement within the Church at the beginning of the 20th century, the situation was so grave that the Biblical Commission, in the interests of Catholic scholars themselves as well as of the Church, had to undertake the task of laying down the boundaries of biblical orthodoxy without killing the spirit of inquiry. Whatever some people may have felt at the time, the wisdom of their decisions has been proved beyond all doubt, (*a*) by the fact that the spirit of inquiry among all Catholics after being warned off a false scent and momentarily checked, has resumed the main path with extraordinary success; (*b*) by the fact that the extremist theories current fifty years ago have now become obsolete and that there has been a general return all along the line towards the Catholic and orthodox position, a movement that is still in full swing. . . .

People outside the Church forget that because she is "the pillar and ground of truth" she can afford to wait a few years or a few decades or even a few centuries in order to form an unbiased judgment. For she will never in any event relinquish the known truth for the sake of a passing fashion or some novelty. They also, quite naturally perhaps, fail to realize how fortunate Catholic scholars are to have an authority to point out the pitfalls of the fashionable folly of the moment, and to recommend suspension of judgment when the data are insufficient to justify a definite opinion.

We therefore see the real purpose of the Biblical Commission is to afford true guidance to the scholar in doubt, without cramping the ardor of genuine scholarship, and Catholics are profoundly grateful to Pope Leo XIII for instituting it.

Certainly the Church has no mechanical method of exegesis, and it would be wrong to regard her as a sort of studious professor of exegesis. She teaches faith and morals out of the two founts of revelation by acts of her ordinary every-day magisterium and sometimes by extraordinary acts of her solemn magisterium. Her judgment on the sense of scriptural texts relating to faith and morals has to mature under the guidance and working of the Holy Spirit, and this happens through the devout study which her Fathers and Doctors and theologians have given and give to the Sacred Page. Authoritative ecclesiastical judgment is given only when the situation is clarified.

(1953)

You cannot make your way into holy Scriptures without having someone to go before you and show you the road. . . . The science of the Scriptures is the only one which all persons indiscriminately claim as their own! This science the babbling old woman, the doting old man, the wordy sophist, take upon themselves; they tear it to tatters and teach before they themselves have learned. . . . Coming by chance to the study of the Scriptures . . . they fancy what they utter is the law of God, not deigning to learn what the prophets and the Apostles taught. Rather they accommodate to their interpretation the most incongruous passages, as if this were something great instead of a most faulty method of teaching, distorting sentences and forcing the reluctant Scriptures to their own whims.

ST. JEROME (ca. 400)

THE FOLLY OF PRIVATE INTERPRETATION

JAMES CARDINAL GIBBONS

No NATION ever had a greater veneration for the Bible than the Jewish people. The Holy Scripture was their pride and their glory. It was their national song in time of peace; it was their meditation and solace in time of tribulation and exile. And yet the Jews never dreamed of settling their religious controversies by a private appeal to the Word of God.

Whenever any religious dispute arose among the people it was decided by the High Priest and the Sanhedrim, which was a council consisting of seventy-two civil and ecclesiastical judges. The sentence of the High Priest and of his associate judges was to be obeyed under penalty of death. "If thou perceive," says the Book of Deuteronomy, "that there be among you a hard and doubtful matter in judgment . . . thou shalt come to the Priests of the Levitical race and to the judge . . . and they shall show thee the truth of the judgment . . . and thou shalt follow their sentence." . . .

From this clear sentence you perceive that God does not refer the Jews for the settlement of their controversies to the letter of the law, but to the living authority of the ecclesiastical tribunal which He had expressly established for that purpose.

Hence, the Priests were required to be intimately acquainted with

103

the Sacred Scripture, because they were the depositaries of God's law, and were its expounders to the people. . . .

In fact, very few of the children of Israel, except the Priests, were in possession of the Divine Books. The holy manuscript was rare and precious. And what provision did God make that all the people might have an opportunity of hearing the Scriptures? Did He command the sacred volume to be multiplied? No; but He ordered the *Priests* and the *Levites* to be distributed through the different tribes, that they might always be at hand to instruct the people in the knowledge of the law. The Jews were even forbidden to read certain portions of the Scripture till they had reached the age of thirty years.

Does our Savior reverse this state of things when He comes on earth? Does He tell the Jews to be their own guides in the study of the Scriptures? By no means; but He commands them to obey their constituted teachers, no matter how disedifying might be their private lives. "Then said Jesus to the multitudes and to His disciples: The Scribes and Pharisees sit upon the chair of Moses. All things therefore whatsoever they shall say to you, observe and do" (Matt. xxiii. 23).

It is true our Lord said on one occasion: "Search the Scriptures, for you *think* in them to have life everlasting, and the same are they that give testimony to Me" (John v. 39). This passage is triumphantly quoted as an argument in favor of private interpretation. But it proves nothing of the kind. Many learned commentators, ancient and modern, express the verb in the indicative mood: "Ye search the Scriptures." At all events, our Savior speaks here only of the Old Testament because the New Testament was not yet written. He addresses not the multitude, but the Pharisees, who were the teachers of the law, and reproaches them for not admitting His Divinity. "You have," He says, "the Scriptures in your hands; why then do you not recognize Me as the Messiah, since they give testimony that I am the Son of God?" He refers them to the Scriptures for a proof of His Divinity, not as to a source from which they were to derive all knowledge in regard to the truths of revelation. . . .

In this very passage our Lord is explaining the sense of Holy Writ; therefore, its true meaning is not left to the private interpretation of every chance reader. It is, therefore, a grave perversion of the sacred text to adduce these words in vindication of private interpretation of the Scriptures.

But when our Redeemer abolished the Old Law and established His Church, did He intend that His Gospel should be disseminated by the circulation of the Bible, or by the living voice of His disciples? This is a vital question. I answer most emphatically, that it was by preaching alone that He intended to convert the nations, and by preaching alone they were converted. No nation has ever yet been converted by the agency of Bible Associations.

Jesus Himself never wrote a line of Scripture. He never once commanded His Apostles to write a word, or even to circulate the Scriptures already existing. When He sends them on their Apostolic errand, He says: "Go *teach* all nations." *"Preach* the Gospel to every creature." "He that heareth you heareth Me." And we find the Apostles acting in strict accordance with these instructions.

Of the twelve Apostles, the seventy-two disciples, and early followers of our Lord only eight have left us any of their sacred writings. And the Gospels and Epistles were addressed to particular persons or particular churches. They were written on the occasion of some emergency, just as Bishops issue Pastoral letters to correct abuses which may spring up in the Church, or to lay down some rules of conduct for the faithful. The Apostles are never reported to have circulated a single volume of the Holy Scripture, but "they going forth *preached* everywhere, the Lord cooperating with them."

Thus we see that in the Old and New Dispensation the people were to be guided by a living authority, and not by their private interpretation of the Scriptures. . . .

A competent religious guide must be clear and intelligible to all, so that everyone may fully understand the true meaning of the instruction it contains. Is the Bible a book intelligible to all? Far from it; it is full of obscurities and difficulties, not only for the illiterate, but even for the learned. . . .

The Fathers of the Church, though many of them spent their whole lives in the study of the Scriptures, are unanimous in pronouncing the Bible a book full of knotty difficulties. And yet we find in our day pedants, with a mere smattering of Biblical knowledge, who see no obscurity at all in the Word of God, and who presume to expound it from Genesis to Revelation. "Fools rush in where angels fear to tread."

Does not the conduct of the Reformers conclusively show the utter folly of interpreting the Scriptures by private judgment? As soon as they rejected the oracle of the Church, and set up their own private judgment as the highest standard of authority, they could hardly agree among themselves on the meaning of a single important text. The Bible became in their hands a complete Babel. The sons of Noe attempted in their pride to ascend to heaven by building the tower of Babel, and their scheme ended in the confusion and multiplication of tongues. The children of the Reformation endeavored in their conceit to lead men to heaven by the private interpretation of the Bible, and their efforts led to the confusion and the multiplication of religions. Let me give you one example out of a thousand. These words of the Gospel, "This is My Body," were understood only in one sense before the Reformation. The new lights of the sixteenth century gave no fewer than eighty different meanings to these four simple words, and since their time the number of interpretations has increased to over a hundred. . . .

One body of Christians will prove from the Bible that there is but one Person in God, while the rest will prove from the same source that a Trinity of Persons is a clear article of Divine Revelation. One will prove from the Holy Book that Jesus Christ is not God. Others will appeal to the same text to attest His Divinity. One denomination will assert on the authority of Scripture that infant baptism is not necessary for salvation, while others will hold that it is. Some Christians, with Bible in hand, will teach that there are no sacraments. Others will say that there are only two. Some will declare that the inspired Word does not preach the eternity of punishments. Others will say that the Bible distinctly vindicates that dogma. Do not clergymen appear every day in the pulpit, and on the authority of the Book of Revelation point out to us with painful accuracy the year and the day on which this world is to come to an end? And when their prophecy fails of execution they cooly put off our destruction to another time.

(1876)

The heretics do away with the true doctrine of the Lord, not interpreting and transmitting the Scriptures agreeably to the dignity of God and of the Lord. For the understanding and the cultivation of the pious tradition, agreeably to the teaching of the Lord through His Apostles, is a deposit to be rendered to God. . . . For neither the prophets nor the Savior Himself announced the divine mysteries so simply as to be easily comprehended by all persons whatever. . . . All things are right to them that understand, says the Scripture: to those, that is, who perfectly preserve His revealed interpretation of the Scriptures, according to the Church's rule.

ST. CLEMENT OF ALEXANDRIA (ca. 150)

THE PROBLEM OF INTERPRETATION ILLUSTRATED

THE REV. ALEXANDER JONES

THE number of texts which have been solemnly interpreted by the Church is little more than one dozen though, of course, one must not forget the implicit interpretations which are latent in her practice. When Scripture texts contain matters of faith or morals the Church's power to interpret them is known as "direct and positive." This means that she is immediately and legitimately concerned with their content for its own sake and is competent not merely to exclude false interpretations but to propose and impose the right one. Over other texts (containing history, science, etc.), it is clear from the discussions at the Vatican Council that here, too, she claims authority. This power, however, is called "indirect and negative." It is indirect because it is not concerned with the content of the text for its own sake (the content is not in itself religious) but with safeguarding the dogma of inspiration and of inerrancy, its consequence. It is negative because it does not propose one interpretation but merely excludes those which she sees to be incompatible with the dogma of inspiration or inerrancy. Perhaps when our non-Catholic neighbors come to understand the economy of this second claim they will come also to realize that the Catholic Scripture scholar is not bound hand and foot. . . .

Well, then, let us not be shy of applying reasoned principles to the Word of God. Why should we? The Saviour of East and West chose to dwell midway between New York and Tokyo. He addressed Pilate, no doubt, in Greek which was familiar to many in Palestine and heard especially in Galilee, but for the most part he accepted the limitations of Palestinian Aramaic. God's written Word, like God's incarnate Word, accepts its limitations. It is written in the tongues of men and, in its defense, man must take up the weapons of reason. The least we claim for the Bible is the justice that would be conceded to any book.

Shall we have this in italics? It is a principle at once obvious, important and forgotten. *The goal of all interpretation is to discover the meaning the author truly intends to convey and truly conveys.* We are not interested, therefore, in what we should *like* the author to say or in what translators or commentators or hecklers try to *make* him say. . . .

The Catholic interpreter is not out to obliterate certain of the bright pictures of our younger days; nor does he assume that everything new is true or that everything ingenious is, by that very quality, proved; nor is he bent on "making things easier"; nor does he intend to impose his interpretation but rather to suggest it. His absorbing purpose is *to discover what the inspired author meant to say.*

With these considerations well in mind we are free to address ourselves to the crossing of the Red Sea:

> *The water was as a wall on their right and on*
> *their left.*   Exodus, xiv. 22. 29

Two high crystalline walls? Possibly. But does the inspired author mean this? It is very doubtful. True, our sentence is taken from the prose account and we do not intend to claim for it the privilege of the poetic form with which it is clothed in the Canticle of Moses (Exodus xv. 5) and in the Psalms (Ps. cxxxv. 15). But it is precisely the prose account that goes out out of its way to tell us that the miracle was worked by means of a "strong east [not 'burning'] wind blowing all night." This suggests no sudden arrest of water but rather a gradual, if rapid, process which does not hint at vertical walls of water. I doubt if the text as it stands gives us the right to deduce more than the recession and return of a tidal wave of some sort, not uncommon in sandy places. I have stood on the railway platform at Grange-over-Sands and watched such a wave advancing with the speed and depth sufficient to overwhelm an armed host.

But the text says "Wall." Am I sure? The Hebrew word used is *Chomah,* from the verb *chamah* meaning "to protect." It is often used to mean "wall," that is true, but sometimes it means no more than "protection." . . . The meaning of the inspired author, therefore, may well be this: the water prevented an outflanking movement by the Egyptian squadron and the speed, violence, depth of its return was enough to overtake, overpower, overwhelm it. In any case, the doubt is sufficient to prevent our identifying the pictures in our "Bible Histories" of long ago with the definitions of the Church. . . .

It all shows, doesn't it, the delicacy and danger of translation? Some have rushed to conclusions, for instance, about the phrase: "the brothers of the Lord" without stopping to ask whether the original Aramaic term (or the Greek, for that matter) cannot include more distant relations without cousins. You see, words catch disease so easily—I mean that we so often contaminate them with our own pet ideas. Since our childhood days the word "angel" has been accumulating fluff and feathers. This is just our way of picturing beauty and speed and, no doubt, is all to the good so long as we remember we are dealing in symbols. For more sophisticated minds it might be better to re-translate the word as "messenger," though even this suggests a bicycle and basket. At the expense of our intellect the imagination clamors for satisfaction where satisfaction is impossible. We are not content to know that an angel is a real but entirely spiritual, and therefore unimaginable, being. We are more interested in the form which he may temporarily have assumed. More often in the Bible angels take human form but not always. When the Lord sends an "angel" to destroy Sennacherib's force (4 Kings xix. 35), are we sure what shape this "messenger" takes? Probably that of a providential plague. (1951)

If we cannot find explanations of all things which require investigation in the Scriptures, let us not seek for a second god beyond the One who is, for that would be the height of impiety. We ought to leave such things to God who is after all our maker, and most justly to bear in mind that the Scriptures are perfect, being spoken by the Word of God and by his Spirit, while we, as lesser beings, and indeed as the least of all, in comparison with the Word of God and with his Spirit, in that proportion fall short of the understanding of God's mysteries.

ST. IRENAEUS (ca. 180)

RESOLVING APPARENT CONFLICTS WITH SCIENCE

THE REV. W. DEVIVIER, S.J.

HOLY Scripture is in no way a scientific book. Even when it touches upon phenomena, the proper subject of science, its end is not to solve problems of geology or astronomy, but to teach the truths of faith and to set forth the facts of religion. Thus when Moses relates the creation, he proposes to reveal and affirm the dogma and the fact of divine creation in regard to all categories of beings; to establish in this way the foundations of natural religion and the obligation of observing the Sabbath. His object is by no means to teach natural history, to formulate a theoretic and complete geogony, to describe scientifically the successive formations of the globe which we inhabit. Hence when we interpret Scripture it must be in this *doctrinal* and *religious* sense, and not for the purpose of seeking formulas to solve the disputed questions of scientists.

Nevertheless, though the intention of the Spirit of truth was not to teach profane science, yet He could not have inspired what is false even upon a subject foreign to dogma and morality, nor have permitted the Sacred Scripture to set forth anything of the kind. Scripture, therefore, cannot present as true things which science proves to be false.

But if the sacred writer is never deceived in regard to the precise object of his statement, there is nothing to prevent his using expressions, metaphors, figures scientifically inaccurate, strictly speaking, but conformable to the genius of the language in which he expresses himself, or to the habit of mind of the people whom he addresses. A few examples will explain our thought.

When Josue wrote that, owing to the miraculous lengthening of the day (due perhaps to a local and atmospheric modification), he was able to achieve the battle of Gabaon, he related a certain fact. But to state this fact, and to be understood by the people, he used a popular term which expressed very clearly what he wished understood: he said that the sun stood still. This is the language of appearances. In this respect, moreover, the example of Josue is still followed by the greatest scholars and even by the Bureau of Longitudes. Notwithstanding the progress of astronomy, we still say that the sun rises and sets; and we should make ourselves ridiculous if, adopting strictly astronomical language, we were to say, the earth sets, the earth will rise tomorrow. It matters little, moreover, whether Josue was or was not ignorant of the scientific truth of this fact. The illustrious astronomer Kepler, referring to these words of Josue, says: "The Scripture in teaching sublime truths makes use of ordinary locutions in order to be understood. It speaks of natural phenomena only incidentally, and in terms common and familiar to men. We astronomers, ourselves, while perfecting astronomical science do not perfect language; we say with the people, the planets stop, the planets return; the sun rises, the sun sets, it rises to the heavens; like the people we express what appears to pass before our eyes, though in reality it is not true. We have less reason to require that Holy Scripture abandon, in this respect, ordinary for scientific language which would perplex the simple faithful and fail to attain the sublime end it proposes." Another famous astronomer, Arago, speaks in the same terms.

Another example. Moses speaks of the sun and moon as two great luminaries destined to light the earth, and he insists less upon the innumerable multitude of stars. The reason of this is that he does not pretend to give an astronomical classification; he expresses himself according to popular ideas; he speaks of nature as the people apprehended it and according to the relative importance of the stars to inhabitants of the earth. Again, when he enumerates the various animals he is not anxious to give a complete scientific enumeration, he is satisfied to make it understood that all were created by God. . . .

The biblical affirmations in regard to facts concerning science, and for which the Church exacts respect, are *very few in number*. The reason is simple and follows from what we have just said: the Bible being a religious and not a scientific book, whenever it touches upon the phenomena of nature it is only to teach men whatever relates, in this matter, to their faith and conduct. By taking successively the principal objections formulated against the Mosaic narration, it would be an easy matter to show that these rare truths are in no way contradicted by the certain conclusions of modern sciences. . . .

In order that there be, on a point touching nature, any opposition between the Bible and science, the union of three conditions is necessary. 1st, the exact and natural meaning of the Scripture must be *absolutely certain,* either because this meaning is completely self-evident or because it is fixed by the infallible authority of the Church. 2nd, the affirmation of science must be *incontestable* and admitted by all judges of undisputed authority. 3rd, there must be, finally, *absolute incompatibility* between the certain sense of the Bible and the result obtained and perfectly demonstrated by science. Now, these three conditions have never been encountered together and never can be.

Apart from the small number of truths clearly affirmed by the authority of the Church, it is difficult to fix in a certain manner the *literal* sense of the Bible in these kinds of passages. We speak particularly of the narration of the creation made by Moses in the first chapters of Genesis, for it is here particularly that objections arise. It is well known that this exposition of the work of creation, of the formation of our

111

earth, has received on the part of the Fathers of the Church and of exegetes, the most varied, not to say the most opposite interpretations. Now it is a fundamental principle of hermeneutics that, in things left by God and by the Church to free discussion, each one must guard against giving his private interpretation as the absolute word of the Bible.

It is beyond all doubt that full certainty accompanies the interpretations of Scripture texts sustained by the unanimity—at least moral unanimity—of the Fathers and Doctors of the Church; provided, however, it is a doctrinal text, that is, contains doctrinal or moral teaching, and that the Fathers gave their interpretation as being that of the Church and imposing, consequently, faith upon the faithful: "In matters of faith and morals belonging to the edification of Christian Doctrine," says the Council of Trent and the Vatican. Then, and then only, are the Fathers and Doctors of the Church invested with higher authority, because in cases of this kind their teaching represents or manifests the authentic teaching of the universal Church, which in virtue of the promise of her divine Founder is infallible. Outside such cases we are in no way bound by the *scientific* ideas of the ancient Fathers. In their exegetical labors they accepted the sciences as they were apprehended in their time; we are as free to avail ourselves, in explaining the Scripture, of the progress which these sciences have made in our day. The condition which we have just specified cannot be verified relative to the Mosaic account of creation.   (1903)

All of them [i.e. scriptural senses] presuppose the literal sense as the foundation. As a building declining from the foundation is likely to fall, so the mystic interpretation, which deviates from the literal sense, must be reckoned as unbecoming and unsuitable. Those, therefore, who wish to make proficiency in the study of the Sacred Scriptures, must begin with the literal sense; especially because from it alone any argument can be brought to prove or declare what is doubtful.... It must be observed, likewise, that the literal sense has been much obscured by the method of exposition recommended and practiced by others who, though they may have said many things well, have yet touched on the literal but sparingly, and have so multiplied the mystical senses as nearly to intercept and choke it.

NICHOLAS DE LYRA, O.S.F. (ca. 1320)
112

SCRIPTURE AND THE LITURGY

E. I. WATKIN

THE liturgy—Mass and Divine Office—is largely (the Office mostly) prayer in words of Scripture, and both Mass and Office provide lessons from Scripture. The liturgical Gospels cover the greater part of the Fourth Gospel, and for a rough guess two-thirds of St. Matthew and a half of St. Luke. Only St. Mark is little read. All the major events of our Lord's life, most of His parables and miracles, a considerable selection from His shorter sayings are read at Mass. Of the Acts, only a few outstanding episodes are read at Mass. Matins, however, provides a larger selection, though chiefly from the first half of the book. The excerpts from St. Paul's Epistles are far too brief to present a continuous exposition of his thought. This, however, would be hardly suitable for the kind of Scriptural reading the liturgy has in view; but most of the passages which contain the heart of Pauline religion are found in the liturgy. This is true of the other Apostolic Epistles. The Apocalypse moves on two planes: the heavenly plane of bliss and adoration, of humanity united to God, and the lower earthly plane where man's rebellious will and proud self-deification produce their catastrophic results. Since the liturgy is first and foremost adoration, it is not surprising that the liturgical excerpts are concerned mainly, though not exclusively, with the higher plane of Divine Reality.

The staple, the substance, of the Divine Office is the Psalter. Its weekly recitation is most commonly broken by a feast, taking Proper and Sunday Psalms. Nevertheless the entire Psalter is recited many times every year, so that every Psalm becomes familiar to those who recite the Office, though rightly enough some Psalms are used much more frequently than others.

Since the Divine Office is essentially the Psalter it is the concentrated essence of the Old Testament. . . .

The Sapiential books provide lessons for Matins during August, the sublime picture of Wisdom read at Mass on our Lady's Birthday, and her Immaculate Conception, many Epistles for Commons of Saints, little chapters for feasts of our Lady and most of the Commons.

From the Song of Songs there are a number of beautiful antiphons for our Lady's feasts, Lessons at Mass for the Visitation and St. Mary

Magdalen and a lovely Gradual and Alleluia for Our Lady of Lourdes; and there are beautiful texts for Our Lady of Sorrows.

Of the Prophets, Isaias is most read. The book provides Matin lessons for Advent, prophecies on Holy Saturday and a considerable number of isolated texts, Introits, Antiphons. A canticle at Friday Lauds and a lesson at the Mass for Advent Ember Saturday gives us the bulk of chapter 45. Chapter 58 is read in two sections on the first Friday and Saturday in Lent, the prophecy of the Suffering Servant on Wednesday in Holy Week, another Servant passage for the birthday of St. John the Baptist, and the picture of the blood-stained warrior returning from Edom, at Mass on the Wednesday of Holy Week. The Epiphany Mass gives us the prophecy of the glory of the Church, the Christian Jerusalem, Ember Saturday in Advent, the prophecy of the wilderness watered and made fertile.

The other prophets are less adequately represented. Jeremias in particular is neglected. Lenten Masses, however, and a prophecy on Holy Saturday, give us some magnificent passages from Ezechiel. Joel's call for penitence and his prophecy for the outpouring of the Spirit are read respectively on Ash Wednesday and the Saturday after Pentecost, and on the Friday after Pentecost a third passage from his prophecy. Friday Lauds for fasting ferias give us Habacuc's Canticle with its picture of God's advent in awful majesty. Candlemas reads Malachias's prophecy of God's visit to his temple.

Lamentations provides the haunting melodies of sorrow which are the first nocturn lessons at Tenebrae; Job, Matin lessons in September and the lessons for the Office of the Dead. The historical books of the Old Testament, including the law, are least read in the liturgy, in part because first nocturn lessons from the Old Testament are suspended from the beginning of Lent until the Monday after Trinity Sunday.

From this summary account it should be clear that, although the liturgy is very far from giving us the Bible or even the greater part of it, it provides what I have termed the concentrated essence or spirit of Scripture. The man whose knowledge of Scripture is confined to the liturgical extracts could not claim to know his Bible. But he could claim to know the essential teaching and the religious truth of Scripture as understood by the Catholic Church well enough, indeed more than enough, to feed his mind and spirit with God's revelation.

We must however be clear what kind of Scriptural knowledge the liturgy conveys and is designed to convey. It is not scientific and historical exegesis. The liturgy does not attempt to inform us, as far as it is discoverable, what was the exact meaning of the human writer in

114

the actual context of his words. Especially, of course, where the New Testament is concerned, this exegetical meaning is often in fact given— but only inasmuch as it coincides with the distinctive meaning the liturgy has in view. And sometimes the exegetical meaning is remote from the liturgical; for example, when Psalms and passages from Job without any reference to a life of communion with God beyond the grave are applied by the Office of the Dead to the holy souls in Purgatory, or when the Psalmist prays for victory over Edom or the Philistines, blesses those who dash Babylonian babies to pieces. Not even is the liturgical meaning the abstract, conceptual and reasoned understanding of Scripture by a scientific, dogmatic theology. The liturgical understanding of Scripture, I need hardly say, *is* theological, thoroughly theological, profoundly theological. But its theology is a concrete intuition of truth, a vital assimilation of truth at a deeper psychological level than abstract conceptual ratiocination. . . .

This use of Scripture is *praying* the Bible. That is what the liturgy does with the Bible; it prays it. The liturgical worshipper prays the Bible, directly when he prays in the words of Scripture, indirectly when he reads or hears a lesson in the same attitude of prayer. He thus combines Bible reading and prayer—as a milk diet combines eating and drinking. He who thus prays the Bible with the liturgy penetrates the letter of the Scripture to its inner spirit to find there Christ, our Lady, the Communion of Saints, the Holy Souls—or again the particular mystery the liturgy on a particular day commemorates; and in and beyond all these the Godhead that can be loved but not conceived. This penetration, however, . . . does not take the shape of the elaborate allegories so dear to the primitive fathers, though the Epistles read on the First Sunday in Lent and Septuagesima are rare examples of this detailed allegorizing. It is effected rather by direct intuition— flashes of illumination which see in and through the text in question a significance more profound or at any rate of wider application than its literal and contextual meaning.

The soul which in and with the liturgy is thus praying the Scripture text makes personal, living contact with the spiritual and personal reality of which it is made aware. When the worshipper, for example, prays or prayerfully hears texts applied by the liturgy to our Lady, to saints or to holy souls, he makes contact with our Lady as she is presented by the text he is praying or hearing, with the saints or with the souls in Purgatory. In the same way he makes vital contact with the mysteries of the Incarnation, not simply as events of past history which he commemorates, but as permanent realities, as real today as when they

115

first happened, sources, ever active, of spiritual power and light, continued, moreover, in all the members of the Total Christ, and therefore in himself. In all these contacts, he makes contact with God thus revealed and incarnate, yet transcending any possible revelation or incarnation. This is to pray Scripture, when the liturgy prays it and as the liturgy prays it; to know it with a concrete, vital, personal knowledge, as the liturgy knows it. For Scripture is the communication of a personal God and as a personal Christ, in and through the Church of persons to the person who studies it, as it is best studied, as the liturgy studies it, by praying it. The liturgical use of Scripture, in short, is in Jean Vilnet's pregnant language *la Bible experimentée*—"the Bible experienced." The Bible experienced is God experienced in all the length and breadth and height and depth of His revelation and communication to man. This experience is imparted to everyone who makes this liturgical use of Scripture his own liturgical prayer, as he progressively enters into that prayer and makes it his own. Scripture, thus prayed, is a dialogue between the spirit of the worshipper and the Spirit who inspired Scripture and who, as the soul of the Church, through her liturgy, unveils its profound, spiritual and liturgical sense.

This deep and manifold significance of Scripture is displayed chiefly by the liturgical selection of texts, such as the Introits which strike the note of the Proper at the Mass, or the Antiphons which are the indicators pointing out the special reference of a Psalm or Canticle, as used on that particular occasion. When Psalm 129, for example, is used at Wednesday's Vespers, its antiphon, the first verse "Out of the depths I have cried to thee, O Lord," tells us that the Psalm is man's cry to God from the depths of his sin, folly, ignorance and weakness. When it is a Psalm for the second Vespers of Christmas and throughout its Octave, the Antiphon "With the Lord there is mercy and plentiful redemption" shows that we are to think of God's answer to that cry, the redeeming Incarnation. When it is a Psalm of Vespers for the Dead, the Antiphon "If thou shouldst search out our sins, O Lord, Lord who shall endure it" indicates that the Psalm is placed on the lips of the Holy Souls agonizing beneath God's searching purification of the least trace of sinful or even imperfect disposition, eradicating the root of sin, the affirmation of self. How rich the wealth of meaning in the Psalm that emerges from this threefold understanding of it!

The same Psalms, lessons or texts may and should be said and prayed from several points of view, each of which supports and enriches what is visible, what is true from another. It may be prayed as the individual prayer of the worshipper, as the prayer of Christ, of the total Christ—

116

the Church—of our Lady or the particular saint whose feast is kept, also in the Office of the Dead as the prayer of the Holy Souls. Or again, a Scriptural text may be understood on different levels, at each of which the principle it enunciates is true, the lower level reflecting the same truth as it is on a higher. For example, the history of Israel with its temporal, its national successes and failures reflects the history of the Church, her spiritual triumphs and defeats. The agricultural fertility for which Psalms 64 and 143 pray—and for which we can and should pray—reflect the spiritual harvest of souls which is the fertility of the Church's agriculture, a harvest which, when the Psalm is used in the Office of the Dead, is the harvest reaped when souls from Purgatory are gathered into heaven. Moreover, the individual and the social understanding of a Psalm or other suitable text may be, as it were, conflated, understood and prayed together.

One text, moreover, in the liturgical use of it, throws light on another text, reinforces it, brings it into a new context of meaning, so that the Scripture read in the liturgy and as so read acquires a compactness, a universal corroboration and harmony; in short, a unity which is indeed present in the Bible as God's unique revelation, but which is liable to be concealed there by the sheer amount of superficial diversity.

Of this close-woven harmony of texts, Pater wrote enthusiastically in *Gaston de Latour,* "All these various offices which in Pontifical, Missal and Breviary devout imagination had elaborated from age to age with such a range of spiritual color and light and shade, with so much poetic tact in quotation, such a depth of insight into the Christian soul had joined themselves harmoniously together."

Two features of the liturgical use of Scripture have contributed most to this contemplative penetration of Scripture, to the mutual indication and harmony of different insights, views of truth from different but complementary points of view. One of these is the frequent employment of isolated *texts;* the other is *repetition* of the same text or passage. The Protestants' love of texts is perfectly Catholic, though their methods of showing it are not always attractive. For the Liturgy is, to a great extent, a Liturgy of texts: Introit, Gradual, Tract, Alleluia, Offertory, Communion, Antiphon, Little Chapter, Response—all these when Scriptural, as they most often are, are isolated texts, on which the Liturgy dwells lovingly, and when fully carried out with the aid of music. As we have seen, these texts often indicate the particular sense of a Psalm the Church has in view. But more generally they isolate from their biblical context particular words of Scripture, place them in the light of their liturgical context and so expose them to the gaze of

117

the liturgical worshipper who prays them. Brooding in this intensive contemplation upon the text, the Liturgy, and the worshipper in so far as he enters into his liturgical prayer, penetrates depths of meaning, evokes resonances, catches sight of relations which render the text an entrance, from a particular approach, into the spiritual and theological storehouse of Catholic truth, nay more, a point of contact with the Divine Personal Truth who is the substance of all religious and therefore af all Scriptural truth.

(1954)

CATHOLIC VENERATION
OF THE BIBLE

THE MOST REV. JOHN J. WRIGHT

CATHOLICS should find in the reading and love of the Sacred Scriptures a source of spiritual refreshment second only to that which is theirs in the Blessed Sacrament Itself. Not a few of our saints or writers on Christian perfection have drawn a parallel between the Incarnate Word of God wonderfully present in the Sacrament of the Altar and the Inspired Word of God given us in the Holy Bible.

Such writers have found it fitting that our forefathers in the early Church should have kept, as they did, both the Eucharist and the Gospels in special tabernacles. To this day the liturgy of the Church reveals the Catholic understanding of the uniquely sacred character of the Bible. The Gospel Book is incensed in Solemn Mass, even as is the Sacred Cross, Tree of our Salvation, and the Adorable Host which hides the very Presence of the Son of God. No other book is incensed because no other book could be of comparable sanctity.

In the Mass there is another striking parallel between the way in which God comes to us through the Word of Scripture and the way in which He comes through the Word made Flesh. The first part of the Mass, the Mass of the catechumens, centers about the Sacred Scripture. It is composed almost entirely of Biblical texts; the Psalm at the foot of the altar, the Versicles and Responses after the Confiteor, the Introit, many phrases of the Gloria, the Epistle, the Gradual and finally the Gospel; all these are straight from Scripture.

When the Mass is solemnly sung, the Gospel is borne in devout procession before it is chanted; it is surrounded with burning tapers and its pages are venerated with a reverential kiss. Thus the rubrics surrounding the use of the Scriptures in the liturgy are not unlike those by which we pay homage to the Sacrament.

In the later parts of the Mass Christ is really present in our midst, but in these opening stages of the divine liturgy He is also somehow present in the Scripture phrases which foretell His coming or proclaim His words and works. And when finally the marvel of the Consecration brings Jesus as truly to our altars as ever the consent of Mary brought Him to Her bosom or the rejoicing throngs led Him to Jerusalem, the words of the Mass become strongly Scriptural in their tone and message. Where could the Church have found accents more worthy to welcome the Word made Flesh than in the written pages of the Inspired Word which is Scripture? . . .

The Bible is so rich a source of spiritual refreshment because Christ, the source of all grace, is found in its every chapter. The Old Testament is the record of humanity's longing for Him and of Israel's vocation to produce Him; the New Testament is the account of His coming and of the first beginnings of the Church's mandate to spread His Kingdom. Jesus is somehow present in every verse of Sacred Scripture. . . .

There is no place in Scripture from Adam below the eastern wall of Paradise to John in ecstasy on Patmos, from which is absent the echo of that prayer: "Come, Lord Jesus!"

To those, then, who read the Bible as the Church offers and understands its inspired pages, there is given that wisdom which comes from God and which is God, the wisdom which is the Word of God. To them Christ Himself becomes a familiar friend, their Redeemer and intimate Guide to God. How pale and lifeless, as contrasted with the living truth of the Gospel story, are those recent romantic fantasies which seek to tell the life of Jesus in fictional form!

It is when we think of the Bible in terms of Christ that we best understand what it is and what it is not. Back in the days when some students, exuberant in their new-found and heady knowledge, used to speak of the conflict between Reason and Scripture, the devout were frequently scandalized because they could not reconcile Genesis and the popular science of the Sunday supplements or the sophisticated lecture halls. Then wise men pointed out to them that the Bible was not written to teach us how the Heavens go, but to teach us how to go to Heaven.

The preoccupations of the moment are more often with economics than with evolution; they are political and sociological rather than concerned with material sciences as they were a generation or two ago.

However, a like warning against misunderstanding of the nature, purpose and use of the Sacred Scriptures is sometimes needed. The Bible was not written to teach us how to grow rich, nor to provide technical advice on how to administer secular affairs. The Scriptures were given us to teach the rich moderation, responsibility and mercy—to tell them how they might pass through the needle's eye which is the Gate of Heaven despite the encumbrances of their possessions. The Bible was written to give the poor hope and patient wisdom; to teach princes God-fearing righteousness and people noble virtue.

The Bible is not a scientific treatise on economics, a book of quotations for the convenience of propagandists or a political textbook for diplomats. It is a guidebook to the spiritual perfection of persons, which, when we have it, contributes mightily to the right order of earthly society but which is primarily a matter of eternal and supernatural considerations rather than of technical questions of a temporal kind. . . .

Catholics love the Bible because it is the history of all their spiritual kinsmen, all who are pilgrims and strangers on the face of the earth, seekers after God, from the beginning of time until time shall be no more. They love the Bible because it is a promise and a prophecy, a constant reminder that the walls of this world are destined to dissolve and that our true fatherland, the Promised Land of our souls, will assuredly be ours if we walk in the ways of our fathers and follow in the footsteps of Jesus.

Catholics love the Bible because it is the Word of God, lifegiving and availing to salvation. They love it because it tells us of Christ and there is no one of us, however imperfect and even base his other loves, who does not live out his days eager to be found with Christ at the end, to die worthy of Christ's love and returning it in some measure.

For Catholics, in a word, as Christ is the King of kings and Lord of lords, so the Bible is the Book of books.   (1952)

TWO

The Old Testament

Thy word is a lamp to my feet, and a light to my paths.

PSALMS, 118:105

IMPRESSIONS UPON READING
THE OLD TESTAMENT

DOM BEDE GRIFFITHS, O.S.B.

I BEGAN to read the Bible. We had each of us obtained an old Black Letter edition of the Authorized Version of the Bible. We began to read them first of all for their literary interest, as part of that great tradition of seventeenth century prose to which we were all alike attached. It soon became part of our regular routine to sit down every day before breakfast round the table with our Bibles spread out before us, while the porridge was cooking on the fire and the candles in winter shed their mellow light on the crockery. I used to read a chapter of the Old Testament and a chapter of the New Testament in this way every day, and in the course of the next year or two I must have read the Bible through two or three times. It now became part of the habitual background of my life; but it very soon ceased to be of merely literary interest.

The life which we were living in this lonely village among the hills, spending much of our time under the open sky and watching the changes of the seasons and the routine life on the farms around, gave to the stories of the Bible an intimate reality. . . . The background of the Old Testament was the background of our own lives, and its people and their story were not a remote past but a living present.

Even as literature it seemed to me greater than anything I had ever read. The stories had all the poetic quality of the *Iliad* and the *Odyssey* and at the same time the vivid historical sense of Herodotus or Thucydides. When I compared this Hebrew literature as a whole with Greek literature as I had known it, I could not but think it was greatly superior. I felt this particularly in regard to the Book of Job. Here was a poem, a poetic drama, a tragedy which could be compared with the work of Aeschylus or Sophocles or Shakespeare. . . . The significance

123

of Job was not to be found in the happy ending which terminated the tragedy, but in the last words of Job: "I had heard of thee by the hearing of the ear; but now mine eye seeth thee, wherefore I abhor myself and repent in dust and ashes." Job had experienced the reality of the divine presence not only in its power to wound but in its utter transcendence, and in the face of this he himself and all his sufferings seemed to count as nothing. Here I seemed to be touching the very heart of the revelation of the Old Testament. It was not a rational explanation of the nature of God in the manner of Spinoza; it was the record of an experience, of a meeting with God, the supreme reality, which had changed men's lives. When God spoke to Abraham, when Moses met him in the Burning Bush, when Samuel heard him calling, these were events of vital significance which determined the lives of men and peoples. They were experiences of the soul which gave a new meaning to existence; that was why they had such a poetic character....

In the Old Testament the reality behind nature and behind the conflicts of human life had been encountered at a level of significance beyond anything that I had known before. These encounters were an experience of the soul in its inmost depths, an experience not of the mind alone but of the mind and will, the imagination and the senses. They issued therefore not in scientific formulae or in philosophical concepts, but in poetry, in dramatic representation, in a living history. It was history because it was the living encounter of men with reality, which changed their lives and shaped the course of affairs; but it was also poetry because it was an experience of the soul penetrating beneath the surface of life and encountering the hidden power which directs and controls it. And this power revealed itself not merely as the Beauty, which underlies all the forms of nature; not merely as the Truth which philosophy discerns beneath the appearance of things; but as a moral power, a power of Good, which made inexorable demands on men and could only be conceived as a living person. Whatever judgment one might eventually pass on this conception, its poetic power could not be denied. It had the reality of authentic experience and had to be reckoned with in any attempt to face the problem of life.

The message of the Hebrew prophets came to me with the force of a revelation: I saw in it a judgment on our own civilization more profound than I had ever envisaged. Our civilization was not merely an offense against beauty and truth, against that rational order of life upon which human culture is based. It was an offense against the moral order of the universe. I saw in the great civilizations of Babylonia and Egypt, of the Greek and the Roman Empires, the exact counterpart of our own civilization. . . . The vision of the prophet looked into the hearts of nations; he discovered the inner meaning of history, the principles which govern the destiny of nations. The source of evil was to be found in the human mind rising up against God and seeking to build up its civilization without reference to God, the supreme arbiter of destiny, whose will was the ultimate source of all human happiness. The error of modern civilization could now be seen to lie not merely in the divorce of the scientific mind from the imagination and the sources of creative life; but in its revolt against the moral order of the universe, in its deliberate rejection of the authority of God. It was but one more instance in the long tale of man's pride and rebellion against God. . . .

The Hebrew prophet had learned that behind the whole movement of history, as behind every human life, there is to be found not merely an abstract moral law, but a personal will, which man encounters when he enters into the depths of his being and upon which the well-being of men and of nations depends.

It would be difficult to say how long it was before this message penetrated into my mind. In a sense, no doubt, it was the work of years, but already, I think, it had taken root. (1954)

THE LESSON OF THE OLD TESTAMENT

ST. AUGUSTINE

TAKE up that Testament which is called the Old Testament, and learn its lesson. The law of God was promulgated then also. Read it, or listen to it when it is read to you, and consider what its promises were. In it an earth was promised to the earth, an earthly country flowing with milk and honey, but still an earth. If, however, we understand it in a spiritual sense, then that earth did not run with milk and honey; the land which *will* flow with milk and honey is something quite different; it is that land of which the Psalmist says, *Thou art my hope, my portion in the land of the living.* Do you seek for milk and honey? *Taste and see how sweet the Lord is.* His grace is signified by the milk and honey; it is sweet and nourishing. But this grace, which is typified in the Old Testament, is revealed in the New.

In short, on account of those who are worldly-wise and seek material rewards from God, and choose to serve Him for the sake of those things which were then promised, that law deserved to be characterized by the Apostle St. Paul as *Engendering unto bondage*. And why? Because the Jews interpreted it in a material sense, for in its spiritual meaning it is the Gospel. It engenders them unto bondage. What men? Those who serve God for temporal goods, who return thanks when they have them, and blaspheme when they have them not. Such worship of God is not that of a true heart. For they look at those who do not serve our God, and see that they have those things for which they themselves are serving Him, and they say in their heart, "How does the service of God profit me? Have I as much as that man, who blasphemes every day of his life?" One man says his prayers and starves, another blasphemes and feasts. He who takes account of these things is human indeed, a man of the Old Testament. But he who serves God in the New has to look for a new inheritance, go farther than the earth, soar higher than the mountain tops, that is, despise the heights of the proud. But in doing this be humble, lest you fall from your high place.

(ca. 419)

"PARTIAL AND INCREASING REVELATION"

THE REV. GERARD ROONEY, C.P.

THE Old Testament should be read for what it was: partial and gradually increasing revelation. We should not look for a definitive statement of man's destiny in the Old. What is there is true, in the way it was meant to be true. But it is not complete. Job should not be read as we would the epistles of Paul or the Gospel of St. John. Proverbs should not be read in the same way that we would read the Sermon on the Mount. The New perfects, brings to fruition the Old. . . .

The *moral law* of the Old Testament is not contradicted by the New. It was indeed inferior to the New. The sanctions arising from the perspective of eternal life were neglected while emphasis was placed on earthly sanctions. Legal purity was stressed more than purity of heart and mind. The minutiae of ritualistic prescriptions gave occasion to mere formalism. The *lex talionis* (an eye for an eye and a tooth for a tooth) is considerably removed from the Sermon on the Mount. There is no doubt but that the Law of Sinai is inferior to that of the Gospel.

But inferiority does not mean immorality or contradiction of what is good and true. The laws in themselves were well adapted to the primitive people for whom they were made. Until Christ redeemed us on the cross, no one could enter into heaven and see the blessed vision of God. The mode of after-existence was left indeterminate in the minds of the Jews, awaiting the full revelation of man's glory and resurrection with the coming of Christ. The sanctions proposed were well calculated to exact obedience and procure justice among the people for whom they were given. As a matter of fact, without the great example of Calvary and the abundance of grace poured out through the Holy Spirit into our hearts, the Sermon on the Mount would have sounded strange on Mount Sinai. The stress on legal purity was adapted to their mentality to impress them with a lofty idea of God's holiness and the necessity for personal righteousness. If formalism crept in, that was an abuse of what was good in itself. The *lex talionis* in pre-Gospel days and in times when the order of society was more dependent on the vigilance of individuals, was in good order. And, compared with its own contemporary social legislation (which is the proper way to evaluate the Mosaic legislation) its moral pre-eminence and grandeur stands out clearly. The niceties of justice, the high ideal of family life and sex relations, of kindness and charity, all stamp it as savoring of divine watchfulness. And yet, its manifest crudities were an acknowledgment of the imperfection and crudity of those for whom it was given. Hence our Lord remarked concerning divorce: "Moses, by reason of the hardness of your hearts, permitted you to put away your wives. But from the beginning it was not so." And yet, generous souls, who wished to love God and their neighbor, could find in the Law a magnificent ideal of godliness. (Cf. Ps. 118. The songs of the psalmists show the fervent heart of Israel at its best.)

It is well to remember, too, regarding Old Testament history, that everything that is related by the sacred author is not thereby *approved by him*. Old Testament history is candid, it deals realistically with human history, and it always had the grand advantage of being written *from God's viewpoint*. Good is good, and evil is evil. Job is rebuked by God for his intemperate language. The Patriarchs are not faultless, and royal politics are often damnable. . . .

The limitations and imperfections of the Old (which were given *for a time*) are far removed from *contradiction of the New*. For, what was imperfect in the Old was made perfect in the New.

Ceremonial law in the Old is not a contradiction of the ritualistic practice under the New Law. The ceremonial ritual of the Old was indeed in keeping with the people for whom it was given. Many customs of worship resembled that of surrounding nations (but were infused with quite a different spirit.) This should be expected, for God deals kindly with people according to their nature. And the Jewish people for whom they were given were a primitive people, at least at the time of Moses and for many centuries thereafter. They were given for a time, and when our Lord appeared and established the New Law they were abrogated, as they gave way to their fulfillment in Christ.

The Old Law reached its fulfillment in the New. Its purpose was served. Imperfection gave way to perfection. Hence, our Lord told the Jews: "Do not think that I am come to destroy the Law or the prophets. I am come not to destroy, but to fulfill." He fulfilled the dogmatic teaching of the prophets by bringing to actuality that which they had in prophetic and often poetic language foretold about the Messias and His work.   (1949)

THE OLD TESTAMENT COMPARED
WITH OTHER ANCIENT WRITINGS

DANIEL-ROPS

IT IS beyond question today that the books in which the Bible describes to us the remote origins of man are drawn from a common source from which many Mesopotamian traditions are also drawn. These resemblances serve to eliminate the mythological theory formerly in favor. The time is past when rationalist criticisms claim to have explained the mystery of Genesis by invoking a solar myth and the faculty for inventing fables with which primitive races are gifted.

We see no reason why the fact that Genesis is the Hebrew expression of a tradition conserved in Mesopotamia should lessen its value. If the facts are true, why should they not have been known before the descendants of Abraham had the idea of giving them form as a

128

narrative? In fact, it is satisfying and reassuring to suppose that in ancient Sumeria they were already speaking of the triumph of Light over Chaos, and that, as the Babylonian priest Berossus recorded three centuries before our era, they explained the creation of man by saying that the blood of a god had animated a body of clay. But two further questions arise: what was the origin of this common source? and what was the original contribution of Israel?

The Bible has, undoubtedly, drawn upon elements anterior to the arrival and customs in Mesopotamia. In the same way as the laws and customs followed by Abraham and the men of the patriarchal period, closely resembling the laws and customs codified by Hammurabi, bear the Sumerian imprint, their religious traditions are strongly marked with pre-Semitic elements. The Bible was to be, through the Book of Genesis, the Hebrew chapter of the great body of cuneiform literature.

What is the source of that cuneiform basis itself? Here human knowledge can do no more than indicate the presence of an uncharted region, in which as yet only a few very tentative explorations have been made. Some authorities believe that we must look for its distant origin beyond Iran to a region between the Caucasus, Russian Turkestan and Central Asia, where originated hieroglyphic writing, to which Sumerian writing is related. This common source would not be an absolute point of origin, but already the product of a long process of human thought. Similarly, as our knowledge of the origins of the Aryan race increases, the more it seems that there is a rich past, a language already perfected for several thousands of years, whose origin was likewise perhaps in that same region of Central Asia, the veritable fountain-head of races. Sir Flinders Petrie, the celebrated English archaeologist, has even based a curious deduction upon this supposition. In the Egyptian *Book of the Dead* it is said that the sun rises over the mountains of Baku and sets behind Tamanu. Now Baku and the peninsula of Taman are the two extremities of the Caucasus. Is it possible that those lakes of fire described in the *Book of the Dead* are the sheets of petrol of the Caspian? (It is to be noted that Mount Ararat, where Noah's ark came to land, is in the same region.)

If we take the statements of Genesis literally, not only the common origin of the human race but also the geographical course of its dispersion is clearly indicated. The race of Shem went towards the south, that of Ham, south-west, and that of Japhet, westwards; that is, the first towards Arabia, the second towards Syria, Egypt and

Africa (the Hebrews were later to call Egypt the "land of Misraim," a son of Ham), and the third towards Europe. All races can therefore claim a part in these traditions of their origin, since they date from before the dispersion. And the coincidences which anti-religious critics have used as a weapon seem rather to be proofs of their veracity. But the implications of these coincidences should not be exaggerated. As yet no single account as complete and coherent as that given in the Bible has been found. We have shown that, for many points (the creation of Adam and Eve, for example), no other is known to exist. And above all, anyone who reads without prejudice the story of Genesis side by side with the cuneiform documents, interesting as these are, will see clearly that there is a great gulf between them.

The originality of the biblical cosmogony lies, in the first place, in its rigid monotheism. In the account of the Deluge, for example, the Mesopotamian text is polytheist, full of gods whose intervention hastened the cataclysm, or who lamented it, feeling themselves also threatened; whereas Genesis attributes everything to the One God. It is the same in every case. The Babylonian cosmogonists attribute different roles to Enlil, Marduk, to the moon-god, to any number of powers; in the Bible, the "Spirit of God" is alone responsible. It is as though the descendants of the Patriarchs in borrowing the elements of the narrative from ancient sources (Sumerian or Asiatic?) had purged them of their idolatry and restored the single God. This confirms all that the story of Abraham tells us of his mission, as he received it and as his people were to preserve it after him.

A second element of originality is of equal importance. This cosmogony is already a matter of history. From the first, the image of the seven days of the Creation, in showing the divine task as being accomplished in stages, suggests that the world has in its distant beginnings a principle of progress, an advance towards the future, a destiny to fulfill. Other accounts of the beginning, that of the Greeks, for example, give the impression that human society has remained fixed in a state of regret for the Golden Age. Genesis holds the promise of a future; its necessary fulfilment is the vocation of the sons of Shem, the special task assigned to them by God.

And that cosmogony itself holds but a tiny place in the great whole. Here is yet another element of originality, one that characterizes the whole Bible, which is a history, the most ancient of histories, the story of human events; man is the essential thing. The relevance of the psychology herein revealed has a meaning that is not so much theological and metaphysical as moral and mystical; the Bible is a book whose scale is that of man. It is not in nature, in appearances, that Israel was to seek for God, but in the human person, to the point of revealing the perfect image, the Son of Man, the Son of God. (1949)

THE HEBREW HISTORIANS

THE REV. E. POWERS, S.J.

THE ordinary reader cannot fail to be deeply impressed by the obvious sincerity of the Hebrew historians. This impression is mainly produced by two remarkable characteristics. The first is their special view of the function of history, which is quite different from that of the modern scientific historian. They see and trace in the facts of history the manifestations of an all-ruling Providence, rewarding good and punishing evil and directing all things according to a divine plan. The moderns, on the other hand, leave Providence aside and only seek to discover the natural causes of events. There is, of course, no conflict between these two different points of view, since each refers to a different order of causality and the Primary Cause concurs harmoniously with the secondary causes in producing the resultant effects. But the Hebrew view of history excludes all deliberate distortion of the facts, since such a mode of procedure would deprive it of its essential foundation and undermine its religious teaching. One might disagree with their interpretation of the facts in some cases, if one had not in the doctrine of inerrancy another and a higher motive for assenting to it, but one could scarcely believe that they knowingly substituted fiction for fact.

The second important characteristic is their truly remarkable impartiality. They know that their people is the chosen people of God, charged with a special mission in the execution of the divine plan, and yet they narrate at length without dissumulation the various instances of their idolatry and moral obliquity, of their backsliding and ingratitude. The sins and scandals of national heroes like David and Solomon are frankly described. Jehu's ferocity and bloodthirstiness and Jepthe's moral and religious deficiencies show us these two deliverers not as idealized figures, but, as they really were, very imperfect human instruments of Yahweh. The error of the prophet Nathan in approving David's plan of building the temple is openly avowed, nor is there any concealment of the very human discouragement of Elias. This characteristic is a natural consequence of the elevated Hebrew concept of history. Alleged instances of partiality can be shown to be only apparent when the special purpose of the sacred writer is considered. Thus the Chronicler's silence about the sins of David and Solomon is explained by the fact that his main interest was in the religious institutions of the kingdom of Judah on which they had no bearing. (1953)

BIBLE'S ACCOUNT OF PRIMITIVE RELIGION UPHELD

THE REV. PAUL HEINISCH

PRIMITIVE religion as contained in the Bible as well as the religious consciousness of Israel regarded the knowledge of one God and the obligation to worship Him, to obey Him and to lead a moral life as an inheritance stemming from most ancient times. . . . If Israel's religion rested upon revelation, we cannot but conclude that Israel's religious leaders had a true conception of primitive religion and did not paint a false picture; for this matter concerns the education of the people on most vital religious truths. No one who regards the Old Testament as the anteroom to the New and the prophets as Christ's heralds can disregard the religious content of Biblical primitive history.

On the basis of material gathered by profane science no convincing proof can be advanced to show that the picture drawn in the Bible of primitive religion corresponds to reality on all points, but science does make it probable. . . . Concerning religion, archaeology gives us little information apart from the fact that primitive men believed in a continuation of life after death. Nor is ethnology able to bolster claims regarding primitive monotheism. . . .

By reason primitive men were able to arrive at the knowledge of a being superior to themselves, a being who created and conferred those things necessary for life. They drew the self-evident conclusion that such a being must be honored by prayer and sacrifice. For this no special revelation would have been necessary. But facts show that most men when left to themselves do not arrive at the knowledge of one God or become very clear upon matters of a religious nature. God aided the people of Israel in a most extraordinary manner by revealing Himself to the patriarchs and to Moses, and later by repeatedly raising up prophets. Should he not also have taught men religion in primitive times? Primitive people say He did, and thereby confirm what the Bible tells about God's relationship to men at the dawn of the human race. (1950)

THE SEPTUAGINT

DR. MICHAEL SEISENBERGER*

AT THE time of Christ and His Apostles the Holy Scriptures were mostly read in a Greek translation made in Egypt for the use of the Jews there. Outside Palestine, and to some extent in Palestine itself, the Jews used this version when they read the Scriptures in the synagogues on the Sabbath. From many quotations in the New Testament it is clear that the Apostles were more familiar with this translation than with the Hebrew text, which did not contain all the sacred books; and, when they converted pagans to Christianity, they gave this version to their converts. Testimony to the respect paid this translation, and to its universal use, is borne by Josephus Flavius (who always used it himself in his writings), and by Justin Martyr, who, in his conversation with the Jew Tryphon, shows that among the Jews this translation was still accepted in the second century, when he lived.

The name Septuagint (LXX) is due to an old story preserved by Josephus Flavius (*Antiq.* XII), and by the ecclesiastical historian Eusebius. It originated in a letter written by Aristeas, an official at the Egyptian court, to his brother Philocrates, in which Aristeas says that Demetrius Phalereus, chief librarian at the royal library at Alexandria, advised his master, King Ptolemy Philadephus, to add the Jewish law to the treasures in his library. The king was pleased with the advice, and in order to procure the book of the law, he set 200,-

* From *The Practical Handbook for the Study of the Bible* by Michael Seisenberger. Copyright, 1911, 1939, by Joseph F. Wagner, Inc.

000 Jews at liberty, and then sent some men, among whom was Aristeas himself, with costly presents to Jerusalem, in order to fetch the book from the high priest. The latter not only gave the book to the envoys, but sent seventy-two learned Jews to Egypt to translate the Thora. They were received honorably in Egypt, and sent with Demetrius Phalereus to the neighboring island of Pharos, where they worked at their translation undisturbed. According to the story, each man was shut up alone in a cell, and made a translation by himself, but when all the results were compared, they were found to be exactly the same.

In ancient times this story was universally regarded as true, but it cannot be correct in every detail, for it contains fabulous additions. The truth probably is that the translation was made by Jews in Alexandria, and supplied an existing need, as the Egyptian Jews mostly did not understand Hebrew. An Egyptian king, probably not Ptolemy Philadelphus (285-247), who banished Demetrius Phalereus soon after his accession, but, according to Clement of Alexandria, his father, Ptolemy Lagi, (323-285), admitted the Greek version of the Jewish law into his library. This occurrence, flattering to the Jews, has been connected with the production of the translation. Possibly the fact that the sacred writings had been rendered into a heathen language displeased some Jews, and a story was invented to calm their indignation.

In any case the report about the translation of the LXX applies only to the Pentateuch. The other sacred books were gradually translated into Greek, in Egypt, and therefore the same name of the LXX was given to them also.

The date of the beginning of the translation may be given as about 300 B.C. Probably it was prior to 286, i.e. to the establishment of the library at Alexandria, for there were many Jews in Egypt ever since the time of Alexander the Great. By 200 B.C. the translation must have been nearly completed, as the translator of Ecclesiasticus knew a Greek text "of the Law and the Prophets and the other books" and mentions it frequently in his prologue.

It is, on the whole, a faithful and often almost slavishly literal [translation]. The Alexandrians frequently translated Hebrew text word for word.   (1911)

DIFFICULTY OF OLD TESTAMENT TRANSLATION

THE REV. FRANCIS P. LEBUFFE, S.J.

MOST of the books of the Old Testament were written in Hebrew. This was the spoken language of the Jews up to the time of the Babylonian Captivity (B.C. 587-539 B.C.). Subsequent to that time it ceased to be a spoken language and was used only as a written or literary language. We say "most" of the books of the Old Testament were written in Hebrew because, e.g. among others, Wisdom and Machabees were written in Greek and some parts of some books were written in Aramaic.

This original Hebrew was written with no space between words and with consonants only and the vowelizing was handed down from mouth to mouth, from generation to generation. This was a difficult task. Suppose, for instance, we wrote in this fashion an English sentence with the consonants only:

<blockquote>
HWSYRFTHR

This might be read

He was your father

or

How is your father?

or

He was your fit (or fat) hero.
</blockquote>

This mouth-to-ear transmission was rendered most precarious when the Jews were definitely scattered out of the Holy Land throughout the world after 70 A.D. Hence, the Massoretes ("Traditionalists"), in the period from the fifth to seventh centuries *after* Christ, determined to "fix" this pronunciation by introducing vowel-signs. In order not to disturb the actual letter-text of the Bible (which letter-text was regarded as peculiarly sacred) they invented dots and symbols—called "points"—which were inserted above, below and within letters.

Prior to this, in order to secure a uniform text the Jewish Council of Jamnia revised the whole Hebrew Bible, and ruled that all other versions of its text should be destroyed.

Prior to the "fixing" of the Hebrew text, the Old Testament had been translated into Greek, the so-called Septuagint (LXX) version being the most famous. Because some of this translation had been done some seven hundred years before the Massoretic "pointing," it often represents a more accurate transcript of the original and is thus superior in places to the Hebrew text. The reason for this is readily seen when one realizes that the Massoretic "pointed" text has suffered a seven-hundred-year oral transmission beyond the Hebrew text used by the Septuagint translators. (1946)

THE CAUSE OF OLD TESTAMENT "DIFFICULTIES"

THE REV. H. J. T. JOHNSON

MANY, perhaps most, Old Testament "difficulties" arise from failure to understand the modes of expression which were current when the Old Testament was written. This is particularly the case when we fail to make allowance for the Semitic love of figurative language. Our own use of it is comparatively restricted and so, interpreting the Bible by modern literary canons, we easily attribute to the sacred writers meanings which they never intended to convey. The Israelite and Jewish methods of recording genealogies differed from our own. Legal parentage figured in them; generations were omitted and families, tribes and nations were personified, appearing in them as though they were individuals. This last point is of special importance in connection with the understanding of the earlier portions of biblical history, though instances of such personification are not confined to them. In the ancient East the individual had not the importance which he has for us and his personality became merged in that of his family or tribe, whose name would cover his own. Thus we find the people of Israel spoken of as "Jacob" and the royal house of Juda as "David." But the whole question of eponymous ancestors is a complicated one and in many cases the "ancestor" is no more than an abstraction, a people personified. The fact that this very often is so has led many anthropologists and biblical critics to regard all or nearly all eponymous ancestors or founders as mythical. But the adoption of such a principle could easily lead us astray. . . .

136

The earliest facts available to the historians of antiquity were those connected with tribal movements. For the memory of these lived on after the exploits of individuals had been forgotten. Now the bulk of the Book of Genesis consists of a record of national and tribal migrations whose object is to show how Israel and the people related to her—Edom, Moab, and Ammon and certain groups of Bedouin Arabs—came to occupy the geographical position which they did in the writer's day. This is done by way of leading up to the story of God's revelation to Moses. But many obscurities arise from the fact that the first book of the Bible is concerned with the twilight age between that in which more or less vague traditions, connected with the beginnings of civilization, and certain memories of tribal movements were all that was remembered, and the age in which the memory of individuals clearly stood out. (1948)

THE IMPORTANCE OF GENESIS

THE REV. H. J. T. JOHNSON

THE Old Testament brings us into contact not with one civilization like the New, but with many. The books of Machabees have for their background the Hellenistic world; Esdras and Nehemias, the Persian one. In the book of Kings we come under the shadow of the great Assyrian Empire; in Exodus we are in contact with the Egypt of the Pharaohs. But of all the books of the Bible there is probably none, for the understanding of which so much extraneous knowledge is needed as Genesis, and for this reason it is the one least adapted for teaching in schools: yet, from the point of view of dogma it is the most important book of the Old Testament, since the doctrine of Christ's redeeming mission is inseparably linked with that of the Fall. The book of Genesis stands, moreover, in relation to the rest of the Old Testament, as does the Old Testament itself with regard to the New. As the Old Testament forms an introduction to the history of the establishment of the Christian Dispensation, so Genesis serves as an introduction to the establishment of the Mosaic one.
(1948)

GENESIS TEACHES HUMILITY

ST. JOHN CHRYSOSTOM

AFTER having said, "This is the book of the heavens and of the earth" he [Moses] again narrates to us with more care the making of man. And because previously he had briefly said, "And God made man, He made him to the image of God," now he says, "And God fashioned man dust of the earth, and He breathed upon his visage a breath of life, and the man was made into a living soul [became a living animal]." What he says is great, and full of much wonder, and surpasses the human understanding. "And God," he says, "fashioned man" taking "dust of the earth." So, just as I said in the case of all visible creatures, the Creator of all things proceeds in a way directly opposed to human nature in order to manifest thereby also His ineffable power; so also we find now in the formation of man. For, see the earth constructed upon the waters, a thing which human reason could not accept without faith, and all things, as we have explained, showing themselves ready to work in a way opposed to the activity proper to them, once He wishes it. The divine Scripture now shows us that the same was the case in the formation of man. "God fashioned man," he says, taking "dust of the earth." What sayest thou? Taking dust of the earth, He fashioned man? Yes, he says, and he says not merely earth, but dust, as if to say, the lowest and vilest thing in the earth. That which is said seems to thee great and paradoxical, but if thou rememberest who was the Maker, thou will not refuse to believe in what was done, but thou wilt admire and adore the power of the Maker. But if thou wilt examine these things with a vain curiosity according to the weakness of thy thoughts, it is likely that it will come to thy mind that with earth a body is not made, but rather a brick or a tile, but certainly not such a body. Thou seest that if we take not into consideration the power of the Creator, and if we do not repress what the great weakness of our own reasonings might object, we shall not be able to grasp the sublimity of these words. For these words require the eyes of faith, and are thus stated with a great condescension for our weakness. For to say, "God fashioned man" and "He breathed" is unworthy of God, but the Sacred Scripture recounts these things thus because of us and of our weakness, condescending to accommodate itself to us, in order that, gratified with the condescension, we may have the strength to raise ourselves toward such a sublimity. "And God fashioned man," he says, "taking dust of the earth." That which has been said so far will give rise in us to no small lesson of humility, if we will be attentive to it. For, when we reflect whence our nature derives the origin of its constitution, even were we to frown ten thousand times, our pride is beaten down, we are humbled, and reflecting upon our own essence we learn to moderate ourselves. It is for this also that God, anxious for our salvation, has thus directed the language of the prophet for our instruction. For, after the Sacred Scripture has previously said, "And God made man, He made him to the image of God," and after He had given him the principality over all visible things, lest, being ignorant of the constitution of his own nature, he should dream of great things, and lest he should exceed his proper limits, Scripture again takes up its narrative, and teaches both the mode of his composition and from whence the first man appeared, and how he appeared. For, if after this teaching, and after recognizing that he derives the origin of his constitution from the earth, from which come the plants and the irrational animals; although his organization and the nature of his soul adorn him, by God's goodness, with a great preeminence, for it is by this nature and because he is endowed with reason that he has received the principality over all things—if, knowing all these things, he who was formed from earth could imagine himself, by the deceit of the serpent, to be the equal of God, then, had the prophet contented himself with his first narration, and not, taking up again his story, taught us everything with care, into what folly should we not have fallen? For this reason it is very important for our philosophical instruction to learn from whence we derived, at the beginning, the constitution of our nature. "And God fashioned," he says, "man," taking "dust from the earth," and "He breathed upon his face a breath of life." Because He spoke to men unable to understand otherwise than we are able to understand, he makes use of such gross language in order to teach us that the goodness of our Creator willed that this thing formed from the earth should also have a soul of rational nature, by which this animal is declared complete and perfect. "And He breathed," he says, "upon his face a breath of life." The breath, he says, adorns that which is formed from earth with a vital act and the latter becomes the substance of the essence of the soul. For he adds, "And the man became a living soul." This formed thing, which comes from dust, having received the insufflation of the breath of life, "was made," he says, "into a living soul." What is meant by "into a living soul"? Acting in him, having the members of the body subjected to its proper activities and governed by his will. . . .

"And He breathed," it says, "the breath of life upon his face and man became a living soul." Here certain ill-instructed persons, relying on their own reasonings, and not thinking in a way worthy of God, and not realizing the condescension of the terms, dare to say that the soul is from the substance of God. . . . If because Scripture says "He breathed into his face" we are to attribute a mouth to God, it will also be necessary to ascribe hands to Him, for it says, "He mouldest man." But lest, thus repeating these follies, we should ourselves be compelled to speak in an indecorous way, let us avoid their folly and manifold madness, and let us follow the object of the Divine Scripture, which interprets itself, but let us not dwell on the grossness of the language, but let us remember that our weakness is the cause of this grossness. For human ears could not receive the things which are said, unless they were tempered in this way. Remembering then our weakness, and also that these things are said of God, let us receive them as it is fitting that they should be applied to God, and let us not reduce God to the form of a body, or a composition of members, but let us think of all things of God as is proper. For the Deity is simple and not composite, and lacks figure, and if from the similitude given to us we should wish to ascribe a composition of members to God, we should fall into the impiety of the Gentiles.

When thou hearest Scripture say "He fashioned man," thou wilt understand the same power as in "Let there be made." And when thou shalt hear "He breathed upon his face a breath of life," thou wilt understand that, just as He had produced the incorporeal powers, so also it pleased Him that this body coming from the dust should have a rational soul, which could make use of the members of the body.

(ca. 400)

GENESIS INTERPRETED AND DEFENDED

THE REV. ALEXANDER JONES

When the Church could no longer deny the facts that scholars put forward, it contrived to retain its power by smilingly adopting science and learning with an air of: "Of course we know all that, and it makes no difference to the truth of Christianity." Symbolism and allegory were again helpful to the Church.

Marjorie Bowen, *The Church and Social Progress,* Thinkers' Library, p. 82.

IT WAS shortly after writing the pages on the Canticle-allegory and the Jonas-parable that I took a holiday, at peace with all the world. But in this warring vale we cry: Peace, peace—and there is no peace. I met Miss Bowen, though not in person, on the Yorkshire coast. My conscience was stirred. There stood I in the bookshop, my hands still red with "symbolism and allegory." One who, a few days before, had smilingly adopted "science and learning"—and not less the villain for smiling. And here was the voice of the Thinkers' Library, no less, denouncing me to the world as "that smooth-faced gentleman, tickling Commodity." Now, since we have to do with the Thinkers' Library, we cannot dispense ourselves from earnest thought. We must roll up our sleeves. But before we begin, may we make one little point clear? The term "Church" coming from a non-Catholic nib—I do not use the word in a colloquial sense—is a wide one. We can undertake to explain the attitude only of that "Church" whose servant we have the honor to be. . . . Things must have been dreadful before the advent of "science and learning." But men did have their difficulties, you know. It is just about seventeen hundred years since Origen put his foot down in the name of commonsense:

"What rational creature would be prepared to believe there was a first, second and third day, morning and evening, before the sun was made?" (*De Principiis.* iv. 3).

You see? The difficulties against the Creation account may be good difficulties but they are certainly not new difficulties. Even third century science could not stomach this.

141

Two hundred years later, Augustine was losing patience with the good old objections:

"What do I care if the heavens are a circumambient sphere and not a sort of dishcover?" (PL. xxxiv. 270).

In the thirteenth century they were still at it. All up-to-date astrologers now knew that some stars at least were bigger than the moon. It fell now to Aquinas to answer the obvious objection drawn from the "lesser lights" that Genesis speaks about. He does so in his usual cool way—he was ice compared with Origen and Augustine:

"Some stars may be bigger than the moon, but the moon means more to us down here; moreover, it looks bigger."
(*Summa Theologica,* I, 70, I ad. 5m).

Clearly this "smiling adoption" business was early in vogue. But how did Aquinas and Augustine and Origen justify themselves? All three, without the slightest doubt, believed in the omniscient and inspiring Spirit. How exempt him from error? None of them seemed to feel any anxiety. Origen, lecturing at Alexandria, was a great allegorist. He certainly did not deny the objective truth of the fact of Creation (see the Preface of his *De Principiis*) but he appealed to a "higher sense," refusing to believe that the Spirit would be bothered with scientific teaching. Augustine followed much the same line:

"When people come along with arguments like this, tell them that the Spirit had no intention of teaching things useless to salvation." (PL. xxxiv. 270).

St. Thomas Aquinas, less curt than Augustine in this, spread himself a little on the subject. He explained that the book of Genesis was addressed to simple folk. For this reason, for example, it did not mention the creation of Air because what the eye does not see the simple heart does not grieve over. (cf. *Summa,* I, 68, 3 corp.).

Now has the Church changed any of these principles under the pressure of modern science? If she has, she may fairly be accused of opportunism and "smiling adoption" and the rest. But she did not change because, to take the meanest view of her, she did not need to change. Aquinas may have had more scientific objections to deal with than Augustine had, but he still used the same answer. He needed no other. In the twentieth century we are in the same case.

142

There is not a new objection; it is an old one re-presented, though not reinforced, with new examples. Like Augustine we still see no reason why God should have favored an inspired author with a scientific revelation. There is no evidence that science has brought man nearer to God in the twentieth century than its pitiful antecedent brought him in the past.

May we explain our position to our opponents? We do not claim that the inspired author of the first chapter of Genesis knew more than his contemporaries about the scientific "how" of the world's becoming. Had you asked him what he meant by referring to the primal abyss of waters when he should have been describing a nebula, he would most certainly have gaped. "If what you call a nebula," we can hear him saying, "is as formless as my abyss of waters, go ahead, call it what you like. All I wanted to say was that God called order from chaos. Didn't you guess I was not writing a treatise on science?" . . .

Now it is important to distinguish the religious teaching of this chapter of Genesis from the framework in which it is presented. Both proceed from an *inspired* author but only the teaching is *revealed*. Here is something of the teaching: the universe did not itself struggle purposefully into ordered existence, as in the picturesque but pantheistic Babylonian account. Nor did the universe spontaneously but blindly evolve—though it so evolved according to the atheistic Phoenician record. On the contrary, it was brought into being (says Genesis) and from being into ordered existence by an intelligent Creator distinct from the universe he had made. The author has something to say about the heavenly bodies, too; something upon which we might reflect even in this great era of science when the newspaper will offer you your horoscope. The lights of the heaven, he says, are there to mark the seasons, not, as for so many Semites, to be adored. As for Man, he is constituted above the rest of creation by reason of a divine act conferring a mysterious "likeness" to God. None of these topics, you will notice, is old-fashioned. Each is of abiding interest and each is beyond the reach of physical science. The author's source of information? Revelation, as we shall see.

So much for the substance. What of the framework? What, for instance, of the *order* in which the different creatures emerged? It is the order of the less to the more perfect, and this is natural enough for the unaided human mind to conceive. It is found roughly the same in the pagan accounts. If this order turns out to be in general accord with the findings of science, we shall not claim that it has been re-

143

vealed. We shall ascribe the agreement to chance, or better, to the fact that human reason is a reflection of the divine intelligence. We believe, with Augustine, that the Spirit was not concerned to reveal information that had no relish of salvation in it. For that sort of information, true to the unchanged principle, we look to the scientist. And if ever in the heat of argument some of us have lost sight of the principle, we freely offer our apologies to the scientist and to the traditional doctrine of the Church which Augustine voiced so well. . . .

What of the "days" of Creation? Did the author think that the world as we see it took only six days to make? What does it matter? The time-element is as unimportant to salvation as the order of creation. We may reasonably assume that the author of this religious passage did not intend to commit himself to a formal scientific statement that had nothing to do with his purpose. For the same reason we may presume that he would have no revelation to guide him. What would he have? Either his own commonsense or the ideas of his contemporaries. To take the second first: what were these ideas? It is hard to discover, but the exciting events of the Babylonian myth could scarcely be crowded into one week. It has even been conjectured that the Babylonians allowed over one million and a half years for the process of "creation." Of course, creation does take longer when you have to fight with other gods. Genesis, with its one God, would get no help from that direction. What, then, of the author's unaided commonsense? What would this tell him? Well, knowing as he did that God created by a word, I should imagine that he thought the whole business instantaneous. Then why "days" at all—and very odd days, too, when there was no sun for the first three of them? Ah, why indeed; unless he wanted the number six. But why should he want six? His choice is clearly deliberate: the obvious number for him to choose was eight because he recounts eight distinct works. It is a personal choice, too; we do not find this number in the Babylonian or Phoenician accounts; the seven tablets on which the Babylonian story is written might appear to suggest the six days' work and one day's rest of Genesis, but in fact these seven tablets are not seven divisions of the creation-work properly so called; this does not begin until tablet four. We must therefore seek an explanation from Hebrew practice. It is there we find, deeply rooted, the six-day working week with the solemn injunction of the seventh day rest (Exod. xxiii. 12). It is reasonable, then, to suppose that the Hebrew author is using an extended anthropomorphism: God's great work is described *in terms* of man's weekly labor.

144

It is further probable that he wishes to present man with a divine model for his work and rest, thus driving home the practice of the Sabbath.

There are popular writers who speak very glibly of the likeness between the pagan cosmogonies and the Genesis story. One sometimes wonders if they have ever read either. You see, the scholars are much more cautious, not to say antagonistic. Listen:

> "But there is no foundation whatsoever for the assertion which has so often been made that the two accounts of Creation which are given in the early chapters of Genesis are derived from the Seven Tablets of Creation described in the preceding pages. The fundamental conceptions of the Babylonian and Hebrew accounts are essentially different." (Wallis Budge, *The Babylonian Legends of the Creation,* ed. Sidney Smith, British Museum, 1931.).

I should say they are! Having just labored again through the wild and wearisome Seven Tablets I turn with relief to the profound simplicity of Genesis. To take just one example of surface similarity combined with deep distinction: it takes the god Marduk one hundred lines of epic to split "like a shell-fish" the hostile goddess who is Tiamat, one half of Chaos, and to push up the top part to form the heavens. Genesis is much less exciting: "And God said: Let there be a firmament made amidst the waters; and let it divide the waters from the waters. . . . And it was so." What if the biblical *Tehom,* the deep, has the same name as the chaotic Tiamat? The *name* is common to all the Semitic languages. (cf. Deimel, *Verbum Domini,* 1923, p. 159), it is the *thing* that matters. If people call the account of Genesis "myth" what word have they got left for the Tablets?

It is proved fact that the serene monotheism and effortless creation of Genesis stand alone in the Semitic world: witnesses have risen from the soil of Assyria to confirm it. This is not a hasty cry of triumph; it is the considered verdict of scholars. The words written fifty years ago by Lagrange (*Revue Biblique,* 1896, p. 403) need no revision in the light of subsequent discovery:

> "The idea of creation by a simple word was never the product of a Semitic mind. . . . and since a transcendental effect demands a transcendental cause, *the most rational explanation of the Mosaic cosmogony is still Revelation.*

This may not make headlines in the sensational Press but it should provide thought for the Thinkers' Library.   (1951)

In the first chapter of Genesis we are not bound to look for scientific exactitude of expression, since it was not the intention of the sacred writer to teach us the innermost nature of visible things, nor to present the complete order of creation in a scientific manner, but rather to furnish his people with a popular account, such as the common parlance of the age allows, one namely, adapted to the senses and to man's intelligence.

THE PONTIFICAL BIBLICAL COMMISSION (1909)

THE PROFOUND SIGNIFICANCE
OF ABRAHAM

THE REV. JEAN DANIELOU, S.J.

THE Old Testament is the story of how God educated mankind to be able to receive the gifts He destined for them. Before He came in the flesh and accomplished fully the mystery of the salvation of the world, and the mystery of the salvation of the nations, the Word of God Himself began by preparing His ways in history. As a first step towards this, God chose Abraham and his race to tell them something of the mystery of Christ, in a way obscure and hidden, but none the less quite real. Men's minds were utterly crude and materialist, and His method was to raise them bit by bit . . . from the worship of idols to a point where they could understand and in part foresee the realities Christ was to bring, so that when Christ at last appeared, and His mystery was revealed, men would be able to understand Him. . . .

Chapter xii of Genesis tells us how Abraham, son of Thare, left Haran in northern Syria, to go into the land of Chanaan, at the command of God: "And the Lord said to Abraham: Go forth out of thy country, and from thy kindred, and out of thy father's house, and come into the land which I will show thee. And I will make of thee a great nation, and I will bless thee, and magnify thy name . . . And in thee shall all the kindred of the earth be blessed. (xii. 1-3). . . .

Thare and Abraham . . . left Ur, the wealthy Chaldean city. They stayed for some time at Haran. And they finally came to the land of Chanaan, which was inhabited by Semites; the latter were related to

146

the Phoenicians of whose civilization and worship we have learnt a great deal from excavations.

Yet this migration, which can be placed as a not specially remarkable historical event, was at the same time an almost unique happening, paralleled only by the Creation of the world, and Christ's Incarnation. It was in the fact the first beginning of God's action in history, just as the Creation was the beginning of His action upon the cosmos, and the Incarnation the beginning of the world to come. It marks the opening of sacred history—perhaps indeed of all history. It is the first appearance of historical action by the living God. With it came a new order of reality which was to fill nineteen centuries. And it is this which gives Abraham's setting-out its unique character. The rest of the Old Testament was, like him, to prepare for and prefigure Christ. But it belonged to him alone to start the work.

There are several aspects of this event. It was, first, an order to leave, to separate. What God commanded Abraham was, in fact, to start something absolutely new, which implied a break with all that had been before in the religious sphere. . . .

This setting forth of Abraham's has echoed through all subsequent religious history. In Jewish-Christian tradition he is the model and archetype of conversion to the living God in the first total act of faith. The Old Testament constantly recurs to this as the origin of the Jewish people's vocation. The New Testament makes him the very pattern of faith: "By faith he that is called Abraham obeyed to go out into a place which he was to receive for an inheritance. And he went out not knowing whither he went" (Heb. xi. 8). The Jewish theologian Philo devoted one of his treatises to the *Migratio Abrahae,* in which he saw a symbol of man's soul leaving visible things to go forward to invisible. Gregory of Nyssa shows him to us as the model of the soul setting out towards God in the darkness of the faith, and in a brilliant commentary on the Epistle to the Hebrews he says in regard to Abraham's "not knowing whither he went" that it was precisely "because he did not know whither he went that he knew he was going right, for then he was certain that he was not being led by the light of his own mind, but by the will of God." Pascal's conversion, on that decisive night, was to be conversion "to the God of Abraham, Isaac and Jacob, not to the God of the philosophers and scholars." To Kierkegaard, and to Chekhov, "the perfect thinker was Abraham, the father of faith, and not Socrates. To Abraham faith was a new dimension of thought, which the world did not yet know, which had no place in ordinary knowledge, and simply broke through the restraining truths of our experience and our reason." And Jean Hering could write: "The model for a Christian is not the princess in exile who longs to return; it is Abraham setting out towards an unknown country to be shown him by God."

But while Abraham's election was an order to leave, a break with the past, it was also a promise, the announcement of things to come. Thus it appeared from the start what was to be the character of the new religion. Cosmic religion recognized God's action in the regularity of the stars' courses and the seasons which God had guaranteed by the covenant He made with Noe (Gen. ix. 9-17): it was a religion of nature. The religion of the Bible, on the other hand, was to be a waiting for historical happenings of the future. . . .

The mysterious object of that promise was the salvation of the nations. "All the kindred of the earth shall be blessed in thee." What is extraordinary here is that at the very beginning of sacred history its end should be set before him. That end, which is the end of the whole set of creation—that is to say, that all spiritual beings were created to recognize and give glory to the Blessed Trinity: *Adveniat regnum tuum* —was set before Abraham as early as this. It was, of course, to be unfolded over the long course of the centuries, through God's great work in the three-fold history of Israel, Christ and the Church. And this threefold history itself was the object of Abraham's faith: he was called upon to believe that he would be "the father of a mighty nation" though his wife Sara was barren; that in his seed, that is, through one of his descendants, God's blessing would be spread over all mankind, which meant that the Messias would be a descendant of his—"Abraham rejoiced that he might see my day,"—Jesus was to say of him (John viii. 56); and lastly that all the kindred of the earth should be saved, which meant the founding of the Church. ("By faith he abode in the land of promise, as in a strange country . . . for he looked for a city that hath foundations, whose builder and maker is God" (Heb. xi. 9-10). But from the beginning, the object of God's promise and the object of Abraham's faith was the salvation of the nations—in fact the very object of missionary work. Thus what Abraham waited for so long we still await. And just as he, alone in an utterly pagan world, believed that all nations should be saved, so, sticking to our faith, even when everything seems to point against it, we must continue to wait, in the Advent of the Church, for all nations to be gathered together in Him who took His flesh in one of Abraham's daughters.   (1950)

GOD'S CHOICE OF THE JEWS

ST. THOMAS AQUINAS

IT MIGHT be assigned as a reason for the Law being given to the Jews rather than to other peoples, that the Jewish people alone remained faithful to the worship of one God, while the others turned away to idolatry; wherefore the latter were unworthy to receive the Law, lest a holy thing should be given to dogs.

But this reason does not seem fitting: because that people turned to idolatry, even after the Law had been made, which was more grievous. . . .

God vouchsafed both the Law and other special boons to that people, on account of the promise made to their fathers that Christ should be born of them. For it was fitting that the people, of whom Christ was to be born, should be signalized by a special sanctification, according to the words of Levit. xix. 2: *Be ye holy because I . . . am holy.*—Nor again was it on account of the merit of Abraham himself that this promise was made to him, viz., that Christ should be borne of his seed: but of gratuitous election and vocation. . . .

It is therefore evident that it was merely from gratuitous election that the patriarchs received the promise, and that the people sprung from them received the Law; . . . And if again it be asked why He chose this people, and not another, that Christ might be born thereof; a fitting answer is given by Augustine (*Tract. super Joan.* xxvi.): *Why He draweth one and draweth not another, seek not thou to judge, if thou wish not to err.*

Although the salvation, which was to come through Christ, was prepared for all nations, yet it was necessary that Christ should be born of one people, which, for this reason, was privileged above all other peoples. (1272)

GOD'S TEST OF ABRAHAM

ST. AUGUSTINE

THE Scripture says that God "tempted" Abraham. Is God, then, so ignorant of what passes and of the human heart that He should require to tempt a man in order to know him? Far be it from us to think so. He tempts in order that a man may know himself. Let us briefly consider this question for the sake of those who are opposed to the Holy Scriptures of the Old Law; for not a few men, when they do not understand, are more apt to criticize than to search that they *may* understand. They become not humble inquirers, but overbearing calumniators, imagining that they may be in the true way, and able to walk properly with only one foot, because they are not scribes instructed in the kingdom of heaven, who brings forth out of their treasures *new things and old.* . . . We say to men of this kind, "You accept the Gospel; the Law you do not accept. But we hold that the terrible Giver of the Law and the most merciful God of the Gospel is one and the same."

What reason does perverse man allege for accepting the Gospel and not admitting the Law? Because it is written that God *tempted Abraham.* . . . Where, then, do we read of Christ tempting? The Gospel records that He said to Philip, *Whence shall we buy bread that these may eat?* And the Evangelist continues, *This He said to try him; for He Himself knew what He would do.* Go back now to God trying Abraham. This God also said to try him; for He Himself knew what He would do. . . . A heretic does not tempt as God tempts. God tempts a man that He may enlighten him; a heretic tempts himself in order that he may shut his eyes to God. . . . If God leaves off tempting, our Master leaves off teaching. God tempts that He may give us a lesson; the Devil tempts in order to deceive. . . . What, then, brethren, do we say? Supposing even that Abraham *did* know himself, *we* did not know him. He was to be revealed either to himself, or, beyond a doubt, to us; to himself, that we might know his own cause for thankfulness; to us, that we might know either what we should ask of God or what we should imitate in man. What, then, does Abraham teach us? To put it briefly, he teaches us not to prefer the gifts of God to God. . . . Therefore, put not even a real gift of God before the Giver of that gift; and if He should choose to take it away, let Him not lose His worth in your eyes, because God is to be loved for His own sake. For what sweeter reward is there from God than God Himself?

When Abraham had accomplished his devoted act of obedience, he heard the words, *Now I know that thou fearest God,* which means that God had revealed Abraham to himself. . . .

Before all things, brethren, we both admonish and exhort you in God's name, to the best of our power, that, in hearing the narrative of the events recorded in Holy Scripture, you first believe that those events took place in the way in which the Scripture tells them, lest, taking

150

away the foundation of the thing described, you seek to build without a basis. Abraham our father was an upright man in those days, believing in God and justified by faith. Sarah bore him a son when they were both old, and the thing was, humanly speaking, impossible. But what may not be hoped for from God, to Whom nothing is difficult? He does great things as He does small things; He raises the dead just as He creates the living. . . . What is difficult to Him Who produces by a word? It was as easy to Him to create the angels above the firmament as to create the heavenly bodies, the fishes in the sea, and trees and living things on earth. Great things He has created with the same facility as small things. Whereas then, it was most easy to Him to create all things out of nothing, is it wonderful that He should have given a son to an aged father and mother? This, then, was the type of man; these were the men whom God used, and whom in those days He made the prophets of His Son to come, that, not only in the words which they spoke, but in their actions, or in those things which befell them, Christ may be sought for and found. Whatsoever the Scripture records of Abraham is at once fact and a prophecy.   (ca. 419)

THE PATRIARCHS: "MYSTICS OF ACTION"

DANIEL-ROPS

This Epic of the Patriarchs, that closes with the death of Joseph, is presented to us in the Holy Scriptures as a page of history and it is a matter of faith for Christians to accept this text. The localities in which it is situated, and the many coincidences that we find, make it seem credible. But it might still be a historical romance, skilfully framed in a background studied by a narrator who was a master of his subject. Is it nothing more than that? Certainly we cannot hope to give, in the present state of knowledge on these distant periods, those precise details that are expected when we are concerned with more recent times; history is always hard to write even when it concerns recent events; when the facts in question cannot be deciphered except in the light of contradictory hypotheses, his muse is ever ready to aid and abet the historian led astray by logic.

Nothing is more dangerous than to claim to explain too far facts that

151

remain scarcely explicable, and to define what is, in its very essence, indefinite. One can suggest approximate dates for the history of the Patriarchs; these vary from one authority to another. It is of no importance whether Abraham lived between 2000 and 1900 B.C., as some suppose, or between 2160 and 1958 B.C., as is stated by others. Based on a whole series of logical deductions founded on correlations with the royal chronology of Egypt, and cuneiform tablets, supported by the evidence of fragments of pottery, these dates remain mere surmises, and one can only smile when one chronology affirms with serene gravity that the departure from Ur took place in the year 2100 B.C. and that Joseph was sold by his brothers in 1645! Modesty compels us to admit that all dates before the seventh century B.C. are hypothetical.

But apart from the dates, what of the people and the facts? This matter has long been open to dispute. For some this story has only the value of a symbol; a theme of religious thought that could be expressed in the course of centuries. Abraham would be a moon god whose voyage from east to west reproduced the celestial migration, and his twelve distant descendants, the sons of Jacob, would be the months. For others the Patriarchs are the epic heroes of the Israelites at the time of their formation as a race. In the same way as we speak of Uncle Sam for the United States, John Bull for England, and Marianne for the Third Republic. The names would suggest anecdotes! For example, Israel, by a play upon the words, Jacob's striving with God. There are other critics, again, who allow the existence of real men named Abraham, Jacob, and Joseph, but who say that around these true facts of history legends have grown up. Here again we are in the field of hypothesis, and no theory carries sufficient conviction for the discussions of the biblical text to be closed, in the absence of further evidence from the field of archaeology.

But it is a very narrow conception of history that sees it as the mere science of facts. There is a human verity that is persuasive, even in the absence of documentation. And this verity shines from every page of the whole epic of the Patriarchs, Abraham, Jacob and Joseph (Isaac less), revealing them as being profoundly alive men who have left their mark on their times, who have engaged the destiny of their people. Each has his own character, his individual way of behaving, and even his own passions. The spiritual change in Jacob after the great crisis of Jabbok carries all the conviction of a conversion; and a portrait of Joseph, in his career in Egypt, is drawn for us by means of a marvelous psychological analysis.

Amongst these psychological traits, one stands out clearly. It is the one from which unfolds, ultimately, the whole history of the people born of Abraham. This trait has been so clearly marked in the character of these Patriarchs that, century after century, men of their race were to strive to keep alive in themselves the same virtue. For we cannot separate this epic from the development that came afterwards. The history of Israel is a progressive history that has a clear meaning and corresponds to an intention. The conviction of being the chosen people was to be, throughout the years, the motive of all their actions; and on what does that conviction rest, if not on the affirmation a thousand times reiterated that the Patriarchs were the repositories of the Promise, that they lived in the presence of God?

These great Patriarchs appear to us, in fact, as mystics of action. If a man may be called a mystic who tries to realize in his life the will and the presence of God—"It is no longer I, but Christ liveth in me," as St. Paul says—Abraham and Jacob, these inspired men, were certainly mystics. All the Patriarchs were in that relationship of sublime familiarity with God that we find, in another period, in St. Joan of Arc or St. Francis of Assisi. Realists they were, like all the great mystics, "men and women of outstanding common sense," as Bergson says; capable of acting in the military and political spheres when necessary, but referring always to the divine intention without the mediation of any priest, practically without any rites, in a direct relationship continually renewed. Mystics, certainly, but mystics of action; they are not isolated and ascetic contemplatives; it is their life that bears witness, their life that is in itself both prayer and contemplation. Their very acts praise God.

Never does the narrator of this history of the Patriarchs miss an opportunity for underlining the intervention of God in the conduct of events. All that is inexplicable is attributed to Him, and frequently men, all unawares, accomplish His designs. From Him comes happiness, fertility, long life. He rewards, but also punishes, towns like Sodom and Gomorrah, or men like Onan. Merciful, he hears the prayers of the just and comforts Jacob in his desolation. This power of God is ever-present. It may manifest itself in a dream, a vision, or under those angelic forms that seem to be the visible images of the invisible that man cannot behold directly; charisms and visions of the great mystics, like those experienced by St. Bernard, St. Teresa of Avila, St. Mary of the Incarnation and many others.

Between man and God, strict relations were established, called in the Bible the "covenant." This is a veritable pact, concluded with precise ceremonial borrowed from the customs of the time. The maker of the sacrifice cuts a victim in half, and passes between the two halves. The Patriarchs, in their own name and that of their people, engage themselves, but in exchange feel themselves to be under the protection and guidance of God.

It is a wonderful thing, this confidence that they all manifest in the supreme Power, a confidant and friend. On all occasions the sacred name is uttered, and prayer rises to men's lips. They consult God, call upon Him as a witness; to bless in His name is a sacramental, irrevocable act. The divine presence literally is everywhere in that patriarchal religion that, across the distance of four thousand years, seems to us so living, so close to the eternal needs of the soul.

There are few rites, few doctrines in this mystical life; nomadic existence does not lend itself to complicated ceremonial; it would be difficult to transport a temple on camels. The Patriarch is himself the priest; he officiates when a sacrifice is to be offered or an oblation or prayer made to God. The religious practices that we find are those that many peoples have practiced in their early days. They go up to the high places in order to implore the supreme Power, in order to be, as it were, more completely alone in that Presence, or nearer to it. The noblest mountains of Palestine still bear the traces of these cults —Carmel, majestic Hermon—and altars of cupped-out stone have been found that are perhaps the same as that to which Abraham led Isaac. Sometimes, also, they raised stones according to an extremely ancient custom, the same as that practiced in our own countries by the neolithic builders of dolmens and menhirs; these were the *massebah,* the sacred steles, an impressive alignment of which has been discovered at Gaza. They also accorded respect to noble trees and flowing water; evergreen oaks and springs play an important role in all these narratives.

But these simple rites, originating no doubt in a secular tradition, were purified in their adoption by the Patriarchs. The fetishism found in the Canaanite and Mesopotamian religions they clearly discarded: if Rachel had the *teraphim,* her husband knew nothing of it. The horrible human sacrifices of Sumeria, long practiced also by the Phoenicians, we find expressly rejected. Nor do we find any trace of the magic that vitiated the otherwise noble contemporary Egyptian religion. And even if we cannot judge the sexual morality of the time of the Patriarchs by our own standards, it is nevertheless clear that license and excess and all violations of the laws of nature were repugnant to them, and seemed to them things condemned by God. Hammurabi, at the same period, set forth his great attempt at theological unification as the simple fruit of ancestral experience; and a little later, when the Pharaoh Amenophis IV carried out his revolution in mysticism, the only authority he invoked was his own. In Israel, everything was a reflection of the will of an all-powerful God, of the Most High.   (1949)

MOSES, MASTER PROPHET

THE MOST REV. JACQUES BÉNIGNE BOSSUET

ALL the prophets who have followed Moses in the Ancient Law and all other sacred writers have prided themselves on being his disciples. Indeed, he speaks as a master. In his writings one notices a very distinctive quality and a certain originality found in no other writing. In his artlessness, Moses strikes a note so sublime and majestic that nothing can equal it. . . .

Some think that he wrote the Book of Job. The sublimity of the thoughts and majesty of the style, render that history worthy of Moses. Lest the Hebrews should have been puffed up by arrogating the grace of God to themselves only, it was proper to let them know that this great God had His elect even in the race of Esau. What doctrine was more important? What more useful subject for consideration could Moses give to the people afflicted in the wilderness than that of the patience of Job? . . . He . . . by constancy shows that a faithful soul supported by Divine aid, amidst the most dreadful trials, and in spite of the gloomiest thoughts the evil spirit can suggest, can not only preserve an invincible confidence, but even raise itself by its own calamities to the highest contemplation, and acknowledge, in the troubles it endures, the nothingness of man, and the supreme dominion and infinite wisdom of God. Such are the lessons taught in the Book of Job. . . . The people of God learn to know what is the virtue of suffering, and to foretaste the grace that was one day to be fastened to the Cross.

Moses had tasted that grace by anticipation, when he chose rather to suffer affliction and shame with his people than to enjoy the pleasures and plenty of the house of the king of Egypt. . . . He drank deep of the cup of Jesus Christ, when, being chosen to deliver that people, he had to bear with their continual revolts in which his life was often in danger. He learned what it costs to save the children of God, and showed afar off what a higher deliverance was one day to cost the Savior of the world.

155

The great man had not even the consolation of entering the Promised Land. He beheld it only from the top of a mountain, and was not at all ashamed to record that he was excluded from it by a sin of unbelief, which, slight as it appears, deserved to be so severely punished in a man who was endued with so eminent a portion of grace. Moses afforded an example of the severe jealousy of God, and of the judgment He exercises with such terrible strictness upon those whom His gifts bind to a more perfect fidelity.

But a higher mystery is set forth to us in the exclusion of Moses. This wise lawgiver, who, by so many wonders, conducts the children of God only into the neighborhood of their land, is himself proof to us, that his "Law brought nothing to perfection" (Hebr. vii. 19), and that without being able to give the accomplishment of the promises, it makes us "behold them afar off" (Hebr. xi. 13), or conducts us at most, as it were, to the gateway of our inheritance. It is a Josue, it is a Jesus, for this was the true name of Josue, who by that name and by his office, represented the Savior of the world; it is that man, so far inferior to Moses in everything, and superior to him only by the name he bears; it is he, I say, who is to bring the people of God into the Holy Land.

(ca. 1675)

THE PROPHETS

DANIEL-ROPS

HERE we enter upon the most magnificent chapter of the history of Israel. The whole of the Old Testament rests finally upon three foundations: Abraham to whom the promise was given and from whom the whole development unfolds; Moses who gave the chosen people the means to survive; the Prophets who, uncovering the true vein of the providential message, formulated the veritable mission of Israel.

For a long time certain individuals had stood out among the Hebrews as being gifted with special powers. In ancient times they were known as "seers." They knew truths hidden from the common run of men. Deborah had been of that line, and also Samuel, who was consulted on every kind of problem, even when a man had lost his she-asses. Clairvoyance was to some extent professional, and there were even

156

colleges of divination. . . . These professional prophets were often false prophets, and Christ Himself was to say of them that it was often hard to distinguish the false from the true.

Nevertheless, in this not always very pure tradition, in these questionable circles, arose the most powerful and admirable religious personalities of the period, those who are referred to as the Prophets, who truly did speak in the name of God. . . .

In the ninth century, the spirit of prophecy found expression in the great personalities of Elijah and Elisha, the passionate enemies of idolatry. From the year 800 B.C. onwards for three centuries, this spirit was to animate a whole series of extraordinary men, among whom was one of the greatest figures of human history, Isaiah: these Prophets are known as *writers,* for as a rule, in the Bible, we possess records written by themselves of the four *major* Prophets—Isaiah, Jeremiah, Ezekiel and Daniel—and of the twelve *minor* Prophets. These men were solitary and non-conformist, guided only by their passion for the absolute. They came from all classes, and their psychology is extremely varied. Amos was a drover, a working man who had educated himself but who still preserved his revolutionary tone. Hosea was a rich peasant with a gentle heart. Isaiah belonged to the ruling class and knew politics from the inside. Zephaniah was even a member of the royal family, and Jeremiah the son of a priest. But there is much in common among them, for they all saw their mission in the same light. Israel saw them come and go, clad in a terrible picturesqueness, dressed in the skins of animals or mantles of goat's hair, living in the most extreme simplicity. They respected no worldly convention. The ladies of the court, painted and perfumed, Amos called "cows of Basham," as a beggar might have called them "bitches." Ezekiel prophesied to them that they would before long be raped. Jeremiah, predicting the Chaldean domination, walked in the streets harnessed like an ass. And Isaiah went naked to show what the condition of Israel was to be in the days of wrath. Nevertheless, they were regarded by the people with troubled respect. Foreign kings—the Assyrians themselves—felt their prestige. They did not like to hear what they had to say, but felt that a redoubtable power spoke through them.

One word accurately describes the essential thing about them, the very word by which they are known: prophets, according to the Greek derivation, are those who "speak on behalf of someone." They are the mouthpieces of God. They begin all their prophecies with the words, "Thus saith the Lord," or "Hear the word of the Lord!" . . .

Their style is elevated by the incomprehensible power that animates them. As with all inspired men, be they Arabs, Greeks or Romans, it falls into the rhythm of poetry.

Not that they ever wrote for the sake of writing. They were men of action and what they said was the means of extending their influence. Their doctrine is never expressed in abstract terms; they reacted to the impact of events as ardent polemicists. But from these phrases, dictated by necessity, arises a sublime poetry.

Therein lies the mystery. These men were inspired directly by God. No one any longer pretends, like certain materialist critics of the past, that there is any question of psychological disorder. . . . As with the great mystics, the secret of the Prophets does not reside in the more or less strange guise under which they are presented to us. Visions and ecstasies are but signs. God is manifest in them according to laws that we do not know; they too have their "dark night," like St. John of the Cross. We can state the results of the fact of prophecy without understanding its mechanism. In this universe that normal men do not penetrate, we sense a grandeur, as of something deeply mysterious and immensely potent.

Into that Israelite society of the time of the Kings, menaced by the worst spiritual maladies, the Prophets were to cut like scalpels into a diseased body. Of all the elements of resistance to disintegration offered by the chosen people, they were by far the most efficacious. Nothing stopped them; they never shrank. Consequently they provoked against themselves the most fierce resistance. Jesus in a celebrated utterance was to say to a Hebrew of His day, "Ye are the children of them which killed the prophets" (Matthew xxiii 31). A passage in the Epistle to the Hebrews (xi: 36) also speaks of the suffering endured by the Prophets —stonings, mockings and scourgings, beheading with the sword—the least of them was imprisonment. Their witness is comparable to that of the martyrs, and for similar reasons. Speaking in God's name, they openly broke with society and convention. . . .

If we consider the religion of the Prophets as a whole (taking into account the variations resulting from individual differences and from an evolution taking place over several centuries), we cannot fail to be filled with admiration for the extension that they brought about in the old Hebrew monotheism. It is true that many elements that they were to develop already existed in embryo, and they no more broke with the spiritual tradition than did Jesus Himself. "Think not I am come to destroy the law, or the prophets: I am not come to destroy but to fulfill," might equally have been said by the Prophets. But they brought into the light of day that moral monotheism whose slow progress we have followed down the course of the centuries and that is, in fact, their fundamental role in history.

For them, Jahweh is not only the One God, the ruler and creator of all things; He is above all, the God within, whose veritable temple is the heart of man and whose justice is absolute. This affirmation was enough to cause a rupture with their contemporaries. What? The God of Israel, who led His people out of Egypt, who had shown an uninterrupted preference for them, could Jahweh abandon and repudiate His children? Yes, the Prophets replied, because Israel had been unfaithful, not only in the letter, but in the spirit, and had violated justice and love. This idea of the punishment and destruction of the chosen people constituted an intolerable offense to public opinion; but even at the price of their lives, the Prophets maintained their position; was not Israel's ruin the best possible proof of the universality of the Almighty?

As they saw it, Israel did indeed continue to be a privileged people, and they even repeated again and again that God has multiplied benefits in their favor. But while the actual conclusion was that Jahweh was bound to give token of outstanding favor, the Prophets dared to say that divine election imposes more duties than it confers privileges. . . .

But what constitutes the greatness of the Prophets of Israel is that several centuries before Confucius and Buddha, and in a way that we may fairly describe as unique, they fully realized the synthesis, already indicated in Moses, between morality and religion. For all their intelligence, the Greeks arrived only very imperfectly at this idea. Therein lies the inspiration of the prophetic message.

Another thing that the Greeks did not discover, and that the Prophets of Israel affirmed in grandiose language, is the necessity of attributing to the world itself, as it exists, a moral significance. Before injustice, violence triumphant, all those violations that make up the stuff of history, the Prophets are those who never are resigned. While classical antiquity on the whole despises misfortune, the Prophets regard it with respect. In speaking of the "poor of God," the "humble ones of the earth," the "oppressed," they use words of infinite mercy. The spirit of poverty speaks through them. Christ praising in the Beatitudes the "poor in spirit," is in line with the perspective opened up by these generous souls. . . .

The time of the Prophets is strictly circumscribed. They appeared and disappeared. The day came, lamented by the Psalm (LXXIV) in which "There is no more any prophet; neither is there among us

159

any that knoweth how long." Doubtless they had spoken their message. And that greater light that they had foretold was approaching. But they had provided for the soul of Israel, hot after sin, "sources of living water" at which humanity has never ceased to quench its thirst.

(1949)

Prophecy implies a certain obscurity and remoteness from intelligible truth; hence they are more strictly termed "prophets" who see through some vision in the imagination; at the same time prophecy through the medium of intellectual vision ranks higher, provided always that it is the same truth that is revealed in both cases. If, however, an intellectual light is infused into a person, not in order that he may know certain supernatural truths, but in order that he may judge with the certitude belonging to divine truth about things which can be known by human reason, then such intellectual prophecy is inferior to that which comes through the medium of a vision in the imagination, and leads to some supernatural truth. All those who rank in the class of prophets had this kind of prophecy; in fact, they are precisely termed "prophets" because they exercised the prophetic office. Hence they were wont to speak in the person of the Lord and said to the people: "Thus saith the Lord," a thing which those who wrote the "sacred writings" never did; for many of these later spoke, as a rule, not in the person of God, but in their own person, yet with the assistance of a divine light.

ST. THOMAS AQUINAS (1272)

THE NATURE AND CONDITION
OF PROPHECY

THE REV. C. LATTEY, S.J.

THE personal side of Old Testament religion is supplied in the main by the prophets; through them comes the direct appeal from the Divine Person to the human, a sublime and spiritual appeal, yet often highly anthropomorphic. Almighty God speaks at times in the language of an emotion no less vivid and personal than that which He seeks to arouse in His people. The prophet is the human instrument by which He manifests His mind, and makes this personal appeal. The distinction between the institutional and the personal side of the Old Testament religion, however, must not be drawn too sharply. Moses the lawgiver was himself a prophet, and the greatest of the prophets up till the very times of Christ; and the later prophets constituted a permanent institution, recognized as such by the Law, in Deuteronomy XVIII, 15-22. . . .

The prophet is the spokesman of God; the very word "prophet" signifies as much in the Greek whence it is derived, and most probably the corresponding Hebrew word also. That he may be God's spokesman two essential conditions are required, revelation and mission: God must speak to the prophet, and also commission the prophet to repeat what He has said. That is the idea of prophecy that we find in the Old Testament, both in the Book of Deuteronomy and in the writings of the prophets themselves. . . .

Revelation and mission are also clearly indicated, for example, in the larger prophetic works that have come down to us. Isaiah, after his vision of the Lord in glory, receives the divine command, "Go, and tell this people" (Isa. vi, 9); to Jeremiah also, like unto Moses in his diffidence no less than in his meekness, it is said, "To whomsoever [or possibly, to whatsoever] I shall send thee, thou shalt go, and whatsoever I shall command thee thou shalt speak . . . I have put My words in thy mouth" (Jer. i, 7, 9). Ezekiel, like Isaiah, beholds the glory of God before receiving his commission; the vision occupies the first chapter, and the commission the second and third, wherein he is told more than once that he is sent of the Lord, and is to speak the words of the Lord. Thus in each of these cases we have clearly the divine message, and the command to promulgate it; but in reality both are indicated every time that a prophet uses the common phrase, "Thus saith the Lord."

In revelation and mission, then, we have the essentials of prophecy. . . . It was not essential that the prophet should commit his prophecy to writing, seeing that we have such striking examples in proof as Elias and Eliseus (Elijah and Elisha). Such records of the prophets' utterances as have come down are guaranteed to us by the fact that they are found in inspired books. . . . The two prophets named worked miracles, by which the truth of their mission was attested. . . . But neither can miracles be called essential to the prophet, valuable as they may be confirmation of his mission. . . .

Even prediction cannot be considered strictly essential to the prophet; but here we have to make a distinction, if I may put it this way with all reverence, between short-distance and long-distance prophecy. The former, to be verified almost at once, may serve as a test of revelation and mission. . . .

Other tests of mission and revelation of course existed besides those already touched upon; the whole life and character of the prophet, the comparison of his teaching with divine truth already known, and so forth.

Such is the broad outline of the Old Testament conception of the nature of prophecy. It is to be found in all the relevant evidence on the subject; it was enforced by the prophets themselves, even by the false prophets, and was accepted by the people at large. Nevertheless, when we come to examine more closely that revelation which lies at the root of the whole conception, it is no longer possible to proceed in peace and security. While Catholics and most believing Christians admit readily enough that the whole subject of immediate communication between God and man is obscure and difficult, those who believe less, or who believe little or nothing, are apt to treat it as a fundamental axiom, a point beyond all dispute, that such immediate communication is entirely out of the question. . . . It is often the fact—more often than not, I should think, among serious scholars outside the Catholic Church as I understand it—that an explanation involving revelation or miracle is looked upon as no explanation at all, but merely a problem still unsolved. . . .

A theory has lately been put forward which I may briefly call the mediumistic hypothesis, which would explain, and explain away, the prophetic revelation by supposing the prophet to be endowed with the same kind of properties as a medium, without however allowing a divine message in the true sense. Let it suffice here to say that the occupation of a medium does not appear to be profitable for mind or body; the prophets are made of sterner stuff. The theory of subliminal consciousness is more often put forward without this accretion; the prophet's pent-up feelings gather in force till they explode with the irresistible conviction of a divine impulse: "Thus saith the Lord!" . . . The prophets themselves, and also those who accepted them as such, would certainly have regarded such a view with horror, as excluding any divine message in the true sense, and putting them on a level with the false prophets. . . .

The modern evolutionary hypothesis supposes the prophets to have developed themselves almost all that was worth having in the

162

religion of Israel, and in order to dispose of any recalcitrant evidence passes them through the same mincing machines as the Books of Moses and Josue. No doubt there is a certain development of doctrine to be observed in the prophetic writings. . . . Yet in the main the prophets enforce acknowledged obligations and established beliefs; most of all they presuppose the clear conception of a personal God without which there could be no question of a revelation or mission. . . .

The function of prophecy, then, with regard to the past was to keep alive ancient standards of faith and religion, and even to infuse into them a life more vigorous still. . . . The prophets were even more responsible for the guidance of Israel in faith and conduct than might at first sight appear. The priesthood of the Old Testament was essentially and almost exclusively a sacrificial and liturgical priesthood; it is astonishing to find how little is said about any teaching function. This latter chiefly fell to the prophets, and was afterwards taken up by the scribes. . . .

Further, the prophets were the guides of Israel even in matters of state; it may be enough to cite Isaiah's warning not to rely upon Egypt (Isa. xxx, 1-7). The Old Covenant is a theocracy wherein is no limit to the divine guidance; yet it would be a mistake to suppose that the Hebrews could not distinguish between religious and civil allegiance. (1921)

There is one solace for my pilgrimage I should like, if I may presume to do so, to beg of you with all earnestness, and that is that you would let me have that copy of the Prophets which Winbert of holy memory—in old days my abbot and teacher—made; there you have the six Prophets all together, written out in clear and plain characters. If God should put into your heart to do this you could not send me a greater consolation in my old age nor lay up for yourself a greater reward. For I cannot in this country get hold of such a copy of the Prophets as I want; now that my eyes are getting dim I cannot make out the closely written characters; that is why I want the copy I mentioned above, it is written in such clear and distinct characters.

ST. BONIFACE (ca. 735)

163

WRITING STYLES OF THE PROPHETS

THE REV. ROBERT A. DYSON, S.J.
AND THE REV. ALEXANDER JONES

THE greater part of the prophetic books are, in all probability, a condensed report of the spoken prophecies. This seems evident from their brevity and their style: from their brevity, because they are compressed and compact in thought; from their style for it displays an art not common in extempore speech. Indeed some of the prophecies, especially those which were directed to Israelites of the future, may never have been delivered orally at all.

In style there is naturally much difference among the writings of different authors in varying periods. Some books, or portions of books are in ordinary prose. . . . Others are poems with the kind of metrical structure which we notice in the Psalms. . . .

The prophetic style of writing is figurative and sublime; the form is determined by the age, conditions of life and environment in which the author lived. The Holy Spirit poured His revelation into the mould of these Oriental minds; the substance of that divine revelation remains unchanged and without error but its shapes are various. Thus in the prophetic writings we find allegory, parable, symbolic images, strange dramatic actions described, all bearing a marked individuality of style and thought.

All who have read the prophetic books agree that they are in great part obscure. Indeed, it would be strange if it were otherwise; books which are over twenty-five centuries old are sure to contain allusions to persons, places, events and customs of which we know little or nothing. But there is a further obscurity which belongs to the passages in which the prophets predict future events. This obscurity existed for the contemporaries of the prophets, even, as it seems, for the prophet himself. It is here that we have the advantage who live after the fulfillment of all that the prophets had obscurely foretold.

The chief reason of this second obscurity is that the prophetic predictions are not a detailed story of future events but merely their foreshadowing. Consequently, the prophets say only as much as is required to prove, after the event had happened, that it had been foretold. The prophets conscientiously passed on the divine message;

if that message had not the fullness of Christ's own life and teaching, if their perception of its complete significance was not perfect, they could do no more; they gave what they received. It follows that if God did not choose to reveal the exact date of the prophesied event, as He rarely did choose, the faithful prophet must content himself with pointing vaguely to the future. Often, indeed, we get the impression that the future of which the prophet speaks is to follow almost immediately on present events. The picture is without perspective like the landscape drawing of a child or like a view of distant mountains. At first sight this would seem a defect, but closer consideration shows that it is not. A more mature study of history convinces us that dates are of no importance for their own sake, but it is of the greatest importance to know how one event leads up to another, to see the chain of cause and effect through the years. In the eternal redemptive plan of God the time-element is secondary— it is more important to know the "what" than to know the "when". . . .

Finally, the revelation which the prophets received was fragmentary. For the individual prophet the veil of the future was only partially lifted. Each prophecy was, so to speak, a stone in the mosaic; only when those stones were fitted together was the picture recognizable. (1946)

Moses, Isaias, Jeremias, and the other prophets, lifted in ecstasy above the natural operations of their minds, by the impulse of the Holy Spirit uttered the things with which they were inspired, the Spirit making use of them as the flute-player breathes into a flute.

ATHENAGORAS (ca. 150)

ISAIAS: THE "ARCH-PROPHET"

DOM HUBERT VAN ZELLER, O.S.B.

THAT Jehovah should bring redemption to His faithless children— that He should Himself *be* that redemption—is the very burden of

Isaias's prophecy. A salvation which is to follow a practical extinction forms the material of all the Prophet's earlier preaching; later he will tell of the manner of that salvation's coming: he will sound the trumpet of the Gospel, he will tell of the Coming of the Christ. . . .

More clearly than any other prophet does Isaias proclaim the promise of the New Law; he seems to see over the shoulders of his own age—over the shoulders, even, of our own—announcing to all mankind the finality of the Gospel sway, universal, vindicated, undenied. . . .

It will be seen (I hope) how much more of an evangelist is Isaias than are his fellow-prophets. Not surprising, therefore, that the Church links together, at the most solemn seasons of the liturgical year, the Old Testament and the New by freely drawing from Isaias's Prophecy. Isaias is the Arch-Prophet, the Prophet whose title rests simply on his "vision," and not on his personality or power of working miracles. . . . It was as an announcer of God's Messianic Message, a more *spiritual* message than any that had been announced before, that Isaias gave the traditional part of prophet a new rendering.

This brings us to what the Prophet actually said that was in any sense new. How did he differ, for example, from the other almost contemporary prophets in Israel, Amos and Osee? Or even from his own countryman, Joel? Like every prophet worthy of the name, Isaias will be heard to thunder against the particular evils of the day: we shall find him accusing the rich of oppressing the poor, we shall listen to his scornful denunciation of the self-indulgent, the smugly satisfied, the outwardly-righteous-but-inwardly-corrupt, we shall see him lifting the veil to expose the rotting judicial system . . . but it is his confidence in God and his confidence in the foundations of Jerusalem—attitudes which are not merely negative—that show us the real Isaias. He is so convinced that the Lord is looking after Juda that it is as much as he can do, when Juda's sins are coming up for censure, to keep to the point. The stone of Sion is God-placed, Jerusalem is rooted for good and all—this it is that marks Isaias from contemporary or future prophets.

So if, in the reading of our Prophet, there is one verse before all others which it would be well to learn by heart (allowing that the reader is willing to follow my finger down Isaias's page) it is v. 16 of ch. xxviii: "Therefore thus saith the Lord God: Behold I will lay a stone in the foundations of Sion, a tried stone, a corner stone, a precious stone, founded in the foundation. He that believeth, let

166

him not hasten." However upset are the fortunes of Israel there is always *that* to be thankful for—Sion is "precious" in the sight of God. Sion is "founded," and God does not waste the foundations He has made. All this is an earnest, surely, of the Messias who is to come . . . and of the Church He is to found. The "stone" of Isaias's Prophecy is a figure which will become still more familiar in the days of the Lord whose advent is heralded here. . . .

This idea, which we might call the "stone-motif," would have been especially acceptable to the Prophet's hearers on account of its association with the building of the Temple. We do not have to know very much about the books of the Old Testament to remember the frequency with which references to ecclesiastical architecture occur; to the Jews the Temple was the symbol of centralization, stability, constitutional religion. The key-thought, then, which the Prophet keeps ever before his remarkably well-stocked mind, is, undoubtedly, that of the *establishment* of the Chosen People; or, to put it in another way and going one step further, his is the doctrine of the Longsightedness of God. Again and again we hear the Prophet reminding his opportunist and expedient-grasping flock that if only they will fix their hopes in *God* and not in political alliances of the moment—or indeed in human securities of any kind—they will be perfectly safe; God cares for them. . . .

"O soul," would be the advice of Isaias to him who would force the pace of God, "remember the centuries that the eyes of God have seen. Recall the generations that are yet to come. Be still, there is plenty of time. Look at life, O soul—your life and the life of mankind at large—through the eyes of God. God's plan frustrated? Oh no! only a long time being realized! What does it matter if you— little, inconsiderable, but infinitely-precious-in-God's-sight *you*— are unable to see the results of your work? For whom is the work being done? Is it not for God? Well, then, results will follow in due time . . . perhaps a fortnight before you die, perhaps, two, three, four centuries after! It doesn't matter, there is plenty of time." So, I think, would Isaias have spoken to us "hasteners." He would have had us understand the massiveness of God, and in the largeness of the Divine Heart he would have had us see our pettiness, our impatience, and our greed. But he would also have had us see our preciousness.   (1938)

THREE NOTABLE MINOR PROPHETS

THE RT. REV. WILLIAM BARRY

OF THE Twelve Minor Prophets of the Old Testament, Hosea, Amos, and Micah stand out as leaders in the movement toward a universal religion which Isaiah celebrates and exemplifies. There is a true sense in calling them the Christian prophets of the Old Testament. Not only do they denounce idols, they uphold the necessity of a moral reformation, of holiness in the heart; and they speak vehemently in disparagement of those who would trust to rites and fasting while no inward change was sought by them. In these minor prophets the strain is audible which we hear as it swells to a world-harmony in Isaiah and Jeremiah. Prophecy does, indeed, revere the Law, but knows it to be spiritual, not a mere outward or carnal observance. And thus we may say of these high teachers that they were the lights also of Psalmody, which by prayer and meditation appropriated the Law to the individual. These three elements of one Revelation are so diverse that in impassioned harangue or argument directed to a single end, they may at times fall into antithesis, particularly under the conditions of Hebrew speech. But a work like Deuteronomy will show us how entirely they agree at last, by its borrowing from each in turn. The Law cannot exist without temple and sacrifice; what the Prophet asks is that these earthly signs should be spiritually apprehended; and the "sweet psalmist of Israel" muses on God's dealings in rites and history that he may attain to the New Covenant that should be written in the heart (Jer. xxxi, 31-33). We perceive, as we follow the growth of Hebraism, that its progress depended on a certain opposition of ideas, to be reconciled when Christ came. He was the Law-giver, Priest and Prophet in one, bringing to perfection the promise of which the Old Testament is the record and the instrument.

(1906)

For no other reason were all the things that we read in the Holy Scriptures written before our Lord's coming than to announce His coming and to prefigure the Church to be, that is to say, the people of God throughout the nations, which Church is His body, in which we are included and numbered among all the just who lived in this world even before His coming and who believed that He would come as we believe that He has come. Christ sent before Him in the persons of the holy patriarchs and prophets some part of His body, with which as with a hand He foretokened His future birth.

ST. AUGUSTINE (ca. 415)

KING DAVID AND HIS SONGS

THE REV. DENIS O'SHEA

THERE is only one David. His name was considered too sacred to be bestowed upon another king. Like the hallowed name of Peter in the long line of sovereign pontiffs, it was never assumed by any of his successors. His memory was most tenderly cherished by his own people after that of their father Abraham. He is described in the sacred pages of Scripture as the man after God's own heart (I Kings 13:14), a unique honor, and such expressions as "the house of David," "the throne of David," "the city of David," "the oath sworn to David," "the seed of David," and, above all, "the son of David" pervade the pages of both the Old Testament and the New, and indicate the permanent mark which he has made upon the minds of both Jews and Christians. The songs which he composed in the pastures of Bethlehem, in the caves of Engaddi and Adullam, on the mountains of Judea, and in the court of Israel became the national poetry. After his death the psalms were sung by countless generations of his race in the solemn service of the Temple, on the days of pilgrimage, on the battlefield, and in private devotions at home. They have had an even wider circulation since they have been adopted by holy Mother Church as her official hymns through which she daily gives glory and adoration to God. By being enshrined in the Church's liturgy they are recited by the lips of all her consecrated ministers, thus bringing hope and consolation to countless souls in lands never heard of by their human author.

(1949)

The Book of Psalms hath this wonder left over and above as peculiarly its own, that it contains the motions, and feels the inner

169

pulsations of every Christian soul, the subtle changes and rectifications wrought out within itself. The Psalms (oh! the wonder of it!) after those great prophecies concerning the Savior and the peoples— why! he that readeth them hears, and he that sings them takes part in them as if written about himself, not as telling a different person something about another, but as himself speaking concerning his very self: thus mirroring to him who reads or sings the Psalms, they are a means whereby he may see himself and his own soul's history.

ST. ATHANASIUS (ca. 350)

THE PERMANENT RELIGIOUS VALUES OF THE OLD TESTAMENT

MICHAEL CARDINAL VON FAULHABER

IT IS a fact in the history of civilization, that among no people of the pre-Christian era do we find so great a number of intellectually prominent men who, by their words and their whole personality, have devoted themselves to the religious guidance of their nation, as among the people of the early Bible. Among no other people do we find a series of writings in which the fundamental truths of the religious life are presented with such clarity, such distinctness and such harmony as in the Mosaic Pentateuch with the simple beauty of its biblical stories; in the books of Kings, classical models of the art of historical writing. . . . In the books of Chronicles with their liturgical prescriptions; in the book of Job with its treatment of the problem of suffering; in the Sapiential books with their maxims of conduct; in the books of the four major and twelve minor prophets with their national sermons; in the books of the Machabees, where the ancient heroism of the faith is once more resplendent. In these days when the history and the literature of other pre-Christian peoples are being investigated, the science of religions is able to make the comparison; and to the people of Israel it will award this certificate: You have excelled them all by the sublimity of your religion; among all the nations of antiquity you have exhibited the noblest religious values.

But pre-Christian Judaism did not produce these values of itself. "Prophecy came not by the will of man at any time; but the holy men of God spoke inspired by the Holy Ghost" (2 Pet. i. 21). The

170

Spirit of the Lord enlightened them; their tongues, as the Psalmist says, were the pencils of God, and therefore their speech was the word of God and their books, as the Fathers of Trent declared, have "God as their author." The French biblical critic (Renan) would have it that these books were the natural product of the Semitic mind. But in that case why did the other Semitic races produce nothing equal or even similar? The Babylonians were masters in the arts of secular civilization, especially in the construction of canals and fortifications; but they have left no heritage to the history of religions. The Arabs, also a Semitic people, near neighbors of the Israelites and closely related to them by blood, were, from the religious point of view, as sterile as the sand of their own desert. Why God should have chosen just this particular people of Israel, in this little corner of the earth called Palestine, to be the vehicle of His Revelation, remains a mystery of the dispensation of His grace. But we give thanks to the Father of light for having preserved their Holy Scriptures for us in texts and versions, as "the book of life."

In particular, human civilization and the Christian religion are indebted to the Old Testament for a pure and elevated conception of the Godhead, the most biblical thing in the Bible; for the revelation of Jahwe, Him who is, the God of Sabaoth, the Lord of armies, the only God, who suffers no strange gods before Him; the transcendent, personal God who by His revelation stooped down from His infinite heights and through His envoys spoke to men, gave them His laws and required that His law should be obeyed; the God who, to use the poetical but unphilosophical language of the Psalmist, has put on praise and beauty, is clothed with light as with a garment, stretches out the heaven like a pavilion, makes the spirits His angels and the burning fire His minister (Ps. ciii, 1-4). The conception of God is the noblest conception that the mind of man can conceive.

The peoples in the neighborhood of Chanaan did not even approach to the high level of the Jewish conception of God: neither the Assyrians and Babylonians with their hymns to the gods, pious enough though they were: nor the Egyptians with their animal idols. Even the Greeks, that highly intellectual people, had an Olympus of gods, and notwithstanding the Neoplatonic expurgations of their theodicy they never achieved so sublime a conception of the Godhead.

I am aware of the objections which are made against the God of the Old Testament: God, it is said, commanded Abraham to offer

171

human sacrifice. God did not require a human sacrifice. He wanted to try the Patriarch, to see whether he could practice faith and obedience, even when the human understanding is at a loss, even when the heart of a father must break. In other incidents Jahwe appears as angry and passionate. The reason is that harsh times call for harsh words. Elsewhere, too, the imagery has an Oriental coloring and there is talk of envy and revenge; or sublime ideas are expressed in elementary guise, so as to be understood by those who were but children in the preparatory school of Divine Revelation.

In the Gospel of the New Testament the ancient conception of God is perfected and fulfilled. Christ came into the world that we might know the Father "the only true God, and Jesus Christ" whom He had sent (John xvii, 3). The men of the Old Covenant spoke as "children"; the New Testament has become a man and "has put away the things of a child" (I Cor. xiii, 11). The same God who spoke from the bush on Mount Horeb had now appeared visibly in the Person of Emmanuel, God with us. Christ called the God of Abraham, of Isaac, and of Jacob "the God of the living" (Matt. xxii, 32), and in the first petition of the Our Father marvellously summed up all the ancient hymns to God. The God of the New Testament is not a different God from the God of the Old. But the idea is perfected and fulfilled in the Gospel in three ways: Here the Divine perfections are more clearly revealed. Here the monotheism in the Old Testament is developed into the doctrine of the Blessed Trinity. This mystery had already been foreshadowed in the triple *Sanctus* of the Old Testament; but here it is openly revealed: "In the name of the Father and of the Son and of the Holy Ghost." Finally, here in the Gospel man is shown the way to God: "No man," says Christ, "cometh to the Father but by Me" (John xiv, 6). . . .

The second great religious value of the Old Testament is the idea of redemption. The Gospel is the "good tidings" of "eternal redemption" (Heb. ix, 12). We read in the Gospel: "Lift up your heads, for your redemption is at hand" (Luke xxi, 28). But throughout the Old Testament the same voice resounds: "I know that my Redeemer liveth" (Job xix, 25). "Let the clouds rain the just; let the earth be opened and bud forth a saviour" (Is. xlv, 8). Compare with this the religious books of the Indians, which preach the end of all in Nirvana: the tidings of despair. A Book which brings the good tidings of redemption—"Shake off the dust . . . Thy light is come and the glory of the Lord is risen upon thee" (Is. lii, 1; lx, 1)—a Book which arouses us from torpor and despair, is a benefactor to humanity.

In the messianic prophecies the portrait of the Redeemer is filled in feature by feature. He is hailed from afar as the conqueror of Satan, as the desired of nations, as the seed of the royal house, as the Wisdom of God, as the light of the Gentiles, as the wondrous child, as the mighty hero, as the Father of the world to come and the Prince of peace, as the lamb at the slaughter. . . . Thus marvellously did the finger of God draw the line that leads straight through the centuries to the Redemption.

Let us venerate the Scriptures of the Old Testament! We do not set the Old Testament and the New on the same level. The Sacred Scriptures of the New Testament, the Gospels, the Acts of the Apostles, the Epistles, and the Apocalypse must hold the place of honor. But the Scriptures of the Old Testament are also inspired, and therefore they are sacred books, precious stones for the building of God's kingdom, priceless values for our religious guidance. And therefore the Church has stretched forth her protecting hand over the Scriptures of the Old Testament; she has gathered the forty-six books of the Old Testament and the twenty-seven books of the New into one volume, and she has used the text of the Old Testament also in her liturgy. . . . These books are inspired by the Holy Ghost, and therefore they are the word of God, they are God's books. The writers of them were God's pencils, the Psalmsingers were harps in the hand of God, the prophets are announcers of God's revelation. It is for this reason that the Scriptures of the Old Testament are worthy of credence and veneration for all time.   (1943)

The New Testament is latent in the Old and the Old Testament is patent in the New.

ST. AUGUSTINE (ca. 400)

THE ROLE OF THE JEWS IN THE REDEMPTION OF MANKIND

F. J. SHEED

IN GOD's plan for the re-establishment of the whole race, a special part was to be acted by one race, the Jews, and because of this God

173

brought them into special relation with Himself. The story is told in the forty-six books of the Old Testament. . . . They treat mainly of God's choosing of the Jews and what followed from it. . . .

The special relation of one people with God begins at a time and a place—the time roughly 2,000 B.C., the place Haran in the land of Chanaan. There had come Abram, with his father and his brothers, from the Chaldean town of Ur. And God said to Abram (Gen. 12) "I will make of thee a great nation, and I will bless thee, and magnify thy name: and thou shalt be blessed. I will bless them that bless thee, and curse them that curse thee; and in thee shall all the kindred of the earth be blessed." In the years that followed, God renewed the promises many times: but it was twenty-five years later that the great covenant was made which constituted the Jews God's people (Gen. 17): "God said to him: *I am*. And my covenant is with thee; and thou shalt be a father of many nations . . . And I will establish my covenant between me and thee, and between thy seed after thee in their generations, by a perpetual covenant: to be a God to thee, and to thy seed after thee." . . .

God then had singled out a particular family, which was to grow into a nation: not for their own sake but for the sake of all mankind: they were chosen not simply for a favor but for a function, something God was to do through them for the whole race. This God made clear again (Gen. 22): "In thy seed shall all the nations of the earth be blessed."

The promises were repeated to Abraham's second son Isaac (he had already had a son Ishmael by a bondswoman) and to Isaac's second son Jacob (for the elder, Esau, had forsworn his birthright). In all this we see the hint of the Redemption—all mankind is to be blessed through the seed of Abraham. And soon comes the hint of a Redeemer, and even of the mode of the Redemption—Jacob, dying, prophesies one who is to come from his fourth son, Juda: "The sceptre shall not be taken away from Juda, nor a ruler from his thigh, till he come that is to be sent: and he shall be the expectation of nations. Tying his foal to the vineyard, and his ass, O my son, to the vine. He shall wash his robe in wine, and his garment in the blood of the grape" (Gen. 49: 10-11). . . .

Upon Mt. Sinai the Covenant was renewed and the Law was given. God gave the Jews through Moses the Ten Commandments and a great mass of moral, ritual and legal precepts covering every detail of their lives. . . .

The Jews were chosen because of something God meant to accomplish through them for the whole world. The essence of their function lay in this—that from them was to come the Redeemer, who should redeem all mankind. Meanwhile, they were to bear witness to truths which were in danger of perishing, which indeed seemed to have perished utterly: the truth that there is but one God, the truth that God will send a Redeemer of mankind. . . .

He sent them the Prophets to bear glowing and glorious witness to the same truth. If they found monotheism difficult, they found not much easier the true doctrine as to the nature of the Messias, the Anointed One, who was to come, and of the Kingdom He was to found. Here again the Prophets were their instructors, and as the centuries pass the picture of the Messias and His Kingdom grows in detail and in clarity.

Yet we should be mistaken if we exaggerated the clarity. There is a vast mass of prophecy, and a magnificence over all of it. But much of it is obscure even to us who have seen its fulfillment; certain elements which now seem most wonderfully fulfilled appear buried in their context, not emphasized as prophetical or especially likely to catch the ear or the eye. The Prophets did not provide a blackboard diagram and then proceed to lecture on it. Indeed our modern use of the word prophet may give us a wrong notion of their office. To prophesy does not mean to foretell but to speak out. They were not there primarily to foretell the future but to utter the eternal and judge the present by it. The Jews not unnaturally found morality harder even than monotheism: the Law had imposed upon them a morality stricter than any known among men, and they fell from it. The Prophets thundered against this as against strange gods. For here too they must judge the present by the eternal.

But precisely because that was their function they did speak much of Him who was to come. Consider how the picture builds up. We have already seen that One who was to be the expectation of nations should come from Juda. From the Psalms (e.g. Ps. 131.11) we gather the further detail that He was to be a descendant of David the King, and this is confirmed by the statement of Isaias (11.1) that he is to be "a rod out of the root of Jesse" for Jesse was David's father: "In that day, the root of Jesse, who standeth for an ensign of the people, him the Gentiles shall beseech: and his sepulchre shall be glorious." There is no explicit statement that this is the Messias: but St. Paul takes it for granted (Rom. 15; 12) and in any event no Jew doubted the Messias was to be sprung from David.

In the seventh chapter of Isaias we read: "Behold a virgin shall

conceive and bear a son: and his name shall be called Emmanuel."
From St. Matthew (1.23) we know that this is a prophecy of the
virgin birth of Christ; yet in the context, one might well think that
the prophecy referred to an event immediately expected and actually described in the next chapter of Isaias, the eighth, as having
happened. In the light of our new knowledge, we can re-read the
eighth chapter and see that though there is some sort of fulfillment
there and then, yet some mightier thing is involved: the language
used is of a grandeur too great for the actual episode.

The fifth chapter of Micheas tells us that the Messias is to be
born in Bethlehem: "And thou, Bethlehem Ephrata, art a little one
among the thousands of Juda: out of thee shall he come forth unto
me that is to be the ruler in Israel: and his going forth is from the
beginning, from the days of eternity. . . . And this man shall be our
peace."

There are other details which we see fulfilled, but which could
hardly have meant so much to their first hearers: thus Zacharias
(9.9) writes: "Rejoice greatly, O daughter of Sion, shout for joy,
O daughter of Jerusalem: Behold thy King will come to thee, the
just and savior. He is poor and riding upon an ass, upon a colt, the
foal of an ass."

Such details as we have been considering—that the Messias was
to be of the tribe of Juda, of the family of David, born of a virgin
and in Bethlehem—are not the primary things about Him. Two
things that matter far more are Himself and what He was to do.
Upon both, the prophecies are fuller and clearer.

As to what He was: there is a central stream of teaching which
shows him a man triumphant, and two parallel streams, one showing Him as more than a man, the other showing Him as less than
triumphant. It would seem that the Jews concentrated on the central stream, and made little of either of the others. Yet these others
are of such vast importance, that missing them one hardly seems Him
at all.

That He was to be more than man, not simply the greatest of
men, is indicated again and again. We have already seen the phrase
of Micheas—"His going forth is from the beginning, from the days
of eternity." The same truth is in Psalm 109—"From the womb,
before the day star, I begot thee." But it is not only by pre-existence
that the Messias seems to be more than man. The hints are everywhere—as for instance the suggestion that He is to be the son of
God in a special way. (It is hard to see how there could be more

than hints: the truth about the divinity of the Messias could not very well be conveyed to a nation that did not know the doctrine of the Trinity.)

The reverse of the medal is the even clearer stream of prophecy that the Messias is to be poor and suffering. The greatest passages are in the Psalm 21 and in Chapter 53 of Isaias. The Psalm and the Chapter should be read most carefully. Here note a few verses from the Chapter, summing all up: "Despised and the most abject of men, a man of sorrows and acquainted with infirmity. . . .

"He shall be led as a sheep to the slaughter and shall be dumb as a lamb before his shearer. . . .

"And the Lord was pleased to bruise him in infirmity. If he shall lay down his life for sin, he shall see a long-lived seed. . . ."

To say that the Jews ignored a great deal of all this is not to accuse them of any startling malignity. The assertion of the Messias's pre-existence, for example, was difficult to reconcile with the certainty that he was to be a descendant of David: one gets the impression that the Jews, faced with two elements difficult to reconcile, simply took the intellectual line of least resistance, concentrated upon the clearer one and left the other in its mysteriousness. Similarly it is hard to see how anything short of what did in fact happen to Christ Our Lord could have shown the fulfillment both of the splendor and the suffering: lacking that cue, they concentrated on the more obvious.

But if their intellect followed the line of least resistance in the picture they formed of the Messias in Himself, their will seems to have followed the line of greatest complacency. They saw it as a Kingdom of Israel in which the Gentiles, if they came into it at all, should be very much in a subordinate place; and they saw it as an earthly and not as a spiritual Kingdom. The Prophets, properly read, supply correctives for both.

Thus they assert that the Messias is coming for a light to the Gentiles and that the Gentiles are to share in the joy of his Kingdom. When Psalm 71 says "In him shall all the tribes of the earth be blessed: all nations shall magnify him," it simply reasserts what God said to Abram in the first of the promises. Isaias is filled with the same teaching: and he indicates the possibility that there may be Jews excluded from the Kingdom and Gentiles admitted. So St. Paul (Rom. 10.22) explains the contrast (Isaias 65) between what God says of the Gentiles: "Those who never looked for me have found me: I have made myself known to those who never asked for word of me," and what He says of the Jews: "I stretch out my hand all day to a people that refuse obedience and cry out against me." But if we find from the Prophets that the Gentiles were to have a place, and a place of joy, in the Kingdom, it was left for St. Paul to utter in plain words the intimate secret of the total equality of Jew and Gentile in the Kingdom, the mystery of Christ "which was never made known to any human being in past ages . . . that through the gospel preaching the Gentiles are to win the same inheritance, to be made part of the same body, to share the same divine promise in Christ Jesus" (Eph. 3. 5-6).

Thus all who belong to Christ are of the seed of Abraham and the promises of the Kingdom are to us. But what sort of Kingdom? The Jews, as we have seen, seemed to expect an earthly Kingdom. The Prophets do not precisely and explicitly contradict them, but they give a mass of teaching which should have made the notion of a merely earthly Kingdom untenable and not even desirable. Thus Ezechiel (36. 24-26): "And I will pour upon you clean water and you shall be cleansed from all your filthiness: and I will cleanse you from all your idols. And I will give you a new heart and put a new spirit within you: and I will take away the stony heart out of your flesh and will give you a heart of flesh. And I will put my spirit in the midst of you." And Zacharias (9): "And he shall speak peace to the Gentiles: and his power shall be from sea to sea, and from the rivers even to the ends of the earth . . . And the Lord their God will save them in that day, as the flock of his people: for holy stones shall be lifted up over his land. For what is the good thing of him and what is his beautiful thing, but the corn of the elect and wine springing forth virgins?"

Indeed it is plain enough, for us who read the Prophets now, that there was to be a spiritualization at every point: even at the point of priesthood and sacrifice where Israel had most scrupulously observed the Law. For the Jewish priests and the Jewish sacrifices were but figures of, and preparations for, something that was mysteriously to transcend them. The Messias was to be (Ps. 109) "a priest forever according to the order of Melchisedech"—a strange phrase, for Melchisedech, who had offered a sacrifice of bread and wine (Gen. 14), was not a Jew. As for the priesthood, so for the sacrifices: "From the rising of the sun even to the going down, my name is great among the Gentiles: and in every place there is sacrifice and there is offered to my name a clean oblation. For my name is great among the Gentiles, saith the Lord of hosts" (Mal. I. 11).

178

Everything in Israel was preparatory, looked forward to something which should complete it. The Law given by God to Moses was not a consummation. It was a preparation: a hard and heavy preparation: not maturity, but a superb training for maturity.

(1946)

MARY AND THE OLD TESTAMENT

THE REV. JEAN DANIELOU, S.J.

THE Blessed Virgin had a most crucial role in the coming of Christ. In her culminated all the expectation of the Jewish people, insofar as all the preparations, aspirations, graces, prefigurations which had filled the Old Testament, all came together and were summed up in her; it is true to say that at the eve of Christ's coming she was the epitome and incarnation of the long waiting of twenty centuries. The whole of the Old Testament seems to come together in her with a more ardent longing and a more complete spiritual preparation for Our Lord's coming. *Omnis vallis implebitur, et omnis collis humiliabitur.* "Every valley shall be filled, and every mountain shall be brought low." The work of the Old Testament was one of education: mankind, rugged, coarse, as yet unformed, still utterly carnal-minded, must be made able, bit by bit, to take God's gifts, to receive the Holy Ghost. It was a long, progressive work of training. And the training culminated in the soul of the Blessed Virgin; and if we can say that in some sense her soul is outside time, and that in her eternity is present, then we may also say that she was prepared by the education of the whole of her people; she is the marvelous flower sprung out of Israel, the final point in the mysterious work of the Holy Ghost in the souls of all the prophets and all the holy women of Israel. All that was done in the soul of Sara, in the soul of Rebecca, in the soul of Rachel, in the soul of Ruth, all that was accomplished in the souls of all the great women of the Old Testament, was brought to its perfect fullness in the soul of Mary. It is, in fact, absolutely true to say that in her "every valley was filled, every mountain and hill brought low." That is to say, in her Our Lord's path was smooth before Him.

What was this education that Israel, and through Israel all mankind, had to be given that it might become a fit path for Our Lord? They must first be given a sense of God. Primitive Israel had no sense of God, or, rather, had a totally wrong and gross conception of Him. To them everything was God, and yet nothing was God. . . .

The first step in the Holy Spirit's education of humanity was, then, to wean it from idol-worship, and lead it to acknowledge and recognize the one true God. Throughout the history of the Jews we feel the tension going on, the people forever hankering after their idols. . . . Throughout the history of Israel God is constantly reproaching His people for being unfaithful, because they went to adore in high places and under every green tree. . . .

It was quite the contrary with the Blessed Virgin; she came at the end of this long, slow process of education, and had the perfect sense of God and His unity. If we compare her fidelity with Israel's infidelity, we see how the mystery of the education of Israel was being perfectly fulfilled in her: she is the *Virgo fidelis*, the faithful virgin, who was never anything else but faithful, whose fidelity was the perfect answer to the fidelity of God; she was always consecrated to the one true God. . . .

This mystery of the education of Israel is the mystery of grace, the giving of divine life to mankind. And we can see that, at the begining, Israel had no notion that this was what was happening. They thought God had chosen them to give them temporal goods, to lead them out of the slavery of Egypt; . . . they thought that God led them across the desert simply to give them the promised land, a land literally flowing with milk and honey. . . . And God, in His goodness and patience, . . . once He had chosen His people, He promised them first a certain happiness on earth; then, having given them various goods, He tried bit by bit to make them understand that these were not the things that mattered, and gradually began to withdraw these things from them; little by little He was putting the mystery of the Cross into the mystery of Israel—that mystery by which He takes from us the things we are too fond of, so that by emptying us of self He can fill us with Himself.

You find this mystery at the very core of Jewish history; it is the mystery of the just man suffering, which we find in the Book of Job, that strange book in the very heart of the Old Testament, the mystery of a soul being tried by God when it does not itself see what evil it has done—a thing both repugnant and meaningless to the Jewish

180

mind. Job himself did not as yet know what the answer was. He could only cling to his knowledge of his own innocence, and adore God's plan which he did not understand. The plan was in fact quite intelligible and extremely wise: God was teaching Job, and through him all his people, that He had never promised His friends the goods of this world. . . . Throughout the history of Israel God was trying to detach His people from material goods, and lead them to see that it was goods of quite a different kind that He had in store for them. . . .

In Our Lady we see the perfectly successful result of this education. Saint Bernard says of her that the only thing she ever asked for was grace. She did not imitate Solomon by asking for wisdom. She asked for grace because grace is the only thing we need. She was, therefore, perfectly wise. . . .

And, finally, God wanted to teach the Jews that He was the God of all men, and not simply of Israel. That is perhaps the high point of the whole drama, that is where the "stiff-necked race" found it hardest to accept God's plan for it; it is certainly the great paradox of that plan. God began by choosing Israel; for nineteen centuries Israel was the only one, and despised all other peoples, who had, indeed, not been so chosen; yet still, bit by bit, God tried to make this people He had chosen understand that He had not chosen them for themselves, but to be an instrument for carrying out His designs in regard to the other nations. At first Israel took this to mean that they were to exercise dominion over the others, that they were always to be in the first place. Only gradually did they see God's plan— that they were to prepare for the Saviour's coming, but that once He had come they were to fade into the background among all the other nations of the earth. And this was what they could not accept; they refused to join the ranks as one nation among all the others.

In Our Lady we see quite the reverse; in her, the fruit of the Jewish people, we see acceptance of the plan, and universal charity. She was not only a daughter of Israel, but she was the one through whom Israel flowed back into the common human current; she was at once daughter of David and of Abraham, and *Mater divinae gratiae,* universal mediatrix, mother of all mankind. She fully realized the promise made to Israel that they would have a special work to do which should affect the whole race. And Mary, born of the race of Abraham, forever a Jewess, is at the same time the mother of all men. She was the one who accepted to be no longer a Jew, who allowed her heart to expand to the bounds of the earth, who renounced the privilege of her birth, only to receive a far greater privilege of universality. The Blessed Virgin, the culmination of Jewish history, is the perfect thing that God intended that history to produce. (1950)

THREE

The New Testament

Many other signs also did Jesus in the sight of his disciples, which are not written in this book. But these are written, that you may believe that Jesus is the Christ, the Son of God: and that believing, you may have life in his name.

ST. JOHN, 20: 30,31

POLITICAL, SOCIAL AND RELIGIOUS CONDITIONS IN PALESTINE IN THE TIME OF CHRIST

THE REV. FRANCIS E. GIGOT

PALESTINE, the scene of Gospel history, has in different ages been designated by the following names: (1) the land of *Chanaan*; (2) the land of *Promise*; (3) the land of *Israel*; (4) the land of *Juda* or *Judaea*; (5) the *Holy Land*; (6) *Palestine*. This last, by far the most common name, was originally applied by the Hebrews merely to the strip of maritime plain inhabited by their encroaching neighbors, the Philistines, hence the name; but ultimately it became the usual appellation for the whole country of the Jews. . . .

Herod

Herod, whose last years of reign mark the beginning of the New Testament history, did not, as was claimed by his partisans, descend from one of the noble Jewish families which returned from Babylon, but belonged to the despised children of Edom, whom the valiant John Hyrcanus had formerly conquered and forcibly converted to the Jewish faith. He was the second son of the shrewd Antipater, who during the rule of the weak Macchabean prince Hyrcanus II gradually became the real master of Judaea under the title of *procurator* conferred upon him by Julius Caesar, and who profited by this fulness of power to appoint Herod, then only twenty-five years old, to the government of Galilee. . . .

On the murder of Julius Caesar (B.C. 44), and the possession of Syria by Cassius, Antipater and Herod changed sides, and in return for substantial services Herod was recognized as governor of Coele-Syria, that is, of the fertile valley between Lebanon and Anti-Lebanon. When the battle of Philippi (B.C. 41) placed the Roman world in the

185

hands of Antony and Cleopatra, the former obtained Asia. Once more Herod knew how to gain the new ruler, and he became *tetrarch* of Judaea, with the promise of the crown if all went well.

Forced the following year, by an irruption of the Parthians, who had espoused the cause of his rival Antigonus (the son of Aristobulus II), to abandon Jerusalem, Herod first betook himself to Egypt, and then to Rome. There, owing chiefly to the influence of Antony, he was declared king of Judaea by the Roman senate. . . .

After an absence of barely three months, Herod was again in Palestine, where, at the head of an army, he soon made himself master of Galilee. He next set himself to take the Holy City. . . . After a siege of six months Jerusalem fell, and a fearful scene of carnage ensued. At length, Herod, by rich presents, induced the Romans to leave the Holy City. . . . Herod, the Idumaean, now ascended the throne of Judaea and inaugurated his long reign of 37 years.

The first part of Herod's reign (B.C. 37–25) was spent in bloody endeavors to consolidate his power. . . . Meanwhile, and also with a view to consolidate his power, Herod neglected nothing to keep up his friendly relations with Rome. To please his then all-powerful patron, Antony, he gave to Cleopatra—who exercised a controlling influence over Antony—a valuable part of his dominions, the fertile district of Jericho. Upon the fall of Antony at Actium (B.C. 31) he succeeded in making a friend of Octavius . . . He received from Octavius a new increase in territory, and afterwards was appointed procurator of the province of Syria. . . .

To establish himself still more in the favor of Augustus, Herod imitated him in great works of peace. He erected a theatre within the Holy City, and without the walls an amphitheatre in which he held games in honor of the emperor with horse and chariot races and the bloody fights of gladiators with wild beasts. He not only embellished the old residence of the Asmoneans . . . but built himself in the upper city a royal palace with wide porticoes, rows of pillars and baths, and for the adornment of which he spared neither marble nor gold. . . . He restored and enlarged the citadel, which he named Antonia, after his former patron. Finally, the most magnificent of all his buildings in Jerusalem was the Temple, which in its former condition was out of keeping with the beautiful recent structures in the Holy City, and which after its rebuilding by Herod became justly the greatest national glory of the Jews.

Herod's love of building naturally extended to other places within his dominion. . . .

In his great desire to please Augustus and appear a liberal and cultured prince, Herod held a court whose splendor and general tone resembled in many ways that of the emperor. Like the Roman ruler, the king of Judaea surrounded himself with men accomplished in Greek literature and art, and many among them were placed in offices of trust or honor. . . . Unfortunately, the Jewish monarch ever remained a barbarian at heart, and his practice of polygamy, together with his suspicious temperament, greatly interfered with the peace and happiness of those immediately connected with him.

Under Herod the upper classes lost much of their hereditary power, and endeavored to make up for it by a life of luxury and enjoyment; yet the high priests continued to form an influential aristocracy.

Amid all his power and glory, Herod himself realized how far he was from enjoying the good-will of his subjects at large. He knew they murmured at his introduction of foreign and heathen practices, his arbitrary setting up and deposition of the high priests, his prodigal expenditure, and his terrible severity against his opponents. Hence he several times attempted to pacify the people by truly generous and liberal deeds; but their gratitude did not last long and time and again serious conspiracies endangered his life.

In consequence of such popular opposition to his rule, as to that of a hated Idumaean and of a direct representative of the foreign and pagan authority of Rome, Herod carefully refrained from interfering with all that the worship of Jehovah in His own sanctuary required in the eyes of the Jews of Palestine and of the Dispersion. Under him, therefore, as under his predecessors, Jerusalem remained the great metropolis of Judaism. It was at the Holy City that the dispersed Jews regularly congregated in hundreds of thousands, bearing their yearly tribute and anxious to worship the God of their ancestors within the sacred precincts of His Temple. . . . It was in Jerusalem that the great masters of Israel, looked up to by the whole Jewish world, expounded the Law and the traditions of the elders, and from the Holy City that all the parts of the Eastern and Western Dispersion received the teachings of their fathers, the regulations for the feast-days, etc. . . . All this had besides the advantage to secure for the capital of Judaea a commerce, an influence, a prestige which it would never have possessed otherwise, and as long as he was able to control it by the free appointment or removal of the head of the Jewish hierarchy, Herod had no direct interest to interfere with it.

That this conduct of the Jewish king was simply the result of expediency is made plain by his manner of action wherever he felt himself free to encourage heathenism. Not only far away, in Phoenicia, Syria, Asia Minor, and Greece, he made himself the ostentatious patron of everything pagan, rearing temples, theatres, porticoes, gymnasia, etc., but also around the central district of Palestine, and even to some extent within its limits, he started to encourage idolatry. Gaza, Ascalon, Dor, Caesarea, Joppe, Samaria, Panaeas were desecrated by heathen temples, altars, idols, and priests. Even in the Temple of Jerusalem the Grecian style of architecture was freely adopted. It is true that in the Temple proper Herod could not venture to forsake the traditional forms; but in the building of the inner fore-courts we see the influence of Greek models. Indeed the king went so far as to place within its sacred precincts a number of trophies, and to display over its main entrance a golden eagle, the symbol of pagan Rome.

It is easy to understand how such unholy changes, forced upon the Jewish patriots and believers by the iron hand of the royal Idumaean, made them long ardently for the reign of the Messias, which their sacred books represented as a future kingdom of righteousness, and which their apocryphal literature described chiefly under the attractive images of material prosperity. False Messiahs made their appearance at the very moment of Our Lord's stay in Egypt, and the message of John the Baptist, a little later, gave a new impulse to the general belief that the Messias was at hand. . . .

According to the popular ideal, the Messias was to be primarily a political leader, a mighty deliverer of His people from the tyranny of its pagan oppressors, and also a restorer of the Jewish institutions in their primitive purity. Issued from David's race and born in Judaea, He was expected to start a world-wide empire, of which Jerusalem would be the capital, and in which the sons of Abraham would be superior in things temporal as well as spiritual to the rest of the world. To be admitted into this Messianic kingdom it would be sufficient to observe the enactments of the Mosaic law, to which the Messias would Himself be subjected. Finally, a large number of Jews believed that if the nation was once engaged in such an extreme conflict with the Romans as to threaten Jerusalem and its Temple with destruction, the Messias must needs appear. . . .

The last period of Herod's rule (B.C. 15–4) was disgraced by scenes of bloodshed still more awful than those which darkened its first years, and the history of his domestic affairs is that of a long succession of intrigues and murders. . . . Herod died in the seventieth year of his age (B.C. 4). At the news of the tyrant's death frightful anarchy prevailed in Palestine. The popular voice, backed up by tumult and riot, clamored for the redress of grievances, such as the diminution of public burdens, the release of prisoners with whom Herod had crowded the dungeons, the abandonment of onerous taxes, etc. . . .

The last will of Herod the Great having, after a time, been confirmed by Augustus, Palestine was divided between three of his sons:

Herod Philip II became tetrarch of Gaulanitis, Trachonitis, Baltanea, and the district of Panaeas. He was a just and moderate ruler . . . from B.C. 4 to A.D. 34. . . .

Herod Antipas was appointed tetrarch of Galilee and Peraea. In character he was unscrupulous, tyrannical and weak, cruel and cunning, though not remorseless. He was a truly Eastern despot, capricious and sensual. In defiance of the Jewish law he had married the wife of Herod Philip—his brother, who was then living as a private citizen in Rome—and this led him to the murder of John the Baptist. It was before this prince that Our Lord appeared at the time of His Passion.

His greatest architectural work was the erection of a city which he called Tiberius, in honor of the emperor. After his banishment to Lyons, in Gaul, his territories were given to Herod Agrippa I, his nephew. He was tetrarch forty-one years, from B.C. 4 to A.D. 38.

Archelaus, like Herod Antipas, was a son of Herod and Malthace. . . . His territories included Idumaea, Judaea, and Samaria. . . . After a rule of ten years (B.C. 4–A.D. 6) his territories were annexed to the Roman province of Syria, and thus Judaea was placed under the *immediate* Roman domination.

The Jews had asked for this *direct* government of Rome at the death of Herod the Great, in the hope that the Romans would allow them to manage their national affairs after their own customs, under their high priests. This hope was revived by the banishment of Archelaus, but it did not last long. Judaea and Samaria were united to Syria, of which Publius Cyrinus was made president or propraetor, while the immediate direction of affairs was given to a *procurator,* residing at Caesarea. The powers of this inferior officer cannot be exactly defined. In general, he was subject to the president of the province; yet, in districts lying far from the main province, he seems to have had a large discretionary power, a considerable number of troops at his disposal, and, in certain cases, the power of life and death.

The immediate Roman domination was exercised over the various provinces of the empire in an irritating, vexatious, and oppressive manner, but it was particularly so in Judaea, on account of the peculiar character of the Jews, which contrasted so much with that of the Romans.

It must be said, however, that under Augustus the rule of Rome over the Jews was fairly tolerable; but the exercise of the Roman power required chiefly two taxes: a *poll* and a *land* tax, the latter tax amounting to one-tenth of all grain and two-tenths of fruit and wine. To establish these taxes a *second census* was necessary. The fiercer spirits in Judaea rebelled at the idea that the *fruits* of a land consecrated to Jehovah should be given to pagan strangers, and that *tithes* to be paid to God alone should henceforth be paid to a heathen lord. . . .

Towards the close of the reign of Augustus the procurators of Judaea succeeded one another rapidly; but his successor, Tiberius, pursued a different policy. During his long reign Judaea had only two procurators: Valerius Gratus (A.D. 15–26) and Pontius Pilate (A.D. 26–36).

Under Gratus things went from bad to worse. He changed the high priests five times in eleven years, and the load of public taxes became so unendurable that the Jews appealed to Rome for relief; but in all probability their entreaties did not bring them any alleviation of misery. The successor of Gratus was Pontius Pilate, the very type of the rich and corrupt Roman of his age. He was a worldly-minded statesman, conscious of no higher wants than those of the present life, yet by no means unmoved by feelings of justice and mercy. But all his better feelings were overpowered by a selfish regard for his own security. . . .

The Pharisees formed the most prominent party or guild among the Jews during the lifetime of Our Lord. As their name indicates, they originally arose as champions of the *separateness* of the Jewish people from other nations. They consequently held fast by the distinctive beliefs of the Jewish race, as, for instance, the hope of a great national deliverer in the person of a Messias, the doctrine of the immortality of the soul, of a divine Providence, of an *oral* tradition equal in authority with the *written* law. Nor were they less zealous in carrying out the external observances of their ancestors, such as fasts, prayers, tithes, ablutions, sacrifices, etc. They were ardent patriots, ever willing to lay down their lives for the national independence, and hating the foreign yoke with a bitterness mingled with scorn. The multitudes, although not actually enrolled among the Pharisees, were under their sway, and zealously adhered to a party so intensely national in politics and orthodox in religion. To the Pharisaic party belonged most of the scribes. Finally, although there were found noble characters among the leaders of the party, self-conceit, arrogance, and hypocrisy had become the general characteristic of the sect.

190

The origin of the Sadducees is probably to be traced to a natural tendency opposed to that which gave birth to the Pharisaic party, viz. the desire to side closely with the ruling party. Their opposition to the Pharisees extended both to religious and to social customs. They notably denied the immortality of the soul, the existence of a divinely revealed oral tradition, etc. They ridiculed Pharisaic exclusiveness, affected Greek culture, enjoyed foreign amusements, and thought it useless to fight for the freedom of their country. They belonged chiefly to the upper and wealthy classes, and formed a kind of priestly aristocratic party in close alliance with the ruling power. . . .

For centuries the Samaritans had been despised by the Jews, as a mixed race descending from the Assyrian colonists who had settled in the land of Israel when the northern kingdom was destroyed in the eighth century before Christ. At the time of Our Lord, the hatred between the Jews and the Samaritans had reached its climax. . . .

The great center of the religious life of the Jews during the lifetime of Our Lord was the *Temple* of Jerusalem. Herod had rebuilt it in its original site, Mount Moria, east of the Holy City. . . .

The persons who had charge of the Temple, and a large number of whom were always in residence, were the priests, whose duty it was to mediate between Jehovah and His people. They formed a sacred order, to which no one could be admitted who did not belong to it by birth; for according to the legislation of the Pentateuch "The Sons of Aaron" were alone entitled to the rights and privileges of the Jewish priesthood. . . .

Although in some cases the priests exercised judicial functions, and were in charge to preserve and expound the Law, their duties were mainly sacrificial. . . . At the head of the whole Jewish priesthood was the *high priest*. He was to be a person especially sacred, hence any bodily imperfection or blemish excluded him from the office. There were, besides, disqualifications, such as illegitimacy, idolatry, etc. . . . Under the Romans this office was too often entrusted to persons who had neither age nor learning nor rank to recommend them. . . .

The position of high priest combined in one and the same person both a *civil* and a *sacred* dignity. To him alone belonged the right to officiate on the great Day of Atonement. He alone could enter the Most Holy Place; he was also the supreme administrator of sacred things and the final arbiter of all religious controversies. At the same time he presided over the Sanhedrim; and in all political matters he was the supreme representative of the Jews in their relations with the Romans.

During the captivity of Babylon the sacrificial services of the Temple were, of course, discontinued; hence, it is most likely to this period that we must ascribe the origin of a religious institution which at the return of the Jews was transplanted into Palestine, and which in Our Lord's time was spread everywhere, viz., the institution of the synagogues. No sacrifices could be offered in these meeting-places; but public prayers were put up, and Holy Writ was read and practically expounded. The synagogues often consisted of two apartments: one for the prayers, preaching, and public worship; the other for the meeting of learned men, and for discussions concerning questions of religion and discipline, and for purposes of education. . . .

The chief interpreters of Holy Writ in the synagogues were the *Scribes,* who far more than the priests, guided and shaped the religious life of the people at large. They belonged to different tribes and families, and also to different sects, although most of them, while being Scribes by office, were Pharisees by religious and political profession. In the time of Our Lord they were spread everywhere, and because of their special skill in the Law and in the other Sacred Writings, they were reputed as men of great learning. They loved the title of *Rabbi,* and required the greatest honors not only from their pupils, but also from the public at large.

By their theoretical and practical interpretation of Holy Writ they had gradually laid a most heavy burden upon the people, for it was their aim to apply the Law to all imaginable circumstances of daily life, and their work in that direction was characterized by slavery to the letter, and by subtle casuistry. . . .

It was in one of the halls of the Temple that, up to about A.D. 30, the *Sanhedrim,* or highest council of the Jews, made up of chief priests, elders and Scribes, met under the presidency of the high priests. . . . This supreme tribunal of the Jews counted seventy-one members of pure Israelite descent and was governed by a president and two vice-presidents; besides there were secretaries and other officers.

During Our Lord's lifetime the power of the Sanhedrim extended to matters of the greatest importance. Among others, we may notice that it superintended the ritual of public worship, regulated the Jewish calendar, enforced the exact fulfillment of the law, punished false prophets, and even exercised judicial control over the high priests. However, its privilege of carrying into effect a sentence of death it had pronounced had been taken away from the Sanhedrim and reserved to the Roman procurator. The supreme authority of the decrees of the Sanhedrim was acknowledged by all Jews dispersed throughout the world.

The social and religious conditions of the Jews in Our Lord's day naturally created many difficulties against the acceptance of His teachings.

One of these difficulties arose from the national antipathies and susceptibilities of Our Lord's contemporaries. The Romans despised, it is true, the Jewish nation and thought they could easily quell any revolt against their domination; yet they were naturally jealous of their authority, and would certainly resent Christ's open assumption of the title of the Messias and His preaching of a new kingdom, for both could easily lead the Jewish multitudes to new uprisings against the hated power of Rome. Again, the Samaritans and the Jews were no less at variance between themselves than the Romans and the Jews; hence, any special favor shown by Jesus to members of either community would certainly tell against the influence of His words and miracles upon the minds and hearts of the others.

A second and greater difficulty to Our Lord's work was to be found in the narrowness or the fears of the Jewish leaders. To be welcome as a teacher to the Scribes and the Pharisees of His time, Jesus should have belonged to the learned class of the "Masters in Israel," and like them He should have pledged Himself to uphold all the "traditions of the elders"; but more particularly, He should have felt bound to comply with the rules of the Scribes and Pharisees, since "all the Jews"—even the Sadducees—carried them out faithfully; and the Gospel record proves that to be faithful to His mission, Our Lord had to set all these traditions aside and to unmask fearlessly the pride and hypocrisy of this the most influential of the Jewish sects. The Sadducees were no less opposed to the work of Our Lord than the Pharisees. His doctrine was in direct contradiction in several points to that of the Sadducees, and His public mission appeared to them most objectionable. On the one hand, these cautious politicians saw that the multitudes were more and more won to His cause, and feared lest they would ultimately crown Him King and rebel against Rome; and on the other hand, they were fully persuaded that Jesus had not at His disposal the forces necessary to cope successfully with the Roman legions. These various elements of opposition to Our Lord's work were all represented in the Sanhedrim, and their ultimate combination against His work and His life led to His trial and to His execution.

It must be said, however, that the greatest difficulty our divine Lord had to contend with in the discharge of His public mission arose from the mistaken notion concerning the Messias, which was so prevalent in the minds of His contemporaries. The Jewish expectations respecting the person and work of the Messias, the nature and conditions of the Messianic kingdom, ran directly counter to what the Redeemer of the world had to be and to establish upon earth.

One of the most remarkable features of the conduct of Our Lord during His public ministry is His prudence of action. During His entire public work we find no trace of the least collision with the Roman power. He usually moves in Galilee, far from immediate contact with the Roman officials, avoids assuming the Messianic title, never shows the least desire for the royal dignity, and when pressed by His enemies to declare whether it is lawful to pay tribute or not, He answers in a manner which had to be distorted in order that it might be brought against Him at the time of His Passion.

Our Lord did not act with less prudence in His relations with the Jewish authorities. Here, however, the avoidance of a collision was an impossibility. His mission of Savior of souls required that He should unmask His opponents to the people and openly contend with them, and this He did repeatedly, with a severity proportionate to the ardor of His zeal. But outside these cases he acted towards them with the utmost kindness. Indeed, it may be said that His conduct was ever in perfect harmony with this most wise distinction between the authority and the person of the Jewish leaders: "All whatsoever they shall say to you, observe and do; but according to their works do ye not."

It is in the same prudent way that Jesus did not go at once against the mistaken Messianic notions of the people, or even of His chosen disciples. He knew that inveterate prejudices must not be handled roughly, and that a gradual light is not only more welcome, but also more effective. Hence He suggested in various ways, but especially through striking parables, the truths regarding the nature of the kingdom of God, its growth, conditions of entrance, etc., which He could not have disclosed openly without hurting uselessly the most cherished hopes of His contemporaries. And it is only towards the close of His work that He fully disclosed His equality with the Father and His true relations to the Jews and to the world.

A second means which Our Lord employed for the fulfillment of His mission is the wonderful power of His words. His discourses are a spirit, an impulse, a direction, not a series of abstract, dry enactments, so that every one of His hearers could at once feel their importance and their beauty. They are also characterized by great originality, for even when He took up the religious truths of the Old Testament revelation, He divested them of their grosser interpretations and gave them a spiritual meaning hitherto unsuspected. . . . So great, indeed, was the power of His words, that the multitudes, in their eagerness to hear Him, pressed upon Him in great numbers, and followed Him everywhere, forgetful of the very necessities of life.

The miracles which our divine Lord performed were, however, the very powerful means by which He won the admiration, gratitude, and authority necessary to cope successfully with the opposition of the Jewish leaders. He multiplied these wonders at each step, and they were such as no man had wrought before Him. . . . Even His presence was not necessary for the performance of such wonders. The most hidden thoughts of His hearers, as well as the most remote events, were equally known to Him. Not only did He perform His miracles Himself, but on different occasions He imparted a similar power to His messengers. It was, therefore, plain to His contemporaries that He was endowed with a perfect mastery over all creatures. The multitudes instinctively felt that the coming Messias could not be expected to perform greater miracles, and were led to consider Him as being Himself the Messias who, as they thought, by His miraculous power was to drive the foreigner from the Holy Land, submit the Gentiles to the Jews, and start a new era of material and religious prosperity.   (1898)

GEOGRAPHY OF THE HOLY LAND

THE REV. S. G. MESSMER

THE land which God had promised to Abraham and his descendants, and where in the fulness of time the divine promises were to be fulfilled (hence the *Land of Promise*), is the small, hilly country of Palestine, formerly called Chanaan. Both names had originally a more limited signification. *Chanaan,* i.e. the low-country, as distinguished from *Gilead,* the high table-land east of the Jordan, was the name of the land in the north-west along the shore of the Mediterranean. Later the whole country west of the Jordan, including Phoenicia, in which the Chanaanites settled, received the same name. *Palestine* or Philistia, likewise, designated originally the low country in the south-west on the sea-shore, inhabited by the powerful Philistines; the Romans extended the name to the whole country.

Palestine is the *Holy Land,* because it is the country chosen by God for His people and His holy temple, where the Messias was to bring redemption to man. It is also called the *Land of Jehova,* because it was His special property, upon which the Jews were only tenants. It is called the *Land of Israel,* or of *Juda,* or of the *Hebrews,* from the names of its inhabitants.

By the river Jordan, Palestine is divided into two distinct sections. The western section extends from the Lebanon in the north to the Arabian desert in the south; the eastern section extends from Mt. Hermon in the north to the river Arnon in the south. At the time of Christ, this eastern section, formerly known as Gilead, was called Peraea. The length of Palestine from north to south is about one hundred and eighty miles, and its width from west to east, ninety miles in the southern, and forty miles in the northern portion, the total area being about twelve thousand square miles, very nearly the same as the State of Maryland. . . .

The natural boundaries of the Holy Land are the Mediterranean Sea on the west, and the Lebanon range on the north, which divides it from Phoenicia and Syria; vast deserts separate it on the east from Syria and Babylonia, and on the south from Egypt. Being a self-supporting country in which Israel was able to lead a secluded life, situated almost in the centre of the ancient world, on the Mediterranean Sea and near the great commercial routes, Palestine was eminently fitted to become the cradle of Christianity. Tyre and Damascus, Petra and Alexandria, the four great commercial centers of antiquity, were its four corner-pillars; Phoenicia, Babylon, and Egypt, the homes of ancient civilization, encompassed it. The road from Damascus to Egypt passed through the entire length, from the plain of Esdrelon via Ramleh (Arimathea) and Gaza; the road from Damascus into Arabia, which joined the north with the south and formed a chief part of the connection between Asia and Africa, ran east of the Jordan, whilst another important highway, from Tyre to Niniveh, ran along its northern boundary. . . .

The following single mountains deserve to be noted:

In the mountain range of Nepthali (Galilee): Mount Thabor, where Christ was transfigured, 1843 feet high, in the north of the plain of Esdrelon. The *Mount of the Beatitudes,* 1080 feet, also called the Mount of Christ and of the Apostles, is a double-crested hill, four miles west of Tiberias. The *Little Hermon,* three miles south of Thabor.

Mount Carmel, a beautiful promontory in the extreme west of the plain of Esdrelon, made famous by the Prophet Elias; its highest peak rises to about 1600 feet. . . .

In the mountains of Juda: *Mount Olivet,* the scene of the agony and the ascension of Christ, with its three peaks, the northern 2,500 feet, the southern 2,100 feet, and the middle one, 2,400 feet, is about a mile east of Jerusalem, *Mount Quarantania,* 1,500 feet, or the mount of the forty days' fast, in the desert between Jerusalem and Jericho. . . .

The *Sea of Genesareth,* or of *Galilee,* or of *Tiberias,* is about twelve miles long and from four to seven wide. Its depth is from eighty to a hundred and sixty feet; its surface is six hundred and eighty-two feet below the level of the Mediterranean. It is oval in shape, and surrounded with picturesque and, in parts, very fertile mountains; the eastern shore is steep; the western was at one time thickly studded with cities and villages, among which Capharnaum, Corozain, Magdala, Bethsaida, and Tiberias are the best known. Jewish writers dwell with enthusiasm on the excellence of this lake, the transparency of its waters, its great abundance of fish, the fertility of its shores, and the sublime scenery of its surroundings. In the Old Testament this water is called the *Sea of Genesareth,* probably from the city of the same name. Much of Our Lord's public life was spent on the shores of this lake. . . .

The principal river of Palestine, the Jordan, i.e. the descender, flows from north to south, down a deep valley in the center of the country, which it divides into two unequal parts, the greater lying west. . . .

Galilee, the region north of Jezrael (Esdrelon), comprised the tribes of Nepthali, Aser, Zabulon, and part of Issachar; it was the region most favored by nature. The gem of the whole territory lay along the western shore of Lake Genesareth. Here stood the well-known towns of Corozain, Bethsaida (the home of SS. Peter, Andrew, and Philip; it must be well distinguished from Bethsaida on the north-east shore, where Christ fed the five thousand), Capharnaum (Our Lord's "own city," Mt. ix. 1, where He finally dwelt during His public life), Magdala, or Magedan, the home of Mary, the sinner (Lk. vii. 37 ff.; viii. 2), and Tiberias, built by the tetrarch Herod Antipas, for his residence, and named after the Emperor Tiberius. The population of Galilee was predominantly Jewish; in Upper Galilee, however, heathen Syrians and Phoenicians were numerous. In central Galilee lies Cana; in lower Galilee, Nazareth; and in the north of Esdrelon, Naim and Endor, where Saul consulted the witch. The Galilean dialect had a peculiar twang, especially in the pronunciation of the gutturals (Mt. xxvi. 73). . . .

Jerusalem (i.e. house of peace), was the chief city of Palestine, and was in succession called Salem, Jebus, Jerusalem, and today also el-Kuds (the Holy).

It lies on a south-easterly spur of the mountain ridge of Juda; it is about thirty-five miles from the Mediterranean, twenty from the Jordan, twenty from Hebron, and thirty-six from the city of Samaria. It is truly a mountain city, as its buildings, in the course of time, covered four hills. . . .

The theatre of biblical events, which, until the coming of Christ, had been chiefly in Palestine, was by the preaching of the Apostles extended to the ends of the then known world. Paul, the Apostle of the Gentiles, in his missionary expeditions, carried the Gospel from Syria over Cyprus into Asia Minor, and thence to Europe, to Macedonia and Greece, and finally to Rome, the capital of the world, which Peter had already made the center of the Church.   (1910)

PROBABLE DATES OF THE PRINCIPAL EVENTS IN THE HISTORY OF THE NEW TESTAMENT*

THE REV. JOHN E. STEINMUELLER AND KATHRYN SULLIVAN

B.C.

8: Birth of Jesus Christ at Bethlehem.

A.D.

August 19, 28–August 18, 29: The fifteenth year of Tiberius.

Spring of 29: Beginning of John the Baptist's mission.

Fall of 29 or Spring of 30: Beginning of Christ's public mission.

April 3, 33: The Death of Jesus Christ.

36: The stoning of St. Stephen.

36: The conversion of St. Paul.

42: The martyrdom of St. James the Greater.

44: The death of Herod Agrippa I.

44/45—49/50: The first missionary journey of St. Paul.

* From *A Companion to the New Testament* by John E. Steinmueller and Kathryn Sullivan. Copyright, 1944, Joseph F. Wagner, Inc.

49: The Decree of Claudius (41–54) expelling the Jews from Rome.
50: The Council of Jerusalem.
50—52/53: The second missionary journey of St. Paul.
53/54—58: The third missionary journey of St. Paul.
58–60: The imprisonment of St. Paul in Palestine.
61–63: The first imprisonment of St. Paul at Rome.
62: The martyrdom of St. James the Less.
66–67: The second imprisonment of St. Paul at Rome.
66–70: The Jewish insurrection in Palestine.
67: The martyrdom of Sts. Peter and Paul at Rome.
About 100: The death of St. John the Apostle.   (1944)

THE CHRISTIAN REVELATION
AND CHURCH ANTEDATED
THE NEW TESTAMENT

HENRY EDWARD CARDINAL MANNING

THE whole revelation of Christianity was given by the Holy Spirit and preached also and believed among the nations of the world before the New Testament existed. The knowledge of God through the Incarnation, and the way of salvation through grace, was revealed partly by our Divine Lord, and fully by the Holy Ghost at His coming. The faith or science of God was infused into the apostles by a divine illumination. It was not built up by deduction from the Old Testament, but came from God manifest in the flesh, and from His Holy Spirit. It was in itself the New Testament, before a line of it was written. . . .

This truth was preached throughout the world by the apostolic mission. They were commanded to "preach the Gospel to every creature," and "to make disciples of all nations." And what Jesus commanded, the apostles did. They promulgated the whole of Christianity. They baptized men into the faith of Jesus Christ. But before they baptized any man he became a disciple: that is, he learned the faith. The Faith was delivered to him in the articles of the Baptismal Creed, as the law was delivered in the Ten Commandments. . . . But what was the source of this perfect science of God in Jesus Christ? It was no written Book, but the presence of a Divine Person illuminating both the teacher and the taught.

And this universal preaching of the apostles was written by the Spirit upon the intelligence and heart of the living Church, and sustained in it by His presence. The New Testament is a living Scripture, namely the Church itself, inhabited by the Spirit of God, the author and writer of all revealed truth. . . .

This revelation was divinely recorded before the New Testament Scriptures were written.

It was written, as I have said, upon the mind of the pastors, or the *Ecclesia docens,* the Church teaching the world; and upon the mind of the flock or the *Ecclesia discens,* the Church learning throughout the world. . . .

The Seven Sacraments of the Church are a Record, or Scripture of God, anterior to the written Gospels of the Evangelists. . . . The Church, its sacraments, and its worship were spread throughout the world before as yet the books of the New Testament were written.

It was not till the Faith had been everywhere preached, believed, defined in creeds, recorded in the mind of the universal Church, embodied in sacraments, and manifested in perpetual worship, that the New Testament was formed. By the inspiration and impulse of the same Divine Teacher who had already revealed the whole Truth to the apostles, it was for the most part put in writing. I say for the most part, because the written Scripture is not coextensive with the revelation of Pentecost, nor with the preaching of the apostles. The written Scripture presupposes and recognizes in those to whom it is addressed the knowledge of the whole Truth. . . .

The most elementary knowledge of Christian history is enough to prove this. The first Gospel, that of St. Matthew, was not written till five years after the Ascension, and then in Hebrew only. In Greek it did not exist for five or six years later; that is, for ten years at least, none of the four Gospels, as we possess them, was written. The second Gospel, that of St. Mark, was written about the same time. The third, twenty-four years later. For the first twenty years there were only two Gospels, and those in Greek. The fourth Gospel, that of St. John, was not written till about sixty years after the Ascension. Where then, till the end of the first century, or for two generations of men, were the four Gospels, which people seem to imagine were distributed by the twelve Apostles to their converts on the day of Pentecost?

The earliest of the Epistles was written about fifteen years after Our

Lord's Ascension—the latest more than thirty years after that event. But all these books are limited in their scope. Even the four Gospels treat only of the Incarnation and earthly life of Jesus. The Book of Acts is but a fragment of the history of St. Peter and St. Paul. The Epistles are local and occasional, and even private and personal in their nature. And all these books for generations were known only by those parts of the Church to which they were dedicated and entrusted. They were not collected into a volume, that is, the New Testament, as men call it, did not exist until a hundred years at least after the Ascension. During all this century, martyrs, confessors, saints, and penitents multiplied in all the world. The apostolic mission had become a universal tradition. The Church on earth rested on the sunrise and the sunset, upon Spain, and upon India. The Heavenly Court had already received the saints of three generations of men. But during all this time what was the source of their Christianity, and what its support? Certainly no book, not even the New Testament Scripture, but the New Testament "in spirit and in truth," the revelation of the day of Pentecost, given and sustained by the presence of the Holy Spirit in the Church, the divine and perpetual Teacher of the world. This is the original, of which the written Scripture is but a partial and subsequent transcript. . . .

This science of God, incorporated in the Church, is the true key to the interpretation of Scripture. It was in possession throughout the world; it was perfect everywhere before the books of the New Testament were written. It bore witness to the whole revelation of the day of Pentecost; it fixed the meaning of the Scriptures by the evidence of divine facts.

The Socinians and Unitarians tell us now, as the Arians and Sabellians told us of old, that the doctrine of the Holy Trinity is not to be read in the New Testament. But it was preached and believed throughout the world before the New Testament was written.

Presbyterians, Independents, and other Protestants tell us now as the Acephali and others told us of old, that a hierarchy, an episcopate, and a priesthood are not to be found in the New Testament; but there was a hierarchy ruling over the pastors of the Church, an episcopate feeding the flock, and a priesthood offering the holy sacrifice at the altar among all nations of the world before the New Testament existed.

There are Puritans of every shade and Anglicans of many opinions, who tell us that the Church is an invisible body seen only by faith and by God; that its unity is only moral, not numerical; that it is

201

divisible into many parts, or branches, and that the New Testament does not exhibit the Church as visible to the eye, numerically one, and indivisible in its unity. But before the New Testament was, the Church had expanded from east to west, visible by its organization, absolute and exclusive in its unity, which the divisions and apostasies of men could neither divide nor multiply.

We are told that there are only two sacraments of the new law, and that they do, or do not confer grace, according as the multiplicity of Protestant errors is pleased to opine; that there is no sacrifice under the Gospel, no real and personal presence of Jesus in the Holy Eucharist. But the Christians throughout the world had received and professed their faith in the seven sacraments of grace, and the perpetual sacrifice and universal presence of the Word made flesh in the Holy Eucharist had already filled the Church with the consciousness of a Divine manifestation before as yet the canon of the New Testament was completed.

Finally, we are told that in the New Testament there is to be read no successor of St. Peter, no vicar of Jesus Christ. But before the New Testament was collected and diffused, all the world recognized one pastor as chief over all, reigning in the place of Peter from his See in Rome.

The faith and the Church then were the key of interpretation. They who read the New Testament, read in the light of the day of Pentecost and within the circle of the universal Church in which they beheld the order of divine truths or facts, which the New Testament Scriptures recognize and presuppose. This was both the actual and scientific key to their true interpretation.

From this it is further evident that the Church is the guardian both of the faith and the Scriptures.

It received both from its divine Head. And it alone received the custody of the divine revelation and of its inspired book. It received from the Church of old, the books of the old law confirmed by the divine witness of Jesus Himself; from the synagogue, the later books; and from the evangelists and apostles, their inspired writings, of which it knew the authenticity and genuineness both by extrinsic and intrinsic evidence. . . .

The Church is not merely the interpretation but the interpreter, and is divinely guided in applying this key to the Holy Scriptures. Before the New Testament was written, it was the living witness for the truth, the organ of the Divine and perpetual voice, which in all nations declared the original revelation. Its authority as a teacher rests upon its commission and its infallibility, that is upon the command of its Divine head, and the assistance of the Holy Ghost. The theory that the Church can err only arises in minds which have lost the faith of what the Church is. Can it be believed that the mystical body of Christ which is indissolubly united to its Divine Head in heaven, should go about on earth teaching falsehoods in His name? Is it credible that the Church, which is the dwelling-place of the Spirit of Truth, should wander from the revelation which radiates from His presence as light from the sun? The Church in the beginning knew the whole revelation of God, and knows it in every age with a perception which is never obscured, and a consciousness which is never suspended. The illumination which pervades its intelligence, unites with the inspiration of the New Testament as two lights pass into one. . . .

The Church so honors the written word of God, that it acts upon its lightest word. It is a strange thing to hear men say that such and such doctrines are incredible because so little is said of them in Holy Scripture. Is truth measured by quantity? How many divine words are needed to overcome the unbelief of men? How often must God speak before we obey Him? How many times must He repeat His revelations before we will submit to His divine voice? Does not every spark contain the whole nature of fire? Does not every divine word contain the veracity of God? The Church of God recognizes His voice in every utterance, and honors the divine will revealed in the fewest syllables. The words "He that loveth father or mother more than me is not worthy of me," has filled the world with disciples. "Whosoever shall lose his life for my sake shall find it," has multiplied the army of martyrs. "Whosoever shall confess me before men," has made the weakest dare the power of the world. "If thou wilt be perfect, sell all that thou hast," has created the state of voluntary poverty. The twenty-fifth chapter of St. Matthew has filled the Church with the orders of active charity. "Mary hath chosen the better part," has created and sustained the life of contemplative perfection. These single words, once spoken, are enough for the disciples of the Church, which is the dwelling place of the Holy Spirit of Truth, the Author of the Sacred Books. It is this profound faith in their sacredness which made St. Paulinus lay them up in a tabernacle by the side of the Tabernacle of the Blessed Sacrament; and St. Edmund kiss the page of the Bible before and after reading it; and St. Charles read it kneeling, with bare head and knees. So the Church cherishes its least jot or tittle, and guards it as a deposit dearer than

203

life itself. . . . The sole guardian and keeper of Holy Writ in all the integrity of its text and meaning, the sole divine witness of its inspiration, the sole, immutable, and unerring interpreter of its meaning is the Catholic and Roman Church. (1865)

MEANING AND USES OF THE WORD
GOSPEL

THE REV. LÉONCE DE GRANDMAISON, S.J.

THE term *gospel,* as applied to a written work, has become familiar to us; yet it is a derived word and one of relatively late appearance.

A gospel was, in classical language, a piece of good news, or, more anciently, the gift made to the bearer of good news. In the second part of *Isaias* the expression which designates the Good News *par excellence,* that of the advent and of the glory of the Messias, is rendered in the Greek of the Septuagint by the word *gospel.* Thence it passed into the New Testament, where it always refers to the message of salvation announced to man by Christ; and the person of Jesus forms an integral part of it, by the same right as his teaching. The Gospel is his whole mission, acts and words; it is indivisibly the divine gift of himself and the divine gifts which he brings.

For the same reason, the Gospel is one. It is only later that, following a well-known law, the container, the book to which were consigned the principal features of the message of Jesus, became insensibly substituted for the contained, and took to itself the name of Gospel. It was only then that one could speak of the "gospels" in the plural. The word is thus found in the plural and with the meaning of a written account for the first time (so far as we can now tell) towards the middle of the second century in St. Justin's first *Apology,* which alludes to "the memoirs of the Apostles which are called Gospels." (1930)

THE FORMATION OF THE NEW TESTAMENT

THE REV. HUGH POPE, O.P.

FROM the very earliest times the question must have arisen: Which are the Books of the New Testament? We can perhaps discern a trace of such disputes in St. Peter's words about St. Paul's Epistles. (2 Pet. iii. 15-16). But the Church must have speedily made up her mind as to the principles which must decide any dispute on the point. The guiding principle was of course that for writings to be canonical, or the norm of faith, they must be divinely inspired. . . . But there still remains the further question: What proof is there that any Book claiming to form part of the Scriptures is really inspired and therefore an integral part of the Canon? . . .

In the formation of the Canon a double process can be traced: the process of accumulation of Apostolic writings, since individual Churches received, for example, St. Paul's various Letters and only gradually made them known to the rest of the world; and the process of elimination of what was not inspired and was therefore not canonical. We have only to examine the formidable list of Apochryphal writings claiming Apostles for their authors to see how vast was the mass of material, and to reflect on the other hand on the seemingly trivial character of such an Epistle as that of St. Paul to Philemon to see how minute was the care taken by the Church in preserving the veriest fragment of Apostolic writings. . . . The Church . . . must have based her decision on no mere critical grounds, but on her own subjective certainty as to her Divinely-bestowed knowledge on the point.

But in another sense the Church's judgment was a critical one. Her pronouncements were not authoritative declarations which disregarded evidence. But the evidence she weighed was the authoritative voice of her representatives scattered throughout the world. In other words she took the votes of those who in the various Apostolic Sees were in a position to declare what was the tradition they had received. Thus, while our knowledge of the contents of the Canon is derived from the Church's authoritative pronouncements, *i.e.* from the official lists of the Canonical Books drawn up by the Pontiffs or by the Councils, it is also true that these latter, *viz.* the various

Pontiffs or Councils, derived their knowledge from the declarations of various Fathers who collectively represented the volume of Apostolic tradition. And it was only by slow degrees that the Church entered into her inheritance in the full Canon of Holy Scripture. For in the first place it is clear that so long as any Apostle survived the deposit of written revelation it could not be said to be definitely completed. Hence it was not till the first century had closed and St. John was dead that the Church could arrive at a knowledge of the fullness of her deposit. And to this knowledge the Churches of Asia, of Europe, and of Egypt had each to contribute their quota. When a Catholic, then, desires to know what are the contents of the Canon he consults the Church's official Decrees, *e.g.* those of the Councils of Florence, Trent, and the Vatican. When, however, he desires to learn on what the Church based these Decrees he consults the writings of the various Fathers of the Church who, either by the use they made of various Books, or by the lists which they drew up, *e.g.* in the case of St. Athanasius and St. Augustine, showed what was the tradition they received and handed down. . . .

The important point to note in reading the statements of various Fathers regarding the canonicity, or the opposite, of the New Testament writings are that (a) we never find any Father saying that some writing which the Church now accepts is no part of the Canon. Thus no Ecclesiastical writer rejects the *Apocalypse* or the *Epistle to the Hebrews*. They may, it is true, throw doubt on the authenticity of such Books, but it is one thing to question their authenticity, quite another to question their canonicity. Thus no one ever wrote more critically of the *Apocalypse* than did Denis of Alexandria; but while he has very strong doubts as to St. John's authorship of it, he has no doubts whatever regarding its inspired character. (b) On the other hand we have no instance of an Ecclesiastical writer insisting on the canonicity of some writing which the Church subsequently repudiated.   (1918)

GOD IS THE SUBJECT OF THE GOSPELS

THE REV. M. J. LA GRANGE, O.P.

ACCORDING to an opinion of the liberal Protestant scholars, we are not to look for anything in the gospels but the *doctrine* preached by

Jesus. But we have only to read those gospels to discover that it was also, and even more, their intention to make known the Person of Jesus Christ. The Christian faithful worshipped Him as they worshipped His Father, without ceasing to regard Jesus as man; and that is how the Gospel represents Him. . . .

Jesus was concerned solely with the religious ideal: He preached it, and His preaching led Him to His Death. Nonetheless the story of His life, as we have read it in the four gospels, has every appearance of truth, on condition we understand how to draw that story from the documents, each of which goes its own way to the goal that is common to them all, documents which are in harmony more by the reality of facts than by any obvious desire for agreement.

At once, however, we are confronted with the objection that this story contains miracles, and the miraculous is impossible. . . . Supposed miracles do not prevent anyone from writing a biography. Phenomena generally taken for miracles are not infrequent occurrences in history, and those who are deemed to have performed them are not on that account blotted out of existence. Ought we, for instance, to be content to remain in ignorance of the history of Rome because Livy has releated a few prodigies? . . .

This history has the stamp of truth, and there is really nothing to be said against the tradition that has preserved its incidents. Just as there have always been men who had the reputation for working miracles, so there have always been some who thought they were entrusted with a divine mission. . . . Now the disciples of Jesus Christ saw with their own eyes that He existed; it is they who have told us, and they were as incapable of inventing His doctrine as they were incapable of inventing the facts of His life. It was on those facts that they based the belief which, as they said, men ought to have in the doctrine He taught. Before many years they expressed all this in writing. . . .

Will it be said that the obsession of a fixed idea, the religious idea, paralyzed the intellectual faculty in Him? But though He has the warmth, even the vehemence, of the prophets, He has the tranquil clarity of a philosopher. What He says about God and the kingdom of God is often expressed in parables such as all ages have acknowledged to be masterpieces of good sense, in which He has adapted ideas of the loftiest character to the capacity of a race of fishermen, farmers and shepherds. Jewish scholars strain every nerve to find parables like these in the Talmud. We do not deny that Jesus spoke the language of His day; but no one used it with the same charm, emotion, almost careless ease, yet with a penetration that reaches the heart. He was severe with Himself without any display of austerity, but gentle with others; no one could reproach Him with sin, and He was merciful toward sinners. . . .

His Gospel gave to the world the notion of God the Father of all men, who desires the salvation of all; consequently all men ought to love Him and love one another as brothers. That is supposed by some to be the entire Gospel, the good news announced by one who is possessed of the most astounding religious genius, who has no equal in the religious sphere, who is a sage, a prophet, a man aided or inspired by God, one most fitted to act as a guide, whose teaching set down in the gospels ought to be listened to and obeyed. But according to this view the Gospel He preached contains nothing at all about His person; it has but one subject, God the Father, and we are told that there is no reason for making Jesus also the subject of the Gospel. Were such the fact He would be less worthy of our respect, for in so far as He made a place for Himself beside His Father He would be so much the less religious. At the very most will these people grant Him forgiveness for having assumed the title of Messiah in order to render His work acceptable; but, they tell us, He is neither Son of God nor God Himself. That would be unthinkable. Such is the language of liberal Protestantism and of those whom without being aware of it, are in communion with that school of thought.

Human reason very loudly proclaims that a man who should make himself a place beside God would be a blasphemer. The subject of the Gospel, therefore, must not be divided; the Gospel has but one subject, and that is God. But Jesus is no other than the Son of God and God like His Father; this He has made known to us because it is our way to salvation. And that is plainly what the Gospel teaches, as may be seen from the four gospels if we take them just as they are. Here we do not mean that we must simply trust their testimony, but that we must understand the manner and significance of that testimony. The Gospel contains a doctrine indeed, but not a doctrine that is expressed in philosophical formula. . . . The Gospel is the representation of something that has taken place, of something that consists of the deeds and words of Jesus, of a fact that is of its nature complex, a fact that has to do with life and is therefore colored by the customs, the manners of thinking and feeling which were current among the Jews of the time of Tiberius. It is not as though Jesus wrote a treatise about God or gave theological lessons;

what He spoke of was the kingdom of God which was at hand and even then beginning. He let it be seen that He was the Messiah. . . .

Anyone who says that the Gospel contains nothing about His Person must either not have read the gospels at all or else have explained them away until nothing remains. If Jesus really lived, preached, was condemned to death, then it was as Messiah, and He acknowledged that He was the Messiah.   (1938)

You who believe what you like of the gospels and believe not what you like, believe yourselves rather than the gospels.

ST. AUGUSTINE (ca. 400)

CHRIST'S GRADUAL REVELATION OF HIS DIVINITY

F. J. SHEED

APART from the Incarnation, man could know of God only in God's Nature. Man could, for example, know God as Infinite Power, creating the universe from nothing, and this is true knowledge and very valuable. But if it is true knowledge, it is undeniably rather remote knowledge. . . . But to see God not simply in His own nature, but being and doing and suffering in our nature, is a very different matter. And reading the Gospels that is precisely what we do see—God obeying His mother, God paying taxes, God receiving hospitality, God receiving insults, God tormented by hunger and thirst, God loving, God angry; and these things we can measure, for we have done them, all ourselves. . . .

Christ Our Lord gives us a great flood of light by what He has to tell us about God, as we shall see in a moment; but with all due reverence we may feel that He gives us more light upon God by being than by saying.

209

This, I think, explains something about Our Lord's way of revealing the primary fact about Himself which puzzles many readers of the Gospels. They feel that He made an unnecessary mystery about it: if He was God, it would surely have been simpler for Him to say so in the plainest words at the very outset of His mission. So people say, believers in His Divinity as an expression of puzzlement, unbelievers as a challenge to the truth of the doctrine. Notice, at any rate, that Our Lord's action in this matter was of set policy: He did, quite deliberately, make a certain mystery about Who and What He was. His enemies felt it. We have the Jews demanding indignantly: "How long wilt thou go on keeping us in suspense. If thou art the Christ, tell us openly" (John 10.24). But it was not only from His enemies that the full knowledge was long held. Between the Birth in Bethlehem and the Death on Calvary there is probably no single episode of Our Lord's life better known than the scene by the lake at Caesarea Philippi, when Peter answered and said: "Thou art Christ the Son of the living God"; and Jesus answered him: "Blessed art thou, Simon son of Jona; it is not flesh and blood, it is My Father Who is in Heaven that has revealed this to thee. And I tell thee this in my turn: that thou art Peter, and it is upon this rock that I will build my Church: and the gates of Hell shall not prevail against it."

In the splendor of this climax, we tend to see what went before it rather in shadow. However often we have read the passage, the mind leaps forward to this, and thus is in danger of missing a good deal of the light in what immediately leads up to it. We remember, of course, St. Peter's great answer. If we press our memory a little harder, we remember what question St. Peter was answering: but it may be doubted if many of us see how very startling a question it was. For Our Lord had asked the Apostles: "Who do you say I am?" Realize that these were the men who had been His inseparable companions so long: and yet so late in their companionship He could ask them Who they thought He was. Clearly He had not told them; just as clearly He had had good reason for not telling them.

The reason, one may in all reverence surmise, why He did not begin by telling either His friends or His enemies that He was God is that they were Jews, and the Jew believed in God. It is only an age deficient in the realization of God's majesty that could be surprised that Christ Jesus should only gradually have led men to the realization of a truth which such men would only find so shattering. I have already spoken of our modern tendency to treat God as an equal, or at any rate to overlook the immeasurable difference between His infinity and our finitude. In such an atmosphere, men think with a certain naïveté of God as an interesting person to meet, and of themselves happily engaging in an interchange of views with Him upon the running of His universe, they making their suggestions and God explaining His difficulties and everybody feeling better for the interchange. In such an atmosphere nothing seems more natural than that God should simply introduce Himself, and with the minimum of ceremony.

I have called this naïve, and naïve it is to the point of drivelling. No Jew of Our Lord's day, however sinful he might have been, would have felt like that for an instant. If Christ Our Lord had begun with the announcement that He was God, and they had believed Him, they would simply have fallen flat on their faces and never got up. To men with their awareness of the majesty of God, the truth that Christ was God had to be broken very gradually or it would have broken them. If we read the Gospels with this in mind, we can see how marvellously Our Lord brought the Apostles to realization. His method was not to tell them, but to bring them to a point where they could tell Him. They saw Him doing things and heard Him saying things—things that only God had a right to do (like forgiving sins and supplementing the law God had given on Sinai), things that only God could truthfully say ("I and the Father are one"; "Before Abraham was, I am"; "No one knows the Son but the Father, and no one knows the Father but the Son"); and they reflected upon what they had seen and heard; and a wild hypothesis began to form in their minds; and at times they felt surer of it as certain things seemed incapable of any lesser answer, and again at times they felt unsure, as certain things could not be fitted at all into their present concept of God. But with endless advance and recoil, the sum of their movement was advance: and at last came St. Peter's confession: "Thou art Christ, Son of the Living God," rewarded so marvellously by Our Lord, as we have seen. Yet as far as the words of Peter go, they contain nothing that has not been said by another Apostle at the very first calling of the Apostles. For Nathaniel had said (John I. 49): "Thou, Master, art the Son of God, thou art the King of Israel."

What difference did Christ Our Lord see between the confession of Nathaniel, and the confession of Peter? Partly, we may suppose, the difference lay in this: that St. Peter's confession was a true act of faith, made under the impulsion of the grace of God—"It is not flesh and blood, but My Father Who is in Heaven that has revealed this to thee." Nathaniel's confession was an act of human reason: Christ had just made a mysterious reference to a fig tree, obviously some incident Nathaniel thought known only to himself, and the only way he could rationally account for Christ's knowing it was to assume that Christ must be more than man. Similarly we find all the Apostles reaching out toward a super-natural explanation when Our Lord calmed the storm with a word; and they said one to another: "Who is this, who is obeyed even by the winds and the sea?" (Mark 4; 40). But bit by bit their human reason was bringing them to see that there could be only the one explanation, was bringing them, that is, to the point where their minds were ready to receive the impulsion of God's grace and make the act of Faith, after which they held the truth not by human reason, which of itself can go on wavering endlessly, but with the sure support of the grace of God. That point Peter reached first. . . .

These were the men who knew Christ before they knew He was God. Had they known from the beginning, they might simply have feared Him, and fear would have made a bar to any progress in intimacy. But by the time they knew beyond the possibility of uncertainty that He was God, they had come to know that He was love. If they had known that Christ was God first, then they would have applied their idea of God to Christ; as it was, they were able to apply their knowledge of Christ to God. The principal fruit for them and for us of their three years of companionship with Him was the unshakable certainty of His love for men; and it was St. John, the apostle He loved best, who crystallized the whole experience for us in the phrase of his first Epistle, "God is Love" (4.8).

We may ask why the Jews did not know this already, for God had shown them His love often enough, and in the Old Testament His love is wonderfully stated: "The Lord is compassionate and merciful, long-suffering and plenteous in mercy" (Psalm 102.8); that is strong enough, yet it is not the strongest thing of its sort. In Isaiah (49.15) there is a phrase which would seem to reach the very limit of divine tenderness: "Can a woman forget her infant, so as not to have pity on the son of her womb? And if she should forget, yet will I not forget thee." The truth is that love arises and abides most easily and naturally where there is community of nature, and until God took our nature and became man that way did not exist: God-made-man could love us with a human love—and this, though a lesser thing than divine love, can be very comforting to our weakness. Nowhere in the Old Testament did it occur to anyone to call God what they were to call God-made-man, "the friend of sinners." The Jews knew that God had spoken to men and done great things for men, but He had not *been* man.

The moral for us is simple: in our approach to God we are helped enormously by seeing Him in our nature; and for the mind this means a continual study of Him whereby the Apostles' experience of Christ becomes our own personal experience, their intimacy becomes our intimacy. . . .

One result of this reading of the Gospels will be to find what Our Lord showed us about God by being God. Another will be to find what Our Lord shows us about God by what He has to say of God. There is a lot to be said for making one's own list of the texts in which Christ Our Lord tells us of God, grasping them in their context and returning to them again and again. (It will be useful later if all texts are noted which tell why Christ came among men.) Most of them, naturally, treat of God in His dealings with and judgments of the human race. Save perhaps in the proportion of statements about God's love to statements about His justice, it would be hard to find among these anything that has not already been told us in the Old Testament. There is a new atmosphere, but if it is impossible not to feel the difference, it is almost impossible to lay a precise finger on it—if one happens to know the Old Testament at all well: everything makes us realize how vast a communication about Himself God had already given His chosen people.   (1946)

ON FIRST READING THE GOSPEL STORY

G. K. CHESTERTON

I AM speaking as an imaginary heathen human being, honestly, staring at the Gospel story for the first time.

Now it is not at all easy to regard the New Testament as a New Testament. It is not at all easy to regard good news as new. Both for good and evil familiarity fills us with assumptions and associations; and no man of our civilization, whatever he thinks of our religion, can really read the thing as if he had never heard of it before. . . . There is a psychological difficulty in seeing those well-known words simply as they stand and without going beyond what they intrinsically stand for. And this difficulty must indeed be very great; for the result of it is very curious. The result of it is that most modern critics and most current criticism, makes a comment that is the exact reverse of the truth. It is so completely the reverse of the truth that one could almost suspect that they had never read the New Testament at all.

We have all heard people say a hundred times over, for they seem never to tire of saying it, that the Jesus of the New Testament is indeed a most merciful and humane lover of humanity, but that the Church has hidden this human character in repellant dogmas and stiffened it with ecclesiastical terrors till it has taken on an inhuman character. This is, I venture to repeat, very nearly the reverse of the truth. The truth is that it is the image of Christ in the churches that is almost entirely mild and merciful. It is the image of Christ in the Gospels that is a good many other things as well. The figure in the Gospels does indeed utter in words of almost heart-breaking beauty his pity for our broken hearts. But they are very far from being the only sort of words that he utters. Nevertheless they are almost the only kind of words that the Church in its popular imagery ever represents him as uttering. . . . A man simply taking the words of the story as they stand would form quite another impression; an impression full of mystery and possibly of inconsistency; but certainly not merely an impression of mildness. It would be intensely interesting; but part of the interest would consist in its leaving a good deal to be guessed at or explained. It is full of sudden gestures evidently significant except that we hardly know what they signify; of enigmatic silences; of ironical replies. . . . I am putting aside for the moment all questions of doctrinal inferences or expositions, orthodox or otherwise; I am simply imagining the effect on a man's mind if he did really do what these critics are always talking about doing; if he did really read the New Testament without reference to orthodoxy and even without reference to doctrine. . . . He would find, for instance, that if there are descriptions that deserved to be called realistic, they are precisely the descriptions of the supernatural. . . .

Now the first thing to note is that if we take it merely as a human story, it is in some ways a very strange story. I do not refer here to its tremendous and tragic culmination or to any implications involving triumph in that tragedy. I do not refer to what is commonly

214

called the miraculous element; for on that point philosophies vary and modern philosophies very decidedly waver. Indeed the educated Englishman of today may be said to have passed from an old fashion, in which he would not believe in any miracles unless they were ancient, and adopted a new fashion in which he will not believe in any miracles unless they are modern. . . . I refer here rather specially to unmiraculous and even to unnoticed and inconspicuous parts of the story. There are a great many things about it which nobody would have invented, for they are things that nobody has ever made any particular use of; things which if they were remarked at all have remained rather as puzzles. For instance, there is that long stretch of silence in the life of Christ up to the age of thirty. It is of all silences the most immense and imaginatively impressive. But it is not the sort of thing that anybody is particularly likely to invent in order to prove something; and nobody so far as I know has ever tried to prove anything in particular from it. It is impressive, but it is only impressive as a fact; there is nothing particularly popular or obvious about it as a fable. The ordinary trend of hero-worship and myth-making is much more likely to say the precise opposite. . . . Now the whole story is full of these things. It is not by any means, as baldly presented in print, a story that it is easy to get to the bottom of. It is anything but what these people talk of as a simple Gospel. Relatively speaking, it is the Gospel that has the mysticism and the Church that has the rationalism. As I should put it, it is the Gospel that is the riddle and the Church that is the answer. But whatever be the answer, the Gospel as it stands is almost a book of riddles.

First, a man reading the Gospel sayings would not find platitudes. If he had read even in the most respectful spirit the majority of ancient philosophers and of modern moralists, he would appreciate the unique importance of saying that he did not find platitudes. . . . He would find a number of strange claims that might sound like the claim to be the brother of the sun and moon; a number of very startling pieces of advice; a number of stunning rebukes; a number of strangely beautiful stories. He would see some very giantesque figures of speech about the impossibility of threading a needle with a camel or the possibility of throwing a mountain into the sea. He would see a number of very daring simplifications of the difficulties of life; like the advice to shine upon everybody indifferently as does the sunshine or not to worry about the future any more than the birds. He would find on the other hand some passages of almost impenetrable darkness, so far as he is concerned, such as the moral of the parable of the Unjust Steward. Some of these things might strike him as fables and some as truths; but none as truisms. For instance, he would not find the ordinary platitudes in favor of peace. He would find several paradoxes in favor of peace. He would find several ideals of non-resistance, which taken as they stand would be rather too pacific for any pacifist. He would be told in one passage to treat a robber *not* with passive resistance, but rather with positive and enthusiastic encouragement, if the terms be taken literally; heaping up gifts upon the man who had stolen goods. But he would not find a word of all that obvious rhetoric against war which has filled countless books and odes and orations; not a word about the wickedness of war, the wastefulness of war, the appalling scale of the slaughter in war and all the rest of the familiar frenzy; indeed not a word about war at all. There is nothing that throws any particular light on Christ's attitude toward organized warfare. . . .

If we *could* read the Gospel reports as things as new as newspaper reports, they would puzzle us and perhaps terrify us much *more* than the same things as developed by historical Christianity. . . . The Christ of the Gospel might actually seem more strange and terrible than the Christ of the Church. . . .

I maintain that a man reading the New Testament frankly and freshly would *not* get the impression of what is now meant by a human Christ. The merely human Christ is a made-up figure, a piece of artificial selection, like the merely evolutionary man. . . . Moreover there have been too many of these human Christs found in the same story. . . . Three or four separate schools of rationalism have worked over the ground and found three or four equally rational explanations of his life. . . . Each of these explanations in itself seems to me singularly inadequate; but taken together they do suggest something of the very mystery which they miss. . . .

Above all, would not such a new reader of the New Testament stumble over something that would startle him much more than it startles us? (1925)

"A LAW INSCRIBED ON OUR HEARTS"

ST. THOMAS AQUINAS

Each thing appears to be that which preponderates in it, as the Philosopher states (*Ethic.* ix. 8). Now that which is preponderant in the law of the New Testament, and whereon all its efficacy is based, is the grace of the Holy Ghost, which is given through faith in Christ. Consequently the New Law is chiefly the grace itself of the Holy Ghost, which is given to those who believe in Christ. . . .

Nevertheless the New Law contains certain things that dispose us to receive the grace of the Holy Ghost, and pertaining to the use of that grace: such things are of secondary importance, so to speak, in the New Law; and the faithful needed to be instructed concerning them; both by word and writing, both as to what they should believe and as to what they should do. Consequently we must say that the New Law is in the first place a law that is inscribed on our hearts, but that secondarily it is a written law.

The Gospel writings contain only such things as pertain to the grace of the Holy Ghost, either by disposing us thereto, or by directing us to the use thereof. Thus with regard to the intellect, the Gospel contains certain matters pertaining to the manifestation of Christ's Godhead or humanity, which dispose us by means of faith through which we receive the grace of the Holy Ghost: and with regard to the affections, it contains matters touching the contempt of the world, whereby man is rendered fit to receive the grace of the Holy Ghost: for *the world,* i.e. worldly men, *cannot receive* the Holy Ghost (Jo. xiv. 17). As to the use of spiritual grace, this consists in works of virtue to which the writings of the New Testament exhort men in divers ways.

There are two ways in which a thing may be instilled into man. First, through being part of his nature, and thus the natural law is instilled into man. Secondly, a thing is instilled into man by being, as it were, added on to his nature by a gift of grace. In this way the New Law is instilled into man, not only by indicating to him what he should do, but also by helping him to accomplish it.

No man ever had the grace of the Holy Ghost except through faith in Christ either explicit or implicit: and by faith in Christ man belongs to the New Testament. Consequently whoever had the law of grace instilled into them belonged to the New Testament. . . .

Although the grace of the New Testament helps man to avoid sin, yet it does not so confirm man in good that he cannot sin: for this belongs to the state of glory. Hence if a man sins after receiving the grace of the New Testament, he deserves greater punishment, as being ungrateful for greater benefits, and as not using the help given to him. And this is why the New Law is said to *work wrath:* because as far as it is concerned it gives man sufficient help to avoid sin.

The same God gave both the New and the Old Law, but in different ways. For He gave the Old Law written on tables of stone: whereas He gave the New Law written *in the fleshly tables of the heart,* as the Apostles expresses it (2 Cor. iii. 3).   (1272)

THE GOSPEL—A TORCH

THE RT. REV. LOUIS BAUNARD

I CALL the Gospel "a torch," and in reality it is the torch, the beacon light of all Christians. Has its light undergone an eclipse during the century I have lived in? It has certainly poured forth its radiance in the midst of great darkness, and the darkness has not comprehended it. But has its own intrinsic brightness failed or even grown fainter? I do not think so. In fact, I believe that just the contrary is the case. I would like to state my impressions on that point—impressions from which my mentality, as a believer, was long ago formed for my entire life. They come to me as distant souvenirs.

Let me think back! I remember Sundays, now so distant, when the saintly priest of our village parish read the Gospel for the day from the pulpit, using for this purpose a large, beautifully gilded volume, ornamented with bookmarks. He then commented on the text, after the custom of the Fathers, keeping the sacred volume open before him, and pronouncing every word of Scripture with an accent of religious authority which made us recognize and revere it as the word of God. I can hear him still. And I, then a little choir boy, used to ask myself: "What is this unusually large and beautiful book the priest incenses at the altar, each word of which is an oracle and before which we are bidden to carry the consecrated candles? I see, also, that everybody rises to hear it read."

I remember, also, long ago, when we boys, pupils of the priests, were obliged, every morning in our grammar classes, to learn, translate, and write at the beginning of our exercises one or two Greek verses from the Gospel of St. Luke. It was a consecration of our work for the day. And I, then a little pupil, used to ponder over the question: "What is this precious essence, the smallest drop of which can thus perfume all that I am to read or write today?"

When the New Testament was given me to read in its entirety, as "the Word of God," I was just graduating from my classical training and about to enter upon other studies which were to be nourished by this divine text. My first impression was one of profound astonishment. How little did this book resemble in form and substance those Greek and Latin writings on which I had hitherto been mentally fed! They had been universally recognized as intellectual works of art, masterpieces of eloquence or poetry, composed, elaborated, and finished for the admiration of centuries. But, from a literary point of view, the book now given me was comparatively rough and unpolished, with an unformed style, of which it was said that "it smacked of the barbarian." Who, then, had written it, and when? Had I not been told it was a product of the great century, the age of the best writers of Rome? What an anachronism! I was puzzled. Moreover, as regards the substance of the book, the dissimilarity was still greater! These singular writers, although contemporaries of Tacitus, Suetonius, and Petronius did not entertain me, as the others had done, with accounts of politics, brilliant wars, victorious heroes, the Caesars, the senate, the army, and the empire, still less with the theater, the circus, refined sensual pleasures, and the great orgies of flesh and blood. Where, then, had I been suddenly transported? Another world had risen up before me, a kingdom of God, a kingdom of heaven, eternal life, divine love, spirit, and grace. All this was circulating under the rough exterior of those letters, like sap which was rising, overflowing, bursting its old vessels, rendering asunder ancient tissues and forms of art, in order to allow the ideal of a perfectly pure truth to flow, like a brimming river, through the world. These were all new writings which spoke a new language through the lips of new men—even rude, simple, obscure, and unlettered men—whom my studies as a humanist had never revealed. . . .

219

Thank God, today the classics—although still endowed with all the honors due their rank—have long since passed into the background of my enthusiasms, while the Gospel has acquired and still holds there the highest place; the place that Jesus Christ Himself will possess in my heart for ever.

The teaching of Scripture was given us in the great seminary by some saintly, white-haired, old men, whose learning drew its inspiration from the best interpreters and commentators of the seventeenth and eighteenth centuries. . . . It was their duty and our security. Rather than doctrine, the priests bade us seek in the Gospel edification, consolation, food for meditation, and a rule of conduct; in a word, the living Spirit of God to vivify our minds and hearts. The Bible was our inseparable companion; we carried it religiously on our persons, and put our lips to it, as a son does to a dear letter from his father, for it was as precious as this to our piety and faith. Has it still the same value in the eyes of our grand-nephews today?

This was the thoroughly simple, but sincere and elevated education, by which our ideas of the Scripture and particularly of the Holy Gospel were formed; and I am not ashamed to confess that the state of soul which characterized my youth in this respect remains today that of my old age. And I understand perfectly why this is so. It is because my old age is so happy in its possession. How and why is this? What sort of experience has caused it? I must confide this to you.

It was only after I had left the seminary, that I was brought to a full consciousness of the question then agitating my century in regard to Scripture. I found that the Gospel and even the person of Jesus Christ had become, alas! a subject of contention. The wind was blowing fiercely on the sacred torch, but the wind that extinguishes a little flame, only augments a great one. What happened? First of all, God be thanked, the torch was held aloft by powerful hands; I mean by representatives of Biblical science among both the clergy and the laity, including authorities of the highest rank in the Semitic and Oriental languages, who made of their Orientalism a stalwart bulwark for the city of God. . . .

At the same time, the other auxiliary sciences of history confirmed the utterances of Orientalism. To mention only those of inscriptions and archaeology, we had, then, the famous Greek inscription of Autun, which a young scholar who later became Cardinal Pitra, had just discovered and deciphered. In this, the dogma of the Eucharist appeared under its ancient symbols. Later on, the similar Phrygian inscription of St. Abercius, called by De Rossi "the queen of inscriptions," was found. The inscriptions and religious paintings of the Catacombs also form, in themselves alone, an entire dogmatic theology, in which not one of the articles of the Creed is missing. . . .

Today, it is modernism that moves about the Gospel with a feline gentleness, in order to salute in it—what? Not an historical book, but what they sentimentally call "a mystical, unreal, and purely ideal conception of the legendary Christ which the Christians of the golden age must have created and transfigured." It is not a history, they say, but a poem! Yet hear the historian himself. The evangelist St. Luke rises solemnly to declare, at the very beginning of his recital, formally, repeatedly, and explicitly the following: "Forasmuch as many have taken in hand to set forth in order a narration of the things that have been accomplished among us, according as they have delivered them unto us, who from the beginning *were eyewitnesses* and ministers of the word, it seemed good to me also, *having diligently attained to all things* from the beginning, to write to thee in order, most excellent Theophilus, that thou mayest know the truth of those words in which thou hast been instructed." Where is to be found in such a narration a place for inventions, poetry, and fantasies? This is actual history, solid history, a temple with a granite foundation and built of hewn stones. Let us enter into it and remain there with confidence!

Let us hear, also St. John: "That which was from the beginning, which we have heard, which we have seen with our eyes, which we have looked upon, and our hands have handled of the Word of life, which was with the Father and hath appeared to us, this we declare unto you."

Now what, on the contrary, do the tardy deniers of a faith of nineteen centuries announce to us? What do they bring in opposition to this firm testimony and to these solemn assertions of the authors themselves? Nothing but hypotheses, scaffoldings, and frail intellectual constructions which speedily collapse on one another. Such were the hypotheses proposed yesterday by Renan—the pretended "hallucinations" of hundreds of witnesses who, sensible and truthful enough when they heard and collected the discourses of Jesus, became deluded creatures, deceived and deceiving, when they saw and reported His miracles, which, nevertheless, had been facts plainly evident to them! Try to comprehend that. Other hypotheses much in favor at one time were those of successive interpolations, which, it is claimed, in the course of time—but when, where, by whom?—slipped into the marvelously unified and compact recital of the Gospel. These intentionally changed the unique physiognomy of Jesus, so harmonious in its features and hopelessly inimitable, that Rousseau said of it: "It is not thus that one invents. Such an inventor would be greater than the hero."

Of the combined attack of France and Germany upon the Gospel, whose advent and whose ending we have seen, what now remains? About as much as remained of the tower of Babel, after the confusion of languages. Of Christ, the Son of the living God, what do the modernists leave us? Only a few traces; not much more than the disciples found in the sepulcher after His resurrection—a winding sheet and some napkins. From these poor remnants, the Christian soul goes sorrowfully away, saying: "They have taken away my Lord, and I know not where they have laid Him." Finally, of Christianity itself—the ultimate product of the evolution of thought and of the progress of humanity through the turmoil of the centuries—what is left of that, according to the modernist theory? About as much as survives the agitation of the sea after a night of storm—a little foam upon the waves.

I come now to true science, to scriptural science, the only serious and decisive one, derived, not from empty theoretical systems, but from the discovery of manuscripts and the revelation of facts. This science, proceeding backward little by little to the farthest limit of the apostolic age, has found there traces of the Gospel. Where the feet of the first disciples trod, beautiful footprints have been discovered under the surface of those distant roads, at the end of which is seen the rising light of Christ. (1930)

There is nought in the Gospels which does not shine and illumine the world by its splendor, so that even things that seem trifling and unimportant shine with the majesty of the Holy Spirit.

ST. JEROME (382)

222

HISTORICAL VALUE OF THE GOSPELS

THE REV. HILARIN FELDER, O.F.M. CAP.

FORMAL portrayals of the life of Jesus are contained . . . only in the *four canonical Gospels*. Precisely for the reason that they proclaimed the Gospel—"the glad tidings"—of Jesus Christ and his salvation, they received already in the earliest times the name: "Gospels of our Lord Jesus Christ, according to Matthew, Mark, Luke and John." The Gospels are, in fact, nothing else than the classic sources of information and the documents of the divine-human life and history of Jesus Christ.

It becomes at once comprehensible, therefore, why ever since the days of incipient rationalism—that is, for about one hundred and forty years—the question of the historical value of these fundamental books of our religion has been always over and over again asked and answered. From this side and from that, out of the conflict of opinions and out of serious research there has grown up an exceedingly rich and almost unlimited literature connected with the criticism of the Gospels. Attack and defense have been renewed innumerable times, in all conceivable positions, and with the sharpest intellectual weapons. Today we can estimate with perfect confidence the results gained, which mean a brilliant vindication of the Gospels. Even if the conflict may enter into many a new phase, another answer to these questions is simply impossible.

The historical value of our Gospels depends, of course, like that of every other source of history, upon two points. One question is, whether they are *authentic*—that is, whether they really originate from an epoch near, and from men who themselves stood in proximity to the events described; the second is, whether they are credible—that is, whether we may rely upon these men and their narrative. . . .

While the Christians were bringing the Gospel to the pagans, the Jews—according to St. Justin—also sent ambassadors into the whole civilized world who calumniated the Christian name to everyone who did not know of it, and accused Christ of the blackest crimes. . . . Wherever a pagan set himself to work to ridicule the Gospels, the Jew also offered him his services in furnishing him with the most childish absurdities about the Gospel history. . . .

However little confidence, therefore, the Jewish tradition about the

223

New Testament writings can inspire, reaching back though it does into primitive Christianity, it is, nevertheless, very important for us, because it never and nowhere dared to cast a doubt upon the genuineness of the Gospels. And yet the proof of their spuriousness would have been equivalent to saving the national honor of Judaism and to an annihilating criticism of Christianity.

The pagan writers at first referred to the Gospels slightingly and contemptuously. Lactantius gives the reason for this. Made fastidious by the brilliant and attractive language and descriptions of the classical writers, the educated pagans felt no interest whatever in the books of the Bible, which were written in a popular style and with a most unusual manner of thought and speech. Moreover, the Christians were anxious to conceal their sacred books from the pagans in order not to expose them to dishonor.

Nevertheless, the Roman controversialists and sophists knew how to get possession of them little by little, and then began the fearful attacks of pagan science on the contents of the Gospels. The eclectic *Celsus,* the Epicurean and satirist *Lucian of Samosata,* the Neopythagorean *Flavius Philostratus,* the Neoplatonist *Porphyrius, Julian the Apostate* and others employed the whole power of their eloquence, the most trenchant acuteness of their logic and the biting sarcasm of their wit, to prove that the Evangelists had written nothing but incredible absurdities. Yet never did the Pagans let a doubt arise as to whether the Evangelists were really the authors of the books ascribed to them. Rather do they everywhere take it for granted that the Christian view of the apostolic origin of their Gospels is based on truth.

Passing over all the others, let us refer to Celsus only, who is not merely hostile to Christianity, and of whom we, at the same time, possess the most definite information. Celsus' book, entitled *The True Word,* was written in A.D. 178, and was refuted by Origen practically sentence by sentence. . . . Celsus knew our Gospels well and studied them. . . . He wishes to argue from the Gospels alone, as the books which form the basis of Christianity, and thus to impale the Christians on their own swords. . . .

Celsus attacks and ridicules only the *contents* and *credibility* of the Gospels. That these *originated with the Apostles,* and that the apocryphal Gospels are merely imitations and counterfeits of the real ones, is for him a certainty. This testimony is crushing. Celsus criticizes Christianity, and especially the Gospels, in the sharpest way, and was able to convince himself as to their genuineness or spuriousness, and must

224

have done so. Proof of their *post*-apostolic origin would have been a veritable death-blow to the hated Christianity.

If, then, he does not produce such a proof, it was only because he felt himself unable to awaken a single doubt of the fact.

Thus do the *non*-ecclesiastical authorities of antiquity assert unanimously that the Gospels originate from the time of the primitive Church, and, indeed, from apostolic circles. . . .

The canonical Gospels themselves indicate with the greatest distinctness their apostolic origin.

The most obvious proof of the great antiquity of the Gospels would, of course, be the existence of the original copies or autographs of the Evangelists. We must, however, give up the idea at once. Not one of the older manuscripts, whether of a secular or religious character, has come down to us as an original manuscript of its author. They were all written on papyrus leaves—the only writing material of that time—unless we except clay tablets and stone inscriptions. The papyrus, however, lasted only a short time, especially since the Gospels suffered greatly by reason of their frequent, almost daily use. Thus the manuscripts of the Evangelists had already disappeared, it seems, before the end of the second century. Only the second and third hand copies of them resisted the ravages of time, and after the end of the third century parchment volumes replaced the papyrus rolls.

Our oldest manuscripts of the Bible date from the fourth and fifth centuries. Nevertheless, even that is of a very great age when we think that the earliest manuscripts of the Greek and Latin classics come to us only with the eighth and ninth centuries. Moreover, the biblical manuscripts of the times immediately succeeding this era are incomparably more numerous than the classical. The latter could be saved only with difficulty and in very few copies, while we possess of the New Testament alone over 3,800 manuscripts.

A comparison of these different manuscripts with one another brings us, moreover, to a time much more remote than the dates at which the individual copies originated. It is true all agree with one another in the immense majority of the texts. The different readings refer almost entirely to small details, and even the most striking variations change neither the least article of faith, nor the most insignificant moral doctrine.

It is, nevertheless, a fact that a great number of these textual discrepancies are found already in the biblical manuscripts of the fourth and fifth centuries, and, indeed, are of such a kind that we must suppose that we have to do here with copies of earlier models which, in their turn also, did not belong to one and the same family of manuscripts, but represent different revisions of a still earlier epoch.

This brings us already into the third or, indeed, into the second century. In this period, however, there existed not merely one or two manuscripts of the Bible; it is true rather, as we can conclude from the works of the Fathers, that the New Testament was spread over the whole Roman Empire. In all the churches it was read aloud at divine services, either in the original Greek, or in the Latin and Syriac translations, which were composed already in the second century.

But in those days the circulation and the multiplication of books proceeded much more slowly than now, because everything had to be written by hand. Plainly, therefore, original models were already existent at the beginning of the second century. The Gospels must, then, certainly go back to the period of the Apostles.

Not only have the latest comparisons of the Gospel manuscripts with the quotations made from them by the Fathers—compiled by Hermann von Soden with astonishing technical knowledge and patience—led to the evident result that the ecclesiastical writers about A.D. 140 already used the predecessors of those Gospel texts and Gospel manuscripts, as we possess them still today, but the interval between the composition of the Gospels and the year A.D. 140 is "so small that scarcely enough time remains for any essential changes in the text." Consequently the *external and critical stability* of the New Testament proves that our four Gospels go back to the apostolic age, and have come down to us from that apostolic era essentially unchanged.

But the *internal features* of the Gospels give us a still clearer and more definite light upon this point. The knowledge of languages and linguistic forms displayed in them is at once characteristic. From these we perceive that the Evangelists, with the exception of Luke, were Semites, *speaking Aramaic*.

The language of the New Testament has been studied thoroughly in recent years, and examined in its minutest idioms. Philologists have analyzed sentence after sentence, and have even numbered and weighed, so to speak, all its phrases; and there has gradually arisen an entire library of dictionaries and grammatical works concerning the New Testament, in which the elements of the Gospel language are established and compared with other contemporaneous writings and documents.

The result of all these labors is that the Greek idiom of the Gospels is proved to rest upon an essentially Aramaic basis. . . . The most exact acquaintance with the popular Greek dialects of that time never fully disclose the meaning of the Gospels. Only a knowledge of the Hebrew-

Aramaic colloquial, popular speech furnishes the key to a complete understanding of the New Testament writings. These are composed in that Hebraic-Greek idiom, which the Jews of the first century acquired from their varied intercourse with Hellenic Romans, and introduced into their literature through their most important scholars. . . .

The Gospels originate, therefore, from the pens of Christian writers who had learned the Greek language more or less accurately, but whose mother-tongue was the Aramaic dialect which Christ and his Apostles used.

If the Evangelists are to be recognized from their speech as Jews, they appear from their acquaintance with their country to be inhabitants of Palestine.

They describe very minutely, with information about innumerable details, the places in which Jesus Christ lived and worked. Geographical, topographical, political, historic and religious conditions are mirrored on almost every page. The Galilean landscape; the lake of Genesareth and life upon its shores; the region bordering on the Jordan; the local peculiarities of the smallest hamlets; the distance from one village to another; the springs, gates, routes and paths; the environs of Jerusalem; the monuments and objects of interest of the Holy City—all these and a thousand other details are clearly delineated. Accordingly, wherever the Palestine of Christ's time is now properly excavated and thoroughly investigated, it is seen that all the statements of the Gospels agree precisely with what has been discovered. Only men who had originated in Palestine, or who, at least, had dwelt or passed some time there could write thus. . . .

Even to the smallest details the Evangelists are fully conversant with those times. The Roman-Jewish census, under the Emperor Augustus and the Governor of Syria, Quirinus; the Greek and Roman coins, which were in circulation together with former Hebrew ones; the famine under Claudius; the expulsion of the Jews from Rome under that Emperor; the tragic ending of Herod Agrippa, the members of the whole Herodean dynasty, as well as other personal conditions, are all well known to the Evangelists. They understand also the complicated dealings of the religious and political parties of those days—the Pharisees, the Sadducees and Herodians, as well as those of the philosophical schools of the Stoics and Epicureans. Before their eyes still stands the magnificent capital of the country, with its monumental belt of walls and buildings of the temple, together with its priests and scribes, its gorgeous ceremonial and intricate observances of the Mosaic Law.

Thus could write only those who had lived in Palestine before the decisive war with Rome, and who, partly before, partly after, the catastrophe of the year A.D. 70 had put their experiences on paper and transmitted them to posterity. John wrote only after the destruction of Jerusalem. . . . The three synoptic Gospels must, however, have appeared before the Jewish war. The prophecy of the destruction of the city and of the rejection of the Jewish people is set forth in these Gospels as still unfulfilled. If the frightful ruin had already stood before their eyes, they certainly would not have kept silent about the event. . . .

From their knowledge of the life and activity of Jesus it is evident that they belonged either to the immediate or collateral circle of the Savior's disciples.

The personality of Jesus, his appearance in public, his discourses and his deeds are drawn from life, and adhered to with striking vividness. The Evangelists conduct us to all the roads and paths trodden by his feet; they accompany us into all the cities and villages where he preached; to the solitary regions and the mountains where he prayed; and into the houses and market-places where he healed the sick and raised the dead.

The whole Gospel story is related not only with astonishing exactitude and certainty, but also with touching candor and simplicity. Nowhere does the narrator obtrude himself; nowhere does he bring out his own personal views and feelings; and scarcely even does he mention now and then the successes of the Savior and the impression which his words and miracles produced. Only that is recorded which transpired before the eyes of the Evangelists, or had been seen and heard by immediate eye and ear witnesses.

No later or foreign historian could have represented that, and in such a way. The Evangelists must themselves have been present, or at least received the verbal accounts or written documents concerning the "glad tidings" from associates and disciples of the Savior.   (1924)

"UNDESIGNED COINCIDENCES"
IN THE GOSPELS

THE RT. REV. JOHN S. VAUGHAN

THOUGH the authority of the Church is all that a Catholic needs to satisfy him as to genuineness and veracity of the Holy Scripture, yet it is always pleasing to be able to point also to other and independent testimonies. . . . We refer to what have been described as the "undesigned coincidences," which are so frequently to be met with in various parts of the inspired volume. Indeed, instances of this kind are scattered up and down throughout the pages of the Sacred Book, and are such as to preclude the possibility of their being the result of design; hence they form a very strong proof of the truthfulness and honesty of the writers. . . .

Now what I propose doing is to set before the reader some examples of these coincidences without design, taken from an exceedingly interesting work by Rev. J. J. Blunt, B.D., who, with infinite pains, has collected quite a considerable number. . . . The object of bringing such coincidences forward at all is to make more manifest the truth, that the various inspired writers described facts and not fancies. . . . The way in which the different Biblical writers support one another, and strengthen each other's narrative, by what, in purely human documents, we should call wholly accidental observations or casual remarks, let fall by the merest chance, is very remarkable, and will strike some minds at least, on account of their very spontaneousness, as the most valuable form of evidence that can be had.

We will take our first illustration from the Gospel of St. Matthew, where we are told that Jesus walking by the sea of Galilee saw "James the son of Zebedee, and John his brother, in a ship with their father *mending their nets:* and He called them. And they followed Him." Here St. Matthew informs us that "they were mending their nets," but he offers us no explanation as to how these nets came to be broken; and but for St. Luke's account of the same call of these fishermen to the Apostolate, we should probably have been left in our ignorance. Now turn to St. Luke v. There he also tells us how our Lord stood by the lake, but then he goes on to describe how "when He had done speaking, He said unto Simon, Launch out into the deep, and let down

229

your nets for a draught. And Simon answering said unto Him, Master we have toiled all night and taken nothing; nevertheless at Thy word I will let down the net. And when they had done this, they enclosed a great number of fishes, *and their nets broke!* And they beckoned to their partners, who were in the other ship, that they should come and help them. . . . Simon was astonished and all that were with him. . . . and so was also James and John, the sons of Zebedee, who were partners with Simon. . . . And when they had brought their ships to land they forsook all and followed him." The circumstances to be remarked is this, "that of the miracle St. Matthew says not a single word; nevertheless he tells us that Zebedee and his sons were found by our Lord, when He gave them the call, *mending their nets.* How it happened that the nets wanted mending he does not think it needful to state, nor should we have thought it needful to inquire; but it is also impossible not to observe that it perfectly harmonizes with the incident mentioned by St. Luke that in the miraculous draught of fishes the *nets broke.* This coincidence, slight as it is, seems to bear upon the truth of the miracle itself. For (1) the *mending* of the nets, asserted by one Evangelist, gives probability to the *breaking* of the nets mentioned by the other; (2) the breaking of the nets gives probability to the large draught of the fishes; and (3) the large draught of fishes gives probability to the miracle." The coincidence does not, of course, prove the miracle, but it forms around it a very strong atmosphere of truth.

We have another instance in connection with the words of St. Matthew, who in describing the Passion of Christ, says: "Then did they spit in His face, and buffeted Him; and others smote Him with the palms of their hands, saying: Prophesy unto us, thou Christ, who is he that smote Thee?" (xxvi. 67). Now any one, unacquainted with the other writers of the Gospel story, would be very much puzzled over these words. He would feel that they were incomplete and that something more was wanted to explain the situation. What could the soldiers mean by asking Him to prophesy who had struck Him? Where is the propriety of such a demand, considering that the offenders stood before His very eyes? Surely He could not help seeing who delivered the blows? Had the records of the other Evangelists been lost, "no critical acuteness could have possibly supplied by conjecture the omission which occurs in this passage," observes Rev. Blunt, "yet without that omission being supplied, the true meaning of the passage must forever have lain hid." But when we take up the Gospel according to St. Luke, the passage grows clear, and the difficulty is solved, for he is careful to tell us that the men that held our Divine Lord, "*blindfolded*

230

Him, and smote His face" (xxii. 64). And it was not *until His eyes were covered* that they sought to make Him prove His power by pointing out to them the striker. Yet St. Matthew makes no mention of that circumstance. "Such an oversight is difficult to account for on any other supposition than the truth of the story itself." . . .

Then another very interesting connection is pointed out between a sentence of St. Matthew and one of St. John. The former writes: "And when he [i.e. St. Peter] was gone out *into the Porch,* another maid saw him, and said unto them, This man also was with Jesus of Nazareth." (xxvi. 71.) Now the strange thing in this sentence is the statement that the maid so readily recognized St. Peter; since he was quite a stranger to her, and had come into the house late at night, and under circumstances of some tumult and disorder. How could she have singled him out at once as a disciple of Christ? Well, St. Matthew throws no light upon this point. True, but then St. John does. If we consult St. John's Gospel (xviii. 16) we shall find that after Jesus had entered, *"Peter stood at the door without,* till that other disciple went out, who was known to the high priest, and *spoke unto her that kept the door,* and brought Peter in." In this way the maid's attention was naturally directed to St. Peter, and thus it was at once explained how she recognized him in the Porch. Here, then, as Rev. Blunt observes, is a minute indication of veracity in St. Matthew, which would have been lost upon us had not the Gospel of St. John come down to our own times. Each Apostle in this instance seems to testify, though quite unconsciously, to the truthfulness of the other.

Here is another excerpt from Rev. Blunt's collection, bearing on the text of St. Matthew xiv. 1: " 'At that time Herod the Tetrarch heard of the fame of Jesus, and said *unto his servants,* This is John the Baptist, who is risen from the dead': St. Matthew here declares that Herod delivered his opinion of Christ to *his servants.* There must have been some particular reason, one would imagine, to induce him to make such a communication *to them,* above all other people. What could it have been? St. Mark does not help us to solve the question, for he contents himself with recording what Herod said. Neither does St. Luke, in the parallel passage, tell us to whom he addressed himself. He baldly states that 'He was desirous of seeing Him [Christ] *because he had heard many things of Him.*' By referring, however, to chapter viii. of this last Evangelist, the cause why Herod had *heard so much about Christ,* and why he talked to *his servants* about Him, is sufficiently explained; but observe, it is by the merest accident! We are there informed 'that Jesus went throughout every city and village, preaching

231

and showing the glad tidings of the Kingdom of God; and the twelve were with Him, and certain women who had been healed of evil spirits and infirmities; Mary, called Magdalene, out of whom went seven devils; and [note] *Joanna the wife of Chusa, Herod's steward,* and Susanna, and many others who ministered unto Him of their substance.' And again in Acts xiii. 1, we read, among other distinguished converts, of 'Manahen, who had been brought up with Herod the Tetrarch,' or who, in other words, was his foster brother. We see, therefore, that Christ had followers from among the *household of this very prince*, and, accordingly, that Herod would very naturally discourse with *his servants* on a subject with which they were much better informed than himself" (Blunt). Thus, we are supplied with a very good reason why he should have taken his servants into his confidence.

These and many other instances of wholly undesigned coincidences seem to set a seal upon the truthfulness and honesty of the inspired writers. . . . As the motion of the merest straw or the bend of a blade of grass may suffice to tell us in which direction the wind is blowing, so the meanest and most insignificant event narrated by Apostle or Evangelist may possess such striking, and yet such clearly accidental relations to other events as to fill our minds with a strong sense of their veracity. To appreciate the value of these relations and connections more fully we must refer to the Book itself. We will satisfy ourselves here with just two concluding quotations. We are told by St. John vi. 5 that when Jesus had reached a certain desert place He "lifted up His eyes and saw a great multitude come unto Him, and He said unto *Philip,* Whence shall we buy bread, that these may eat?" Now the question that naturally arises in our mind is, "Why should this question have been directed to Philip in particular rather than to Peter or James or John or to one of the other more prominent Apostles? If we had the Gospel of St. John and not the other Gospels we should see no particular propriety in this choice, and should probably assign it to accident. If, on the contrary, we had the other Gospels, and not that of St. John, we should not be put on the inquiry at all, for they make no mention of the question having been addressed *expressly to Philip*. But by comparing St. Luke with St. John we discover the reason at once. By St. Luke, and by him alone, we are informed that the desert place where the miracle was wrought was *belonging to Bethsaida* (ix. 10). By St. John we are informed (though not in the passage where he relates the miracle, but, which is worthy of remark, in another chapter altogether independent of it, *viz.* i. 44) that *Philip was of Bethsaida*. To whom, then, could the question have been directed so properly as to him who, being of the immediate neighborhood, was the most likely to know where bread might be bought?"

Our last excerpt concerns the Ascension of our Lord into heaven. So great and marvelous an event must have impressed itself very vividly upon the minds of all those who had witnessed it. St. John, whose love for his Divine Master seems to have surpassed even that of the other Apostles, must have treasured up the memory of that consoling and encouraging ascent even more than all the rest; yet, strange to say, St. John's writings contain no history whatever of the Ascension. Are we to conclude then that he did not know it, or that it was untrue? Nothing of the kind. Quite the contrary. We gather from his own words that he was so fully conscious of the miracle, and took it so completely as a recognized and undisputed fact, that it no more occurs to him to gravely relate the circumstances of it than it would occur to a present-day historian to burden his pages with a long description of the rising of the sun. Hence, though he omits to describe it, he alludes to it and mentions it, though quite incidentally, as a fact familiar and well known to all. Thus he refers to it when he observes that "no man hath *ascended up to heaven,* but He that came down from heaven, even the Son of Man who is in heaven" (iii. 13). So in another place he asks: "What if ye shall see the Son of Man *ascend up* where he was before?" (vi. 62). Again in xx. 17, when describing the meeting between St. Mary Magdalene and our risen Savior, St. John describes Him as saying to her: "Do not touch Me, for I am not yet *ascended* to My Father, but go unto My brethren, and say to them, I *ascend* to my Father and to your Father, to My God and to your God." No man, and least of all such a devoted and loving Apostle as St. John, could have recorded such words without realizing their bearing on the stupendous miracle of Christ's glorious Ascension into heaven. The very fact that these sentences bear only indirect and accidental allusions to the fact renders them all the more striking and convincing. For it is clear from their whole setting that St. John was fully acquainted with this crowning miracle in the life of our Lord.   (1904)

THE "SYNOPTIC PROBLEM"

THE REV. L. C. FILLION, S.S.

EVEN a rapid persual of the Gospels leads one to observe two striking phenomena. It is certain that the Gospels according to St. Matthew, St. Mark, and St. Luke, compared with St. John's, form a group or family apart. Notwithstanding undeniable resemblances, when we pass from this group to the Fourth Gospel, we seem almost to enter a new world, so notable do the divergences appear to be. . . .

A second and less remarkable phenomena consists in the family likeness, impressing one at the first glance, between the Gospels of Matthew, Mark, and Luke. It is for this reason that they are called the "Synoptic" Gospels. . . .

This resemblance constitutes only one phase of what has been called the "Synoptic Problem." It is also easy to note a multitude of divergences which create an interesting complication, though difficult of explanation. Like the differences, so, too, the agreements concern both the substance and the form of the narratives. We will point out merely the chief ones.

First, as to the *resemblances*. In subject-matter, the three Synoptic Gospels have the same historical, doctrinal, and moral basis, the same series of events and discourses, numerous episodes in common. The preaching of the Precursor, the Baptism and temptation of Christ, His ministry in Galilee, His journey to Jerusalem for the last Passover of His earthly life, His Passion, death and Resurrection, these items constitute the theme treated by all the Synoptics. When we think of the enormous abundance of material to which the Apostle St. John alludes (John xxi. 25), this resemblance in subject-matter is doubly remarkable, since the authors had an embarrassing wealth of matter from which to choose in order to vary their accounts. Moreover, with the Synoptics, these various elements are nearly always coordinated in the same way. Our surprise increases when we examine a particular incident related by all of them.

In the matter of form or style, our observations are still more astonishing. Not only do the three Evangelists use the same Greek dialect called Hellenistic, quite distinct from classical Greek, introducing a certain number of expressions borrowed from the Aramaic language then spoken in Palestine; not only is the tone of the narrative identical in all three—simple, popular, and dramatic—but the similarity in diction extends even to sentence structure and word arrangement, to peculiarities of spelling and grammar. Rather often it even goes to literal identity, especially, as we might expect, when reporting Our Lord's sayings and discourses. "At the side of these resemblances, these same books present characteristics quite opposite. The diversity is sometimes even more remarkable: the order of events may be found inverted, the elements are displaced and arranged in a different way, the expression changes, the color alters, numerous omissions and additions render now one, now another of these collections more complete in its material, more precise in detail." (Reuss, E.) These differences are manifested in every direction. Thus St. Mark entirely omits the account of the Savior's infancy; St. Matthew here and there groups the miracles and discourses of Christ according to a logical order, while St. Luke follows rather a chronological sequence of events. Each of the Synoptists introduces into his narrative some episodes or details which are not recorded by the other two. Each of them has his own style or manner, his favorite expressions, his characteristic turn of mind. It happens that, after a passage where their resemblance goes to the point of verbal identity, they suddenly part company, though it be only by the use of a synonymous word. Most of the time these differences are of small account and concern matters of quite secondary importance in the narrative; but they also occur in graver matters, sometimes even constituting apparent contradictions.

We should not fail to note that in itself there is nothing surprising in the existence of resemblances and differences between three historians writing on the same subject. What constitutes the "Synoptic Problem" is the complexity of the phenomena that we have just indicated, carried to an extraordinary degree, in the matter of contents, arrangement, and language. There is nothing analogous in sacred or profane literature. In fact, if there were only resemblances between the three sacred writers, such similarity would be explained by saying that they had made use of the same sources; if there were merely differences, we would say that they had recourse to distinct documents. How, then, does it happen that we find such a similarity of material and form along with such a multitude of differences?

The Fathers and early Doctors of the Church were, in general, but little concerned with this problem. They were satisfied with explaining the apparent contradictions to which we have just alluded. The same line of action was followed in the Middle Ages and up to recent times. But for the last one hundred and fifty years or so, the Synoptic Problem has become a subject of endless discussions, big and little dissertations almost innumerable. The problem is closely connected with the questions regarding the origin of the Gospels, questions which during this same period have been a matter of violent dispute.

At first the Protestants, and especially the Rationalists, were almost the only ones who raised the question and sought to solve it after their own fashion. The circumstances helped to imprint upon it at first an unfortunate direction. Catholic exegetes entered the lists only somewhat later. Even then it was with moderate zeal, for they at once understood, in the first place, that the Synoptic Problem is morally insoluble and, in the second place, that, even though its study might render a genuine service by throwing into relief the mutual relations of the first three Gospels, it is not of any appreciable usefulness for interpretation. Moreover, the schemes invented to account for the problem are so numerous and complicated that they produce darkness more often than light. Not infrequently they are plainly arbitrary and extravagant. . . . Too often it has been forgotten that we have no right to neglect tradition when studying the Synoptic Problem, nor to revel in conjectures devoid of any basis and in contradiction with the facts.

The many systems to which we have just referred all branch off from three principal ones. There is the hypothesis of a written tradition, that of an oral tradition, and that of the dependence of one Evangelist upon the one or two who preceded him.

The hypothesis of a written tradition assumes that St. Matthew, St. Mark, and St. Luke, each in turn according to his own purpose and particular needs, made use of a primitive Gospel, which had been published before the Aramaic text of St. Matthew and which served all of them as their principal documentary source. In this way the numerous resemblances would explain themselves. As for the differences, they are explained by supposing that this primitive Gospel had undergone successive revisions and that each of the Synoptists had before him a different revision.

If for the words "written tradition" we substitute "oral tradition," and if we suppose that tradition to have undergone gradual modifications, we shall have the general elements of the second theory, which starts from the undeniable fact that the Gospel was preached orally long before being consigned to writing. From numerous passages in the New Testament and from information handed down by the earliest ecclesiastical writers, we can readily understand that the Savior's life, especially His public life, His Passion and Resurrection, formed the habitual subject of Apostolic preaching, as also in general of the preaching of the first Christian missionaries. By virtue of being often repeated, and probably also as a result of a previous understanding between the Apostles and their helpers, this subject before long acquired a well nigh fixed form. Yet it was not absolutely rigid, nor was there any hesitation in subjecting it to some modification according as the hearers were Jewish or pagan, Greek or Roman, barbarian or civilized. Thus, quite naturally, a traditional groundwork of the Life of Christ was formed, which, while remaining substantially the same, offered rather considerable variations, according to difference of country, preacher, and other secondary circumstances. In this oral tradition, identical and yet varied, we would have the key both to the resemblances and to the characteristic differences that exist among the first three Gospels.

The hypothesis of mutual dependence, or of reciprocal utilization by the Synoptic Evangelists, has also found many partisans. It can be summed up in a few words. The second Evangelist in the order of time made use of the work of the first; the third composed his work by using the Gospels written by the two earlier authors. The digressions or differences occur whenever the sacred writer exercised his freedom by following other sources.

If we here take up the Synoptic question *ex professo* we should have to express a conclusion, with its supporting reasons, in the matter of all these theories and the multitude of variations that have been grafted on each of them. For our present purpose it will suffice to say that they all offer advantages and difficulties. But none of them is able by itself to furnish an adequate explanation of the problem. It is by combining them in various degrees that we obtain the most satisfactory solution, bearing in mind the data of tradition relative to the composition and chronological order of the first three Gospels.   (1928)

SCRIPTURE INTERPRETS SCRIPTURE

MARGARET T. MONRO

By "READING the New Testament" is meant reading it all, or nearly all, as distinct from reading selections, such as the Gospels and Epistles at Mass. And the object of the reading is to get an idea of the New Testament *as a whole*.

To grasp the whole of anything is usually an enjoyment in itself, besides doubling or trebling one's enjoyment of each of its parts. For much of the pleasure a thing can give us comes from the way it all fits together. The difference between good and bad taste in dress, for instance, is entirely a question of whether the outfit is a whole, to which every detail contributes. In the same way, a well-designed car or well-built house or a well-laid-out garden is a source of pleasure, for it is a whole which gives each of its parts a meaning and function it could not have alone. The same is true of all arts, including literature. The marvelous thing about the New Testament is that eight men could pen twenty-seven pieces of writing, in the course of nearly sixty years, and yet the result be a whole. That is because there was another Author concerned besides the eight men, no less than the Holy Ghost Himself. God is always a great Artist—you can see this by looking at any lovely stretch of country or at the sky by night. Hence when God gives us a Book, that Book is a real work of art, which is another way of saying a real Whole. The first step towards appreciating any work of art is always to try and see it as a whole. Therefore our first *aim* is to see the Book God has given us as a whole. . . .

It never did anyone any harm yet to discover that there are difficulties in the Bible: the real harm would be to fancy we understood it all. The mere fact that the Bible is a Divine book means that it must have much to puzzle our understanding. The real marvel is that so much of it speaks home to us, giving support and enlightenment in the actual circumstances of our lives.

In feeling discontented with our powers of understanding we are in very good company. Even St. Peter admitted that he sometimes found St. Paul a little difficult! And since then a long series of Fathers and Doctors of the Church have confessed that Holy Scripture held for them many insoluble problems. We are thus in the Mind of the Church if, in the measure of our own much smaller attainments, we feel the same. In this as in everything else there never comes a time when Christians can begin to feel pleased with themselves. They get something much better than self-satisfaction—growing knowledge of Him who alone can satisfy. And that makes for self-discontent.

The best practical advice about difficulties is: Treat them like fishbones. Leave them at the side of the plate while you make your meal of the very much larger part which you can digest. Above all, never *gnaw* a difficulty, any more than you would gnaw a fishbone. Bones, as we have learned in war, have a number of important uses, and in peacetime they may serve as manure for our fields. A thing is not useless because we do not know its use. There are things in the Bible which specialists find of great value for their work, though we cannot directly use them for our spiritual food. Our concern is with what has immediate and obvious food-value for our souls.

In any case, as we go along we shall find that some of our questions begin to answer themselves. Scripture is the great interpreter of Scripture; simply because the Book is a whole, the parts shed light on each other. The first thing then is to get an idea of the whole. Once that is done, everything you read in the Bible, or about the Bible, will help to clear up some of the things which at first seem puzzling.   (1945)

THE SIMPLICITY AND GRANDEUR
OF JESUS' WORDS

THE REV. JOSEPH HUBY, S.J.

IN THE transmission of the Lord's doctrine, the essential point in most cases was knowing what He had said, not where or when He said it. It was of little importance that such a word had been pronounced in a valley or on a mountain, on a highway or in a house, especially since Jesus may have repeated the same words under several different circumstances. He did not necessarily hold Himself to proclaiming only unpublished ideas; on the contrary, preaching an absolutely new doctrine to poor illiterates, slow to open up their minds, He must often have repeated the chief points of His message.

The grouping of these utterances in a sufficiently broad chronological order had the advantage of facilitating the task of the evangelistic preacher by simplifying the work of the memory. Utterances grouped by subjects were more easily kept in mind than *logia*, disconnected like unstrung pearls, and this system of gathering Jesus' teaching to definite points was calculated to produce a greater impression on the listener.

But this word-of-mouth transmission of the Lord's teaching raises a question in the modern mind. Accustomed as we are to receiving the opinions of our predecessors in writing, we ask if it was possible for the Apostles to preserve an accurate recollection of Christ's doctrine and to assure its faithful reproduction. If we attempt to revive in our minds the definite circumstances under which Christ ministered and under which the Apostles preached, we will not hesitate to answer yes. Needless to say, it is not a question of crediting the Apostles with a word-for-word repetition of the Lord's speech, a *ne varietur* rubber stamp. Why introduce a miracle where it has no point? But it is not extravagant to ascribe to the first disciples a faithfulness which, while safeguarding the inner sense of the evangelic message, has regarded its form in the most characteristic features and has often transmitted the speech of Christ very nearly in its original phraseology. Jesus preached the kingdom of God to a people with whom the word-of-mouth tradition was the great means of instruction, with whom it was "through the channel of the ear that teaching or revelation came into the heart, seat of the intelligence." Such a method takes for granted a high development of the power of memory. Renan recalls this fact precisely on the subject of the conservation of Christ's utterances in the early Church: "We have remarked many times that our power of memory is in inverse ratio to the habit we have of writing. It is hardly necessary to point out what the word-of-mouth tradition was able to retain at a time when people did not rely on notes they had taken or pamphlets they possessed. A man's memory was a book in those days; it knew how to reproduce even conversations at which its owner had not been present." One of the keenest critics of the radical ultra-Rhenish school, Johannes Weiss, has taken hold of the same point to justify the historical value of Jesus' teaching as it is passed on to us in the gospels. "We must not forget that Jesus's listeners had much fresher and more practiced memories than we children of paper." . . .

Jesus, for His part, had made the work of memory easy for His listeners by using manners of speech best suited to the genius of His people. Péguy's remark that there is not an abstract word in the whole Bible, applies with special fitness to the New Testament. Christ's teaching, even when it treats of the profundities of the divine scheme, takes a living and concrete form in language as simple as the voice of a child, as transparent as a clear April morning. "Jesus is often mysterious; His subject requires it. But He is not obscure, obscurity being weakness and poverty. With Him in word as in action everything is simple, direct and luminous. No scholarly subtlety, no bookish figures, but images drawn from the immediate realities of the country;—the narrow lives of the people who knew nothing beyond mending a garment, sweeping out a house, grinding

240

a measure of grain; to whom the loss of a drachma or the disappearance of a sheep meant an emotional crisis; the life of the laborers who sowed and reaped, separated the good grain from the tare, gathered the wheat into barns and the new wine into skins, with now and again a marriage feast to vary the monotony or the less agreeable surprise of a bullock fallen into a well; the life of the fishermen of the lake of Galilee, mending their nets on the shore or grading the fish on their return from the boats. An intensive spiritual growth tends at times (as in the case of St. Bernard) to weaken the specific or aesthetic feeling for visible things. We do not have to regret this incompleteness in the Saviour; Francis of Assisi himself was not more a friend of nature. The gospel shows this on every page. The whole of His Galilee is mirrored in it, with its sorrows and its joys, its skies and its seasons, its flocks and its vineyards, its harvests and its fleeting vesture of anemones, its beautiful lake and its robust population of fisherfolk and contented farmers." (L. de Grandmaison, *Jesus Christ,* Vol. 11) Just as the Son of God took bodily form and veiled Himself in our flesh, so His doctrine is veiled in these humble details, incarnate in this luminous imagery.

But that is not all. The material side of Jesus' discourses, the words, images, parables, is turned out into moulds made familiar to the Jews by many centuries' tradition of oral teaching. The best known among these methods, for it strikes every reader of the Bible, and the principal one as well, is the parallel. Just as the jeweler likes to make the facets of a precious stone gleam in the sunlight, so the Semite enjoyed presenting the same idea under different forms, holding it up under varying images which made resplendent its value, lighted the depths of its meaning, showed the detail of its beauty. The mould may seem stiff and uniform, but Jesus knew how to use it with marvelous suppleness. If we recite His sermons aloud, especially those in Matthew's gospel, we will see that a living intricacy plays under rhythms which we recognize even in our Greek version and the more so if we retranslate into Aramaic. Sometimes the parallel is reduced to its simplest form, a rhythmic scheme with two or three contrasts balancing one another, sometimes it is developed into strophes, or to use a better suited term, into recitatives, marked out by sentry-words, responses, refrains, ornamented with assonances, guides and stimulants for the preacher, fastening points for the memory of the listener. . . .

These methods, traditional among the Hebrews, but treated by Jesus in an incomparable manner—never did man speak like this

241

man—did not result merely in exciting among His hearers the approving murmurs that the Oriental gives spontaneously to the successful cadence or to the gracefully phrased proverb. Just as the rhythms of the oral style had their origins not in literary conventions, but in physiological and psychological conditions imposed on all declamations intended to perpetuate a spoken lesson, so their usage, while charming the listener, was intended first of all to aid the memory and to assure the certain transmission of the doctrine. As it has been said, the rhythms of the oral style are above all a mnemonic expression of the thought and we may be sure that among the disciples of Jesus, drawn as they were from a people with whom the spoken word was the customary means of instruction, there were some who hearing the essential doctrines of the evangelic message impressed them on the living tablets of their memory with a boldness of relief which they would not lose. And this preservation, this "keeping," was the more easy because Jesus, while using the traditional rhythms and word forms, filled them with a new meaning, gave them an absolutely new authority, force and brilliance. From His very first preaching in the synagogue of Capharnaum "they were astonished at His doctrine. For He was teaching them as one having power, not as the scribes . . . and they were all amazed, insomuch as they questioned among themselves, saying: What thing is this? what is this new doctrine?" (Mark, I. 27). A newness not confected from eccentric originality, but flowing from an incomparable union of simplicity and grandeur. . . . To lively, familiar and paradoxical manners of expression, Jesus did not fear to add even the extravagant and the hyperbolic. "It is easier for a camel to pass through the eye of a needle than for a rich man to enter the kingdom of God." (Mark, X, 25). And that other utterance of which we may well say, as of the parable of the prodigal son, that it remains driven "like a nail of tenderness" in the hearts of the faithful and unfaithful alike: "I say to you, even so there shall be joy in heaven upon one sinner that doth penance more than upon ninety-nine just that need not penance." (Luke, XV, 7). Whoever has heard them even once can forget the warnings against scandal, keen and biting as a steel blade? . . . Mordant words which after nineteen centuries still preserve the living impress of the Master who wrought them. . . . By their very extravagance they pique our curiosity, provoke our thoughts, shake our lethargy, make us stronger than ourselves. . . .

Because they do not understand this hyperbolic nature of Jesus' utterances it happens that some Occidentals (an Oriental would be less deceived) are upset by reading the gospel. They feel a discomfort and as it were a vague uneasiness in the presence of these words which throw a light on a single aspect of reality as if there were no other. And when they compare the Sermon on the Mount with the Christian morality as propounded in wise and measured words by the Church today, it seems to them that there has been not harmonious growth but deviation, or rather correction, that the Church corrects rather than continues the gospel. And nevertheless this is not so; the Church does not have to correct the gospel; she interprets it, she does not change it. The necessary limitations are set by Jesus Christ Himself; they are in the gospel, but in the gospel taken in its entirety. Alongside of a formula which seems absolute in one sense, you have another absolute in the opposite direction. Place them in juxtaposition; they balance one another, limit one another, explain one another. From their antithetical relation their true interpretation will come out.

Should we give examples of these words which illuminate and discipline one another? Jesus enjoins His disciples to edify their neighbor in order to bring him to give glory to the heavenly Father. "So let your light shine before men, that they may see your good works, and glorify your Father who is in heaven" (Matt. V, 16). And to the same disciples He gives this warning: "Take heed that you do not your justice before men, to be seen by them: otherwise you shall not have a reward of your Father who is in heaven" (Matt. VI, 1). It is one thing to do good in order to give glory to God and to have it given; it is another to perform externally good works with ostentation in order to draw the attention and praise of men.

(1931)

St. John put on Our Lord's lips about 8,000 words. SS. Matthew, Mark and Luke about three times as many.

To speak slowly and distinctly, all the words of Our Lord recorded in St. John would take less than one hour, the words given in the Synoptics about two and a half. Now the Gospels give us to understand that during His Public Ministry Our Lord spoke practically, day by day, for many hours. If Our Lord spoke only one hour a day in public, His public speeches would occupy say one thousand hours, but Our Lord did not merely speak in public. He spoke continually in private to His disciples. His longest recorded speech in St. John, xii-xvii, was spoken entirely in private to His disciples. Considering that, apparently, Christ devoted all His time to speaking and teaching, somehow, His twelve Apostles must have heard Him for thousands of hours, and what is contained in the Gospels is in consequence not one-thousandth part of what they heard Him say.

THE REV. J. P. ARENDZEN (1929)

THE LITERARY PERFECTION OF THE GOSPELS

THE REV. DANIEL A. LORD, S.J.

THE Scriptures are so often treated in small, isolated, chopped-off sections that one misses the tremendous onward sweep of the story of the Gospels. One never realizes that here, rising in a series of sharp climaxes, are the adventures of the world's most fascinating hero meeting the most subtle, open, and concealed enemies, struggling against overwhelming odds, charming as no character of fiction has ever been charming, throwing into a single episode the staggering achievement of clearing out the Temple and in almost the next breath speaking sentences that are the essence of poetry.

We have used the Scriptures as a series of isolated texts with which to point a moral and adorn a tale. We have seen Christ as a signpost for virtues and moral precepts instead of as a man who never did a stupid or dull thing and never uttered a thought that was not saturated with meaning and phrased in perfect rhythm, in exact words, and with a power of condensation and vividness of imagery that put His style beyond all possibility of imitation.

And to us who have to live surrounded by writers who worship only one thing, style, style, style, the glorious point is that the content of His literature is true. Half of our popular writers today don't care whether or not the thing they say is true, provided only it is brilliant. They would slay the truth for an epigram and kill a fact to make a

244

phrase. They would rather be clever than right, amusing than honest, smart than true.

Probably never before in modern times, perhaps not since the Greeks went mad over form, have we had such perfection of style. There is no trick of words that we have not learned. We can swing sentences in a fashion to make literary men of other ages blush with envy. We know all the architecture of form. We have the great masterpieces, and we pull them to pieces so that we can copy them from cornerstone to highest pinnacle.

And into this lovely form, what are the authors of the present day packing? Clever lies, smart dirt, sophistical defense of the very things that would overthrow society, brilliant characterizations of people right from the gutter and the lowest night clubs, morality that reeks of the pigpen and the barnyard, philosophy that would cause an ancient Sophist to hide his lead, and such a vague uncertainty about everything that we long for an honest yes and a candid no.

And then we turn back to Christ, the man of letters and the man of sublime truth. His literary form is beyond compare. But it is only the chaste setting for truth that has stood the refining test of ages and human experience. His style is magnificent; but His thoughts warm the heart, lift the eyes, puts humanity on its feet, and turn the soul up from the earth to heaven, in which dwells a merciful Father.

Nothing can be more painful than truth limpingly expressed. Nothing can more easily drive clever people away from that truth than the sight of truth dressed in tawdry raiment or walking about in literary rags. But to Christ the master of thought and style, the creator of a new message of faith and hope, and the maker of an incomparable literary style to contain it—to Him we can bring the most brilliant mind, the most widely read critic, the most cynical traveler down the world's literary highways and know that not only will they be charmed by the beauty of His language and style, but when they leave, their hearts will burn within them, not because of the style of His thought, but because of the burning love, the boundless hope, the tremendous depths of truth revealed.   (1932)

The style of the Gospel is admirable in so many ways, and among the rest in hurling no invectives against the persecutors and enemies of Jesus Christ. For there is no such invective in any of the historians against Judas, Pilate, or any of the Jews.

If this moderation of the writers of the Gospels had been assumed, as well as many other traits of so beautiful a character, and they had only assumed it to attract notice, even if they had not dared to draw attention to it themselves, they would not have failed to secure friends, who would have made such remarks to their advantage. But as they acted thus without pretense, and from wholly disinterested motives, they did not point it out to anyone; and I believe that many such facts have not been noticed till now, which is evidence of the natural disinterestedness with which the thing has been done.

BLAISE PASCAL (1661)

A GOSPEL OF LIFE AND OF DEATH

THE REV. B. W. MATURIN

THERE are two words that constantly keep ringing the changes throughout the teaching of Our Lord and His Apostles. One is "Life," and the other is "Death." And different people, according to their difference of temperament and training, take up one or the other of these words as the keynote of their spiritual life.

The Gospel of Jesus Christ, say some, "is a Gospel of Life. It breathes with the vigor of a fresh energetic life from beginning to end. 'In Him was Life and the Life was the Light of men.' 'I am come that they might have Life, and that they might have it more abundantly.' 'They will not come unto Me that they might have Life.' 'I am the Resurrection and the Life. He that believeth in Me shall never die.' 'I am the Bread of Life.' 'The Law of the Spirit of Life hath delivered me from the Law of Sin and of Death.' From first to last it is full of this thought of living rather than dying, of giving forth rather than restraint, of letting yourself go in energetic action rather than holding yourself back in timid self-repression. What we need is not to die but to live and to live more abundantly, to die to sin by living to righteousness, conquering evil by good. If we thought less of ourselves and gave ourselves out more to others, we should

246

get rid of a multitude of faults bred of self-analysis and morbid self-repression."

And so these men tell us that the Gospel is a Gospel of Life; and in Life not death, in action rather than in mortification we are to find the remedy for our needs. And as we hear them speak, still more as we watch them live, we feel that they certainly have not got the whole of the truth, and part of a truth is often very misleading. There is too much talk about life and living to be healthy, too much of the very self-consciousness that is deprecated, too little taking in —it all seems to be giving out, and a good deal of it is a waste of energy. Somehow such people, though they may quote the words of Our Lord about living, seem very far from reproducing the calm strong life that He lived and taught.

And then there are others who read the teaching of Our Lord very differently, who say: "Nay, but His Gospel is a Gospel of Death, its message of hope and joy is only for those who are ready to give up all and to die for it. 'If any man will come after Me let him deny himself and take up his cross daily and follow Me.' 'He that saveth his life shall lose it, he that loseth his life shall find it.' 'Unless the grain of wheat falling into the ground die it remaineth alone, but if it die it shall bring forth much fruit.' 'We are buried with Him by Baptism into His Death.' 'If ye live after the Flesh ye shall die, but if ye through the Spirit do mortify the deeds of the body ye shall live.' 'I die daily,' says St. Paul, 'I bear about in my body the dying of the Lord Jesus.' The Gospel of Christ is a Gospel of death. We must die to everything that is of earth that we may gain the things of heaven. We must mortify every earthly passion, every human feeling and desire. The very beauty of this fair earth has its subtle danger; better turn our backs and close our eyes to it and wait for the beauty of that land that lies beyond."

And as we listen to such words, and watch the lives of those who teach them, we feel, again, they may have part of Our Lord's teaching, but certainly have not the whole. And in their lives we feel the chill and the rigor of death, but a death that has little cheer or hope and still less love. We must always respect the sincerity and courage of those who are ready to deny themselves, and who reduce life's pleasures and comforts to a minimum. But we do not feel inclined to follow them, or to believe that they have the true secret of that Gospel which sets men's hearts on fire. God has not given us things *merely* that we should give them up, or powers *merely* that we should not use them.

For the fact is, that each of these has taken but one side of Our Lord's teaching and ignored the other. These two words, Life and Death, ring out with equal distinctness and ever-recurrent rhythm, one always following close upon the other. Now He seems to be speaking about that Life which He came to give, and which He would have us live, and, lo, He is speaking of Death; and again, He is speaking of the Cross and the Tomb, and behold it is of Life He speaks. They are never separated in the teaching of Our Lord. Neither life stands alone nor death alone. And it is the part of those who would follow Him to reconcile these two principles in their own practical lives.

(1915)

THE PERFECTION OF THE PARABLES

MOST REV. ALBAN GOODIER, S.J.

NOT enough account is usually taken of the most essentially Asiatic character of the New Testament, and especially of the Synoptic Gospels. The writers of these books did not think as we think; they had not our idea of order, much less had they our historic sense; they had little use for definitions, truth to them was something which could not be confined within the narrow limits of mere human reasoning. The European mind, especially the modern European mind, tends to reject any truth which it cannot prove; the Asiatic mind, ancient and modern, tends to look upon proof, or evidence appealing to the senses, merely as the starting point for its leap into the infinite. If anyone will compare Asiatic literature of any kind, Chinese, Indian, Persian, Semitic, or any other, with the literature of the West, Greek or Roman, or those which have come from them down to our own time, he cannot fail to be struck by one great difference between them; that is, the essentially figurative thought and language of Asia as contrasted with the abstract and reasoning mind of Europe. The Asiatic thinks in symbols, he argues by means of symbols; he has little use for the Western syllogism even in his philosophy. Indeed, usually, he does not argue, he sees; and when he wishes to bring home a truth to another, he does not attempt to prove it, but states it in a sentence and pictures it in some way that the other may see it. Hence he delights in allegory, in stories with or without a moral, in picturesque proverbs which express a truth in a single sentence. . . . Plato, the Wise Man of the West, wrote dialogues, discussing and arguing to a conclusion; the Son of Sirach, or the contemporary Wise Man of the East, heaped sentence on sentence, proverb on proverb, expressing in a hundred ways, by example, by illustration, by antithesis, the truth he wished to drive home, letting it be seen from many angles. This is the one distinguishing feature of the Books of the Old Testament, especially the Major Prophets and the Wisdom Books, as contrasted with the literature we have received from the Greeks and Romans, not excluding the philosophers.

Now Our Lord, as Man, was strictly one of His own race, country and generation. He made use of the material His circumstances provided, not only in His manner of life, but also in His way of thinking, and in the language in which He expressed His thoughts. Though He was God Almighty, He was in all things like to man; He did not improve on the methods of His day, He invented no labor-saving machinery, still less did He work a miracle, to help Him in His daily task as the Carpenter of Nazareth. He did not attempt to correct the standard ideas of His time in science or philosophy, or history, but accepted and used them as other men used them. His way of thinking, and of teaching, was not that of the Greek Aristotle, or of the Latin Cicero, or even of the Hellenized Jew, Philo of Alexandria; it was that of the Jew of Palestine, such as was common in the synagogues of the provincial towns and villages, as well as in the schools of the more learned rabbis in Jerusalem. . . . He had a Jew's, or an Asiatic's, neglect of mere logic; with them, He used the more telling method of making the truth vivid and alive. There is not a syllogism anywhere in all His addresses; instead, He argued with His enemies, if it can be called arguing, on the same lines as they argued with one another; with His friends He brought home His points, not by what we call proofs, but by making their truth evident, almost to the sight. He was expert in asking questions; but that was seldom, as with Socrates and the Greek philosophers, for the sake of opening a discussion, most often it was to close one; the answer was usually so obvious that there was no need to put it into words, or to argue further. Above all His language teemed with the vivid color characteristic of His people, from the moment He began to preach the kingdom, till He uttered His last lament: "If in the green wood they do these things, what shall be done in the dry?"

Were it not that we are used to the language of the Gospels, we would be compelled to wonder, as were the Galileans on the mountain-side above Capharnaum, at this richness in color of our Lord's teaching; it is safe to say that there is not in all literature any example to compare with it. Moreover it is always spontaneous; it is not the result of the poet's careful pruning, it is uttered freely and naturally, as if the speaker could not express Himself in any other way. Sometimes a word or a phrase will serve His purpose, as when He calls Simon a Rock, or John the Baptist no "reed shaken by the wind," but "a voice crying in the wilderness," or Herod "that fox"; or when He tells His disciples that they are "the salt of the earth," or "the light of the world," or "a city set on a hill," or when He describes Himself as "the good shepherd," or "the door of the fold," or "the vine." Sometime He speaks in well-known proverbs, as when He quotes "Physician, heal thyself" to the doubters of Nazareth, and replies to their objections by reminding them that "a prophet is not received in his own country"; or when He defends Himself against the gibes of the Pharisees: "They that are well have no need of the physician but they that are sick." Sometimes His symbolism rises to a picture, as when He defends His healing on the Sabbath Day: "What man shall there be among you that hath one sheep; and if the same fall into a pit on the sabbath day will not take hold on it and lift it out? How much more is a man than a sheep!" Or again when He denounces hypocrites with biting irony: "When thou doest an alms-deed, sound not a trumpet before thee, as the hypocrites do in the streets, that they may be honored among men. Amen, I say to you, they have received their reward." When He speaks of His Father in Heaven His picture rises to pure lyric: "Behold the birds of the air, for they neither sow nor reap, nor gather into barns; and your heavenly Father feedeth them. Are not you of much more value than they?" Perhaps the most striking example of all is the conclusion of the Sermon on the Mount; where others might conclude with a summary of what has been said, or an exhortation for the future, our Lord embraces both in a vivid picture: "Every one, therefore, that heareth these my words and doeth them shall be likened to a wise man that built his house upon a rock. And the rain fell, and the floods came, and the winds blew; and they beat upon that house. And it fell not, for it was founded on a rock. And everyone that heareth these my words and doeth them not, shall be like a foolish man that built his house upon the sand. And the rain fell, and the floods came, and the winds blew; and they beat upon that house. And it fell; and great was the fall thereof." Last of all, His picture sometimes rises to a story. The first instance occurs at the table of Simon the Pharisee, spoken in defense of the Woman who was a Sinner: "A certain creditor had two debtors: the one owed him five hundred pence, the other fifty. And whereas they had not wherewith to pay, he forgave them both. Which, therefore, of the two loveth him most?"

This example at least brings us within sight of what we commonly understand by a parable. Many authors would include under the heading of "parables" all these more elaborated pictures, but I have preferred to keep them apart chiefly because, at a certain moment in the life of our Lord, the Gospels themselves make the distinction. However symbolic, or parabolic, our Lord's language had always been, there came a time in His career when He began to alter His method of teaching. Then, St. Mark tells us, "He taught them many things in parables," and after relating some of them he concludes: "And with many such parables he spoke to them the word, according as they were able to hear, and without parables He did not speak to them: but apart he explained all things to his disciples." The change of method was so marked, and so sudden, that the disciples themselves were taken by surprise. In the evening of that same day they came to Him and asked Him: "Why speakast thou to them in parables?" They also asked what these parables meant. His reply was very explicit: "Who answered and said to them: Because to you it is given to know the mysteries of the kingdom: but to them it is not given. For he that hath, to him it shall be given, and he shall abound: but he that hath not, from him shall be taken away that also which he hath. Therefore do I speak to them in parables: because seeing they see not, and hearing they hear not, neither do they understand." Immediately after, quoting His favorite prophet Isaias, He gave the reason for their deafness: "For the heart of this people has grown gross, and with their ears they have become dull of hearing, and their eyes they have shut: lest at any time they should hear with their ears and understand with their hearts and be converted, and their sins should be forgiven them: and I should heal them!"

Naturally, to the more literal European mind, these words of our Lord have given rise to much discussion. Did He really mean what He said? Did He really wish that some of His hearers, indeed the great majority of those who listened to Him on the lake-side at Capharnaum, should not understand what he taught? I would venture to say that no Asiatic would think that, neither in His time or now. He would say that this passage is but an instance of that hyperbolic way of speaking which is common in the East; he would also add that the parable, requiring application on the part of the hearer, was the normal way of teaching. The language of Palestine had no superlative, and had to use other devices to express it, one of which was the hyperbole. . . .

Consequently, when our Lord spoke of concealing His doctrine, everyone who heard Him would know that He concealed it only from those who no longer had "ears to hear"; moreover, in teaching by parables He was but using the favorite weapon of the scribes, mainly against themselves. But it is also important to notice, what is often passed over, that this hiding of His doctrine in parables referred to one set of parables only; of all the others it is obvious that the very opposite is their purpose, as we shall see. Our Lord Himself expressly confines His meaning to one set alone when He said to His disciples: "To you it is given to know the mysteries of the kingdom of Heaven; but to them it is not given." In other words it is what are known as the parables of the kingdom of Heaven whose meaning is concealed from unadapted ears; those who had refused that kingdom, who persisted in demanding a kingdom according to their own ideas, would never understand the parables of the kingdom that He had come to found. In the Gospels these are eight in number. All are prophetic, telling something of the kingdom that the future would reveal; all add a further detail to the concept of the kingdom on earth. It is also perhaps worth noticing that, unlike the other parables, none of them are narratives; they are just descriptions of events within the experience of those who heard them, so that to many they would seem to be of no significance at all. There was (1) the description of the Sower of Seed; without application it could not have been immediately clear that that this referred to the preaching of the word and its results. There was (2) the description of the Cockle growing up among the Wheat; it concealed the prophecy of the efforts the enemy of the human race would make to destroy the work of Christ, and their ultimate failure. There was (3) the example of the Mustard Seed; showing how, from the tiniest of beginnings, the kingdom would grow till it covered the whole world, and would include every type of human being. There was (4) the Leaven, a perfect illustration of the process by which the Kingdom would influence the human race and would build up a new civilization. There was (5) the picture of the Seed growing of itself while the sower slept, telling how the spread of the kingdom would depend on the grace of God alone, how man of himself was but a tool. There were the two illustrations (6) of the Hidden Treasure, and (7) of the Pearl of Great Price, showing how the kingdom was worth all the world besides, and how any price should and would be paid to acquire it. Last, there was the parable (8) of the Draw Net, telling how not all in the kingdom of heaven on earth would be saints, but how it would still contain both worthy and unworthy members, good men and bad.

This first group of parables is given by the evangelists all together, which seems to confirm the view that the warning words of our Lord belong to them alone. All deal with the same subject, each adds something to its development; all are prophetic, and therefore would be the less intelligible to their hearers; one might say they were spoken more for us of the twentieth century than for the people of the first, though there are still those who have not eyes to see nor ears to hear. For a long time after this series the Gospels do not give us any more parables of the stricter kind, though, of course, the highly figurative language never ceases. But when Jesus leaves Galilee, and sets himself to His final task in Judea and Jerusalem, parables begin again. And now they are not, as in the first series, all gathered together and made to supplement one another, developing, as it were, a certain definite thesis, but they are given as they are spoken, here and there, on the roadside, at table in private houses, in the city street or the Temple court. Secondly, these fresh parables differ altogether from those of the kingdom spoken in Galilee. The Galilean parables were little more than descriptions of ordinary events which might occur in any Galilean experience; the Judean parables are mainly complete stories, dramatic scenes illustrating some practical truth or virtue. The Galilean parables had a double purpose, to enlighten some and to leave others in ignorance; the Judean parables are expressly given to drive home some lesson, and are therefore so clear, so easily interpreted, that not even the most obstinate enemy can fail to understand them. More than that, to make sure they are understood Jesus often follows them up with a test question. In Galilee, again, the parables were confined to one subject, the kingdom of Heaven, which was doctrinal rather than practical, having no immediate application to ordinary life; the Judean parables taught lessons of charity, perseverance, humility and other

253

virtues. The Galilean parables taught the kingdom, the Judean parables described the life of the children in the kingdom.

The number of parables in this second series is sixteen. All are short stories; each describes the life within the kingdom from a different angle. Many are not interpreted, but are left to tell their own tale; none need more than the slightest change for their application. (1) The story of the Good Samaritan teaches the virtue of effective charity, even to a stranger. (2) That of the Merciless Steward emphasizes the obligation to forgive as we are forgiven. (3) The Importunate Guest at Night illustrates the efficacy of perservering in prayer. (4) The Rich Fool lays bare the folly of glorying in earthly possessions. (5) The Barren Figtree warns us against resisting the grace of God. (6) The Rejection of the Invited Guests shows the danger of neglecting divine inspirations. (7) The Lost Sheep and (8) the Lost Drachma bring before us the longing of God to save the most abandoned soul. (9) The Prodigal Son, the longest of all the parables and the most detailed, tells of this infinite mercy for the repentant sinner, and His rebuke, however gentle, for the jealousy of the just. (10) The Unjust Steward teaches that the good things of this world must be used with a view to eternity. (11) The Rich Man and Lazarus describes the nature of the recompense hereafter. (12) The story of the Judge and the Widow assures His disciples that they shall be protected and their cause vindicated. (13) The Pharisee and the Publican contrasts false and true devotion, the one founded on self-complacency, the other on humble contrition. (14) The Laborers in the Vineyard vindicates the right and justice of God in awarding His elect. (15) The Pounds, and (16) the Talents, which may be the same parable differently worded, warn us again of the use to be made of the gifts of God.

Almost all these parables are given as spoken on the spur of the moment, without any preparation, suggested by a question that has been asked, or a casual circumstance; yet all are complete in themselves, perfect for their purpose, one might say impossible to improve. . . .

We come next to a third series, which ought to be taken apart. They are four in number, and they were spoken by Him on His two last days in the Temple, that is, on the Monday and Tuesday in Passion Week. They were the days of His final appeal, and of His final condemnation of those who had rejected Him, and yet were the representatives of Israel. The parables correspond; they rise to the highest pitch of tragedy, they ring with the bitterness of the Agony in

254

the Garden. Their significance is so clear that there is no possibility of misunderstanding, and our Lord makes sure they are not misunderstood by questioning His hearers about them. (1) He tells the story of the Two Sons sent into the vineyard, one of whom said he would not go and went, the other said he would go and did not. Immediately He asks: "Which of the two did his father's will?" And when He has received from them the only possible answer, like Nathan with David, before they have time to recover or defend themselves He applies the lesson: "Amen I say to you, that the publicans and harlots shall go into the kingdom of Heaven before you." (2) Next, after this preparation, He gives the parable of the Laborers, who murdered their master's son that they might seize his estate. Again immediately He asks: "When, therefore, the Lord of the vineyard shall come, what will he do to those husbandmen?" There is only one reply, and He makes them give it themselves. They say to Him: "He will bring those men to an evil end, and will let out his vineyard to other husbandmen, that shall render him fruit in due season." He takes up their words; He speaks to them in their own language, which is that of the Old Testament; when He has ended they know without a doubt that they have condemned themselves. "And when the chief priests and Pharisees and the scribes had heard his parables, they knew that he spoke of them." We would venture to say that nowhere in the Gospels does Jesus stand out in greater majesty than in this scene in the Temple. He boldly tells His enemies, as they cower beneath His gaze, what He knows they will do to Him before three days are over. (3) There follows the parable of the Wedding Feast, which again ends in tragedy. But this time it is tragedy confined to a single case; there rings nevertheless the triumphant note that in spite of rejection and in spite of contempt the room was "filled with guests." (4) Last of all, later that same day on the slope of Olivet, as a kind of conclusion to all He has said, He gives to His disciples apart a last warning on the need of prayer, in the parable of the Wise and Foolish Virgins. . . .

On the one hand we have the evidence of the evangelists themselves that the parables they have recorded are but a few of those spoken by our Lord; on the other hand, while with Him they were so abundant, we have not one coming from any other. Neither Paul nor Peter, nor Luke nor John, nor any other of the inspired writers of the New Testament ever attempted to write a parable. This, surely, is internal evidence enough that the parables of our Lord are authentic; the disciples did not put in His mouth stories which they were unable to invent for themselves. . . . The parables came from Him in all their perfection as spontaneously as the rest of that figurative language which was characteristic of Him from the beginning to the end of His career. Swift, terse, clear-cut as a diamond, with every word considered, the parables shine out with a brilliance which scholars of every kind have acknowledged to have no equal in the whole history of literature. What may we conclude? A doubter had to say of him: "Rabbi, we know Thou art a teacher from God." His enemies were compelled to own: "Never did man speak as this man hath spoken." But a follower could say: "Lord, to whom shall we go? Thou hast the words of eternal life." There is that in the parables alone, even in their very form, which should convince the eye that would see, and the ear that would hear, that He who spoke them was more than man.

(1938)

"THE IRON OBJECTIVITY OF THE GOSPELS"

ARNOLD LUNN

IT IS difficult to imagine the impact which the Gospels would make upon the mind of a man who was reading them for the first time. How would you react, reader, if you stumbled by chance on the story of the Christ child born in a manger, "because there was no room for them in the inn"? What other religion has had the audacity to begin with God in a stable? Try to read the story of the woman taken in adultery as if you were reading it for the first time, then turn to the no less wonderful tale of the woman who was a sinner, the woman who washed Christ's feet with her tears. Then read the parable of the Prodigal Son, and you will find it difficult not to echo the exclamation of men for whom custom had not staled the infinite variety of Christ's words, "Never man spake like this man.". . .

The attention of one who was reading the Gospel for the first time would be focused so intensely on the central figure that he would find it difficult to spare a thought for the lesser miracle of the biographers. Who were these men? What were these men?

256

That they were not creative artists, finished masters of the written word, this is certain. Nothing could be more certain. The effect which they produce is due to the theme, not to the artistry with which that theme is presented. It would make too great a demand on our credulity to credit the artlessness with which the tale is told, artlessness which has its own literary appeal, to conscious art. The Evangelists make all the mistakes that a conscientious beginner, tutored by modern handbooks on the writer's craft, would avoid. They spoil some of their most effective scenes by the failure to bring down the curtain. Their scenes often fade into another by awkward transitions. The stories often begin and end abruptly. They report the most bewildering sayings without the least attempt to explain them, thus violating a canon of sound fiction which ordains that every problem raised should have its solution, and that characters should run strictly true to type. But the aim of the Evangelists is not artistic fiction, but history. They are ambitious to report what Christ said and what Christ did, and these unsolved conumdrums fall into place as the recollections of men who were often mystified by their Master. The Gospels are full of loose ends, of incidents which remain unexplained. Indeed, the cheerful casualness with which the Evangelists leave unsolved even those problems to which they could supply an answer, proves how far their treatment is removed from the treatment of a modern biographer or modern novelist. Consider, for instance, the last scene in the Garden of Gethsemene. The disciples have forsaken Christ, and the darkness is lit only by the torches of the guard. One young man still continues to follow the soldiers, and the guard turns on his heels with an angry exclamation—so one reconstructs the scene—as if his nerves had been frayed by vague rumors that the populace might attempt a rising in support of Jesus. The guards lay hold of the young man. The linen cloth wound about his naked body comes away in their hands, and the naked man escapes into the darkness. The modern biographer, if he recorded this strange incident, would speculate on the identity of the young man, would, at least, attempt to explain his singularly inadequate wardrobe. If tradition be true, St. Mark had good reason to know the answer to this riddle. St. Mark was the young man in question, but he throws no beam of light across the darkness into which the young man has fled.

If the Evangelists make many mistakes which a conscientious beginner would avoid, it is no less true that they avoid most of the mistakes which a beginner would make. The surest sign of immaturity in a young writer is a certain weakness for labels. He wishes to convince you, we will suppose, that his hero, Sir Harry Tremayne, was famous for his caustic wit. Instead of allowing us to infer from witty dialogue that Sir Harry is a wit, he tediously insists that his *bon mots* were quoted from one end of Mayfair to another. The experienced writer avoids labels. He does his best to convince you with his dialogue, and allows us to infer wit from the remarks which he reports. He does not tell us that his hero is brave, but he shows his hero proving his courage in action.

One of the first facts about the Gospels which strikes anybody who has ever tried to write, is the remarkable absence of labels. The Evangelists do not try to describe Christ, they show Christ in action, and report what Christ said. Seldom do they add a comment of their own, as if they realized that although a biographer might try to interpret a human subject, biographers of Christ would do well to confine themselves to what Clough calls "the mere it was."

Interpretations of Christ from those who did not know him in the flesh may be forgiven, for it is a natural instinct which makes the Christian seek to expand the meaning of Christ's words, and to illustrate them in relation to modern problems. But the men who were fortunate to walk with Christ were too modest to believe that their readers would be interested to learn what they felt or what they thought. Their sole concern was to provide the world with an authentic record of what Christ said and what Christ did. Their theme was so tremendous that they dared not intrude their own poor comments into a divine tragedy. To quote Francis Thompson with due alteration, they feared

"To mar immortal melodies
With broken stammer of the Earth."

Men who have passed through supreme experiences are drained of emotion. Words are poor things to describe what they felt, so they content themselves with reporting what they saw and what they heard. Thomas Herbert, who accompanied his royal master, Charles I, to the scaffold, has left a record of those last hours as moving as it is simple. On the way to the scaffold Charles handed Herbert his watch, "which Mr. Herbert keeps accordingly." Nothing more. What more is there to say? Is it really necessary to add that Herbert never looked at this watch without a poignant memory of the master he had loved so dearly, and served so faithfully. "Which Mr. Herbert keeps accordingly" tells us all that we need to know.

The iron objectivity of the Gospels is more impressive, for their theme is infinitely more tragic than the execution of a king. Read the story of the crucifixion and remember that familiarity with the subject inclines us to forget that it hurts to be crucified. How easily this record might have degenerated into sentimentalism. To quote only one incident, it must have been difficult to resist the temptation to describe what the mother of Jesus felt during those long hours when she watched the slow agony of her son. Yet how pitiably inadequate any words must be to express so terrible a grief. "Now there stood by the cross of Jesus his mother and his mother's sister." Nothing more, and for nineteen centuries Christians have been trying to find words to translate and art to represent what his mother and his mother's sister felt.

The engraver's knife moves across the plate. A few sharp lines, and the picture has taken shape. No dry point burr softens the hard outline which emerges.

"And they crucified him . . . and sitting down they watched him there . . . I thirst . . . and straightway one of them ran and took a sponge . . . but when they came to Jesus, and saw that he was dead already, they brake not his legs. . . ."

Those who believe that religion should never degenerate into sentimentalism or emotion into emotionalism will find support in this conviction in the bleak poignancy of the crucifixion story.

That the Gospels are the work of eye-witnesses is indicated not only by the things which they record, but by the things which they do not record. The Gospels are full of homely details which an eye-witness would have recorded, and are full of gaps which a fiction writer would have filled in. Read the most perfect short story in literature, the story of the woman taken in adultery. The great masters of the short story might have invented that sublime touch, "Jesus stooped down, and with his finger wrote on the ground," but they would not have been content to leave us ignorant of what Christ wrote. It is contrary to the canon of fiction to arouse the reader's expectation without easing his curiosity. Had Tolstoy invented this touch, Christ would have written something very telling in the dust, something very telling indeed, but nothing half so telling as the silence of St. John.

Reticence is the keynote of the Gospels.   (1933)

259

THE MEANING OF "SUBSTANTIAL ACCURACY"

THE REV. HUGH POPE, O.P.

INSPIRATION is not revelation, neither is it dictation. But unless it ensures the substantial accuracy of the account it fails of its purpose. Jer. xxxvi. 32 serves as an excellent commentary on this. But what is "substantial accuracy"? St. Augustine has developed this point very fully in his treatise *De Consensu Evangelistarum:* thus, after pointing out that Matt. iii. 11 makes the Baptist speak of himself as unworthy so much as to *carry* Christ's shoes whereas the other Evangelists report John as saying he was unworthy to *loose* them, St. Augustine draws a first conclusion:

"If, then, we are asked what precise words the Baptist used . . . Whosoever grasps the fact that it is ideas in themselves which are necessary for arriving at a knowledge of the truth—no matter what words be used to express them—will realize that it is idle to waste time over such a question."

He then dwells on the way in which the Evangelists tell us of the same events but in different words, and he concludes:

"Moreover, and this especially affects sound doctrine, we must realize that we have to look for and embrace the truth of *things* rather than of *words* when we note with approval that those who use not the same expressions yet stand in the same truth since they do not differ in *things* and *ideas*."

But Augustine is nothing if not thorough. Consequently he now proceeds to point out that these expressions "to carry" and "to loose" differ not merely in words or their order or mode of expression, but "to carry shoes" and "to loose the latchet of a shoe" are two distinct *things*. After suggesting that John might have used both expressions and that one Evangelist remembered one, another another, Augustine lays down the following broad principles:

"If, however, when John spoke of the Lord's shoes he *intended* nought else save to set forth Christ's excellence and his own lowliness, then whichever of these expressions he used, whether 'loosing the latchet' or 'carrying the shoes,' he held to the same *idea,* and whosoever expressed this same feeling of lowliness in the words wherein he refers to the shoes did the same, and consequently did not fail to express the same *intention.* We have, then, a useful rule and one we should commit to memory when treating of the harmony of the Evangelists; there can be no question of lying, since—even when one says something which he did not say of whom he narrates it—he yet expresses the speaker's *intention* as much as he who does give his actual words. Thus we learn this profitable truth: that nought else is to be looked for save what he *meant* who speaks."

St. Augustine lays down precisely the same principles when discussing the apparently conflicting accounts of St. Peter's denials. Nor can we argue that St. Augustine is here speaking of the words used by the Baptist or by Apostles and that he would not apply the same principles to our Lord's words. For when discussing Christ's prediction that Peter would deny Him "before cock-crow" he insists on the various forms in which this prediction is given in the Gospels and concludes:

"If we look for the precise words which the Lord spoke to Peter, they cannot be found, and it is idle to seek them. For His *meaning*—which the words are meant to make known to us—can easily be gathered from the Evangelists' words howsoever different they may be."

This, then, is the meaning of "substantial accuracy": the written record infallibly sets before us what our Lord *meant* to say. (1918)

THE MIRACLES PROVE CHRIST'S DIVINITY

THE RT. REV. MSGR. RONALD A. KNOX

You will hear people say, "We, in our day, believe the Gospels in spite of the miracles it records, not because of them. To us, miracles make it harder, not easier, to accept the Christian faith." Now, if you examine that statement for a moment, you will see that it rests on a very silly confusion. In order to believe the Gospels, you must do two things. You must first of all convince yourself that the narrative which the Evangelists have left us is true; and then you must decide whether the Church is right in inferring, from the narrative, that the Hero of the story was Incarnate God. Now, it's quite true to say that the miracles which are recorded in the Gospels don't make it easier for us to believe *in the truth of the narrative*. But then, who ever thought they would? Who ever, in his wildest dreams, imagined that a document was MORE likely to be historically accurate because it represented its Hero as walking on the water, instead of walking on the land? The suggestion is ridiculous. No, the value of the miracles comes in when we reach the second process, the process of proving that the Church is right in representing the Hero of the Gospels as Incarnate God. Now, is anybody going to be such a fool as to tell us that miracles make it harder for us, instead of easier for us, to believe that? Is anybody going to say: "What! Did Christ walk on the water? Then of course He can't have been God! Did Christ rise from the dead? Then of course He can't have been God"? Obviously, if the Gospels give us satisfactory evidence that our Lord walked on the water and rose from the dead, then that is the best possible proof that the claim He made was true.

I will go further, and say, it is the only *adequate* proof that His claim was true. I will not speak dogmatically here; I will simply record my own religious state of mind. I will simply say that if it were not for the miracles which the Gospel records (including among those the fulfillment of Old Testament prophecies) I would not, personally, be a Christian. I should think it a treachery to my reason to accept the divine claim of an unmiraculous Christ. I know that there are people who will tell you that even if Our Lord had done no miracles on earth they would have accepted, and would have felt bound to accept, His assertions of His own Deity. For myself, I could not accept it, and should think the worse of others if they did.

But, you say, was it not enough for Our Lord's contemporaries to see His face enlightened by a charity not of this world, to hear His gracious speech, to watch His unfailing meekness and patience, His sympathy with the poor and the outcast? With such evidence before their eyes, was it not their duty to hail Him as a God? Theirs perhaps; but mine? No artist has put on record for me, even if I could trust the skill of artists, that heavenly beauty of which you speak;

262

the accents of that gracious speech had faded from the world before my living memory; the record of His actions which is left to us is very far from complete, and, at this distance of years, it is not different in kind from other records of sanctity, the record of St. Francis, the record of St. Philip Neri. It is a biography to which even the most cynical of readers is bound to pay homage, as the story of an amazing human career; but do we dare to say that the Hero of it is self-evidently God?

But at least (you insist) if that living revelation of a human Character which was enough for His contemporaries is not enough for you, sundered from it as you are by the centuries and by the changing fashions of human thought, have not His own words been put on record for you; and do not *they* attest His Divinity? "Never man spoke like this man"—that was the verdict of His audience, and has not the written word power to move our hearts as well? Once more I say, they are words whose spiritual beauty even scoffers have recognized, even His enemies have been unable to traduce. But is there anything He said which a merely human teacher *could not* have said? . . .

Our Lord did not come to earth unexpected and unannounced; He made no sudden intrusion into our world. He came to people who had been taught to expect His coming. . . . The Messiah Who was expected was a Messiah Who should come with miracle. And that was the popular expectation of Our Lord's own day. "When the Christ comes," they said, "will He do more miracles than these?" The Jews were expecting, and expecting with justice, a miraculous Messiah. . . .

Another point. Our Lord Himself claimed to do miracles, and pointed to His miracles as the evidence of His Divinity. "If I had not done among them the works that no other man had done, they would not have sin." "Or else believe for the very works' sake." And, in answer to John's question whether He was the Messiah, "Go and tell John what you see and hear; the blind see, the lame walk, the lepers are cleansed, the deaf hear." . . . Above all, He pointed forward to the crowning miracle of His Resurrection. Deliberately He flung out a challenge to His critics; let them kill Him, and He would prove them in the wrong by triumphing over death. "Destroy this temple, and in three days I will raise it up." . . . When He foretold His Passion to His disciples, He foretold that on the third day He would rise again. He issued a challenge; and if He never fulfilled the terms of that challenge, if it was only some pale Ghost that left the tomb on Easter morning, can He blame us, can He condemn us, if we fail to believe?

I say, then, that if ever there was an occasion when it was antecedently probable that God would signalize His Almighty power by miracle, it was here. A revelation came from Him which claimed to be an unmistakable revelation; and it could not be unmistakable, unless it were accompanied by miracle. He had foretold it through His prophets, and had foretold that it would be accompanied by miracle. Finally, He Who came to make that revelation pointed to His miraculous powers as evidence of His Divinity. And now, what are the historical facts?

We have four records of the Incarnate Life in question. Everybody admits that they were all in circulation a hundred years or so after the events they record; that two of them at least were in circulation forty years after the events they record. Three of them at least were written by simple men who set out merely to report the facts which they had witnessed with their own eyes or heard from eyewitnesses; had no theological thesis to defend, no theories to maintain. There is no conceivable reason why those records should not be accepted as unreservedly as, let us say, Caesar's commentaries. No reason whatever, except one. They report miracles. . . .

Where they report miracles, in so far as they report miracles, these records are discredited by the critics of today—why? BECAUSE they report miracles. Was there ever such madman's logic? We prove to them that Almighty God can do miracles. We prove to them that He is likely to do miracles, given sufficient cause. We prove to them that the revelation of Himself which He made to the world not merely gave sufficient cause for miracles, but demanded miracles if it was to be a revelation at all. And then we say, Here are the miracles; here is the record of them. And they say, Oh, but we can't accept that record. Indeed, we say, and why not? Why not? (they answer) Oh, because it reports miracles.

Of course, if you found a chapter in Caesar's commentaries which purported to describe how Caesar fed the Tenth Legion with five loaves and two fishes, you would do right to suspect that that chapter was spurious. Not because miracles are impossible, but because in such a case the conditions are absent which make miracles probable. Caesar made no claim to supernatural powers, needed no argument, save the sword, to support his authority. But the Gospels deal with a situation in which miracles are not only natural; they are necessary. Our Lord was not proving that He was a prophet, was not proving that He was a man entrusted with a divine mission. He was proving that He had been personally present when the foundations of the earth were laid, when the morning stars sang their praises together, and all the sons of God made a joyful melody. He was proving that He had existed from all eternity, the Co-equal Word of the Omnipotent Father. Was he to prove this by earnest moral exhortations, by devoted missionary zeal, by patience endurant of indignities? Put Raphael down at a street-corner as a pavement-artist, what proof can he give of his identity but to paint like Raphael? Bring God down to earth, what proof can He give of His Godhead but to command the elements like God? (1928)

That the dead really were raised and that those who penned the Gospels did not invent this, is very apparent from the fact that if it were a figment they would have told us that many more were so raised and would have made out that they had remained much longer in the tomb.

ORIGEN (246)

THE QUALIFICATIONS OF THE EVANGELISTS TO REPORT WHAT THEY WITNESSED

THE REV. HUGH POPE, O.P.

IT IS the custom to speak of the Evangelists as "uneducated fishermen" who would be incapable of appreciating evidence, and who would be only too easily carried away by their emotions and by their personal devotion to their Teacher. Yet what ground is there for supposing them uneducated? Their writings should be sufficient dis-

265

proof of this notion, for—leaving on one side the indubitably literary Third Gospel—we have in Matthew, Mark and John narratives of undeniable charm even if we cannot claim for their very simplicity a high standard of literary composition. The men who penned these "living" documents cannot have been uneducated in the ordinary sense of the term. And as a matter of fact the entire Jewish tradition is opposed to it. The Jews themselves have always been educationalists and we can trace back their efforts in this direction to a very early date. . . . It is true that this education was almost, if not quite, exclusively Biblical. But what finer education could men have? St. Paul makes it a matter of special commendation to Timothy that he has received such education. We see its effect in the way in which the Evangelists are steeped in the Old Testament; it is the same with the Saints of the time of Christ. When Zachary, Simeon and the Blessed Virgin break into song their Canticles are little more than a cento of passages from all parts of the Old Testament; it is the same with St. Stephen's speech. How insistent was the regular teaching by the Scribes is clear from the numerous references in the New Testament; and though this teaching was not elementary, yet there is no indication that it was confined to a limited audience. As for individual Evangelists their educated character is vouched for in the case of St. Matthew who would hardly have sat at the seat of custom had he been lacking in the ordinary requirements of a man of business. That St. Luke was educated goes without saying. As for St. John, even if it could be shown that he had not received a good elementary education, we should still have to reckon with the long years of his life, his travels and his intimate experience of men. St. Mark can hardly be an exception; at any rate both St. Peter and St. Paul found him useful as a secretary.

The Evangelists, then, had first-hand sources of information. Moreover they were far from being prejudiced witnesses, they had no axe to grind, they had stubbornly resisted the evidence for Christ's Resurrection, as some also of the body of disciples had found the doctrine touching the Holy Eucharist "a hard saying." But just as St. Thomas' doubts serve to render our faith the stronger, so too the fact that the Evangelists were "slow to believe" renders their grudging witness the more effective. Further, the very independence of their individual narratives, together with the apparent want of harmony in their accounts of certain events, cries out against the idea that their stories are fictitious. The same must be said of the unaffected simplicity of style which so offended St. Augustine and on which Lactantius remarks more than once. Yet this same simple style served as a vehicle for the profoundest doctrine, a doctrine which at the same time revolted and yet won the world. The Evangelists died, their Evangels remained. False Gospels appeared in profusion, but they have hardly endured as the treasures of museums, while the Canonical Four, despite their lack of adornment, are and always will be fruitful in the divinest thought for all men and for all time.

Hence the "Majesty" of the Gospels; hence the custom of swearing by them; hence, too, the place of honor assigned to a copy of the Gospels in the Councils of the Church.   (1918)

ST. MATTHEW'S GOSPEL

THE REV. LÉONCE DE GRANDMAISON, S.J.

ALL the ancient witnesses agree in telling us that St. Matthew's Gospel was aimed at the Jews; it was amongst them that he composed it on behalf of those of them who believed and against the others. The only date handed down to us for its composition is approximate. Matthew wrote, says St. Irenaeus, "when Peter and Paul were evangelizing Rome and founding the Church," which would bring us to the years preceding the persecution by Nero (64).

Certain features [of St. Matthew's Gospel] strike us at once. The most obvious of these is the Judaic nature of the book. Matthew himself drew attention to it when he spoke of the "scribe perfectly instructed in all that concerned the Kingdom of heaven," and capable in consequence of drawing from his treasure things both new and old.

As regards the old, that which concerns the religion, the spiritual outlook, the manners, the customs, and the language of the educated rabbis of his time, none of the New Testament writers knew more than he himself. His work is Jewish to the backbone and, we may say, to its very marrow. Without this clue nothing in it is intelligible, its allusions, its vocabulary, its literary mannerisms, its narrow horizon, its method of argument, or its controversies. From the very beginning we are plunged into the atmosphere of the Old Testament:

"The Book of the Generation of Jesus Christ, son of David, son of Abraham" and the whole genealogy, deliberately simplified, which follows: "So all generations, from Abraham to David are fourteen generations. And from David to the transmigration of Babylon are fourteen generations: and from the transmigration of Babylon to Christ are fourteen generations."

And this Christ is the Messias, the son of David, foretold by the Prophets. He comes to preach the Kingdom of Heaven; he comes to fulfill the Law, not to abolish it; He is sent to the lost sheep of the House of Israel; he condemns neither the ceremonial side of the Law, nor the observance of the Sabbath. He does not even dispute the authority of the Scribes when it is contained within just limits; and the reward of his faithful disciples will be that "when the Son of Man shall sit upon the throne of his glory" they also "shall be seated, judging the twelve tribes of Israel."

It was for these twelve tribes, in fact, that the book was written. Its readers are presumed to be familiar with the history of God's chosen people, with the language of the prophets, and with the Palestinian customs of the time. They know "what was said to the ancient"; they are more familiar with the whole gamut of rabbinical judgments, "of the tribunal, of the sanhedrim, and of gehenna," than the most learned modern exegete, and know, as well as he knows, the form and the shape of the characters of Hebrew writing. Nor are they ignorant of any of the ruses by which they can, under color of piety, refuse to help their aged parents or swear without thereby committing themselves irretrievably. There is no need to explain to them what is meant by "an adulterous generation," a proselyte, or "a child of hell."

So also they can equally well appreciate as connoisseurs that art, immemorial among the Jews, of developing the leading idea through opposition and parallelism, and then establishing it by a kind of rhythmic cantilena or ballad which stresses certain salient words. Veritable landmarks for verbal development, these words sharpen the memory, and almost automatically bring to the lips of the reciter a given passage or antithesis. They made possible for the scribes of those days, as for the oriental-story-tellers of all time, feats of improvisation and of recitation which our analytical methods make not only difficult, but almost incredible to us.

Suggested on almost every page of the New Testament, and easily discernible by those who have made themselves sensible to them, these rhythms are especially numerous in St. Matthew's Gospel. In it they, as it were, run neck and neck with the text, and to point them out it would be necessary to transcribe whole chapters. From the beginning the sermons of Jesus bore this stamp, and probably they were passed on by the Master in person to the ears and the lips of his disciples without change.

Another Semitic mannerism, related to the first, consists in distributing the matter in a certain number of fixed frames, in groups of two, three, five, seven, or ten. Such arrangements, intended to help the memory and also, no doubt, sought for their own sakes, are to be found throughout this Gospel: in the narrative portion no less than in the discourses. A case in point occurs in chapter ii, in which the story of the Magi and the subsequent events down to the return from Egypt are distributed in three sections each of which is begun by a genitive absolute (ii, 1, 13, 19); the first two are in their turn divided into two paragraphs beginning with the same words: "Then Herod" (7, 16); and the essential climax (the departure of the Magi by another route, frustrating the evil design of Herod and exciting his rage) is stressed by a characteristic key-word which acts as a link between the two halves of the story (12, 13).

But if there is nothing in the Gospel that would seem foreign to a Jewish reader, the whole of it gives him occasion for serious, even moving, reflection. For true as it is that the Messias "came to his own," it is equally true, if we consider them in their leaders and in their mass, that "his own received him not." And on this scandal, this infidelity, no one insisted so much as St. Matthew. His Gospel is like the book which a mysterious hand offered to Ezechiel: "And behold . . . he spread it before me. And it was written within and without: and there were written in it lamentations and canticles and woe" (Ezech. ii. 9). Peace to the Israel of God which recognized its Messias and chanted "Hosanna to the Son of David!" But woe to the rest! When we look at the Gospel today, we see in it from beginning to end, like the watermark in a sheet of paper, the tragic story of God's appeal made to all the people, and heard only by the elect, obeyed by a minority comparable to the "holy remnant" so often spoken of by the prophets of old. So it is true of Israel at this critical hour: "Many are called, but few are chosen"! But for all that, the divine plan will not be frustrated; in place of the sons of the Kingdom, those invited from outside will sit at the Messianic feast.

It is significant that the genealogical table which sketches in broad outline the story of the race of Abraham and of David mentions only those women who were sinners, all of them foreigners: Rahab the Chananite, Ruth the Moabite, and the wife of Urias the Hittite. And even in his cradle Jesus was recognized by the wise pagans who had come out of the East, while the prince of his people pursued him. At the beginning of the public life of the Savior the temptations of the Evil One take the form of the popular Messianic expectations which closed so many eyes to the pure light of the Christ. And all the way through the Sermon on the Mount, which was the charter of the New Kingdom, the Gospel stands in contrast to the human traditions which were then dominant in Israel. The miracles worked by Jesus suffice for men of good will, notably for the pagan centurion, more faithful than the Jews, and the true son of Abraham, of Isaac and of Jacob; but they were a dead letter for the leaders of the people, the Scribes and the Pharisees. Like infidels, these demand prodigies, "signs in the heavens," contrary to the designs of God. The towns where their influence prevails are the most hard-hearted and will receive more severe treatment than Sodom and Gomorrha. And worse still, they attribute the divine works of Christ to the Prince of Devils, and the simple are deceived by this sinister device. . . .

Moreover, the inner meaning of the parables is understood only within the apostolic circle, and only a handful of men recognize in Jesus, "the Christ, the Son of the Living God." And from thence onwards there is the road to the abyss foretold in the Master's prophecies, in which the princes of the people, the leaders, and the learned, are ever seen taking part against him and delivering him over to the Gentiles. And this is the clearly-expressed message of those last days: "the first shall be last"—the sons of the Kingdom shall be supplanted by heathens come from the four quarters of the earth. Woe to the Pharisees, "the blind leading the blind"! Woe to the false shepherds, to the husbandmen who exceed even the malice of their fathers by slaying the Heir of the chosen vineyard! The corner-stone which these wicked laborers reject will fall upon them and crush them. But first they will have their hour, for the Scriptures must be fulfilled. Jesus accordingly is condemned by Pilate, but behind the Roman there is the chief culprit, and he is not only Judas. Just as guilty are the leaders of this mob, and it is "all the people" who cry out "Let his blood be upon us, and upon our children!" . . .

And all this pathetic story is told in a manner worthy of its subject. Where we speak of history it is not in order to drag in a comparison with the classic types of literature: apophthegms, memoirs, lives,

270

and themes are of little assistance here, for this book, written in sufficiently good everyday Greek, is in no way hellenized. But if it is perhaps useless to search for the models our author sets before himself, or to discover whether he has any models at all, it is, on the other hand, easy to see what he has done. No complete biography, no mere collection of maxims and edifying anecdotes, the Gospel presents the elements of a sufficiently adequate Christian initiation. It replies to the questions which a Palestinian Jew of the period before the great catastrophe in A.D. 70 would, if he were touched by the apostolic preaching, naturally put to himself on the person of Jesus, the essentials of his message, and the reception given to this message by Israel.

Considered from this point of view, the work is admirable. It is not only, as all admit, the most complete of our Gospels, but it is also the best balanced. (1935)

ST. MARK'S GOSPEL

THE REV. ALOYS D. DIRKSEN, C.PP.S.

THE author of the Second Gospel was known either by the Hebrew name of John or the Latin name of Mark. . . . In Acts he is called "John who was surnamed Mark." . . . Although his cousin Barnabas was a native of Cyprus, Mark was probably born in Jerusalem, for his mother Mary resided there. She seems to have been fairly well-to-do. Her home served as a place of assembly for the Christians of Jerusalem—possibly the "upper room" of the Last Supper and of the Descent of the Holy Spirit. In 44 A.D. Mark left Jerusalem for Antioch in the company of Paul and Barnabas. In the following year he accompanied them on the missionary journey through Cyprus, but upon reaching the mainland at Perge in Pamphylia he returned home to Jerusalem. He seems to have been considerably younger than Paul and Barnabas. Hence, it was probably the dread of further physical hardships rather than a dispute over methods or principles that induced their assistant to abandon the missionaries. In any case Paul was greatly offended by Mark's desertion. In 50 A.D. Mark was again in Antioch, probably having returned with Barnabas after the Council of Jerusalem. In the same year he accompanied his cousin on a second missionary journey in Cyprus. Thereafter we lose sight of him for a few years. We find him, however, in Rome during both of St. Paul's imprisonments in that city (61-63 A.D., 66-67 A.D.). During this same period he assisted St. Peter, who, writing from Rome, calls Mark his "son." This may be either a term of affection or may signify that Peter had given him spiritual birth in Christ through baptism.

That St. Mark wrote the Second Gospel should be beyond question. Some fifty years ago the theory of a "proto-Mark," a writing upon which the present Mark was thought to be based, was current; but today the Marcan authorship of this Gospel is supported not only by Catholic scholars but by many non-Catholic critics. Tradition has never associated the authorship of the Second Gospel with anyone but Mark. . . . If we read the Gospel itself, we soon see that the author was a Palestinian Jew, familiar with Palestine and with the customs and institutions of its inhabitants. His own Semitic mentality is plainly reflected in his thought and language. All this fits Mark admirably.

The oldest and by far the most important testimony concerning the origin of St. Mark's Gospel is the statement of Papias (c. 120 A.D.), which has been preserved for us by the Church-historian Eusebius. The immense importance of this testimony lies in the fact that Papias himself is merely quoting the words of the "Elder," who is commonly believed to be none other than St. John the Apostle. The statement of Papias is as follows: "This also the Elder used to say, 'Mark, having become the interpreter of Peter, wrote down accurately, although not in an orderly arrangement, the sayings and deeds of the Lord, as far as he recalled them. For he himself neither heard the Lord nor was He His follower, but he was later on, as I have said, a follower of Peter. The latter used to deliver his instructions as circumstances required, but not like one who draws up an orderly arrangement of our Lord's activity. Hence Mark did nothing wrong in thus writing down certain things as he remembered them. For his sole purpose was to omit nothing of what he had heard and to falsify nothing in recording this.' "

From these words we might rightly conclude not only that Mark wrote an account of Christ's ministry according to the preaching of St. Peter, but also that this account is identical with our Second Gospel. For, (a) this Gospel lacks the "orderly arrangement," i.e., the artificial disposition of material according to subject-matter, that is seen so clearly in the First Gospel and in part also in the Third; (b) the choice of subject-matter and its general chronological arrangement are exactly the same in this Gospel, which was intended primarily for Gentile Christians, as they are in Peter's discourse to the Gentile centurion Cornelius (Acts 10, 36-43); (c) the many graphic details that are recorded in this Gospel come from one who was an eye-witness of these scenes; (d) the most distinctively Petrine touch, a tribute to the humility of Peter's preaching, is seen in the fact that in this Gospel such things as might redound to his honor are lightly passed over by Mark, whereas those of little or no credit to him are mentioned, even where the other Evangelists omit them. Considering all these facts, we are not surprised to learn that St. Justin (c. 150 A.D.) called this Gospel simply "the Memoirs of St. Peter."

Since Mark's main purpose in writing was merely to give a faithful reproduction of St. Peter's preaching, his Gospel is by far the most primitive of all, even though the Aramaic Gospel of St. Matthew was written at a somewhat earlier period. Mark's language is the ordinary *koine* Greek of every-day life as spoken by the Jews of the Diaspora. He does not make the slightest pretense at composing a piece of "fine literature." Yet there is a certain great charm and beauty in this very simplicity. His style is direct, vigorous and characterized by a realism that one would expect to find in a primitive narrative. The uneven structure of the sentences, the frequent use of the historical present, the vividness and graphic touches that are seen throughout, all show that this is essentially an oral narrative of an eye-witness. Nevertheless, we should not conclude from this that St. Mark acted merely as an amanuensis who mechanically records the speeches of another. Mark and not Peter is the true author of this Gospel; he alone was inspired by the Holy Spirit to write down this story which Peter had told over and over again to the first Christians.

From the nature and origin of this Gospel, it follows that Mark's scope and purpose are identical with Peter's scope and purpose in preaching these truths, i.e., to show that Jesus of Nazareth is the Christ, the Son of God. For this reason Mark emphasizes mainly the deeds and miracles of Christ to prove His divine mission. No other Gospel so forcefully depicts the divine power of Jesus, which is shown especially in His power over demons. But at the same time no other Gospel gives us such a vivid picture of the true humanity of Christ, for Mark is pre-eminently the historian of the earthly life of Jesus. Since an account of Christ's teachings would distract somewhat from this main purpose, Mark records very little of the words of Christ—not much more than a few parables and a part of the Eschatalogical Discourse. Hence his Gospel is much shorter than the others, even though it is generally longer and more complete than Matthew and Luke in the narratives which he had in common with them. . . .

The Second Gospel was written at Rome and intended primarily for the Christians of that city. Early tradition attests that it was written at the express request of the faithful of Rome. These consisted principally of Greek-speaking Gentile converts. The internal evidence confirms the truth of this tradition. For, (a) Mark's language is typical of the Greek spoken at Rome, as its Latinisms and even words borrowed from the Latin prove; its Semitisms and a few Aramaic words are relics from the original oral Gospel of St. Peter; (b) Mark directs his Gospel principally to Gentile readers for whom he often explains Jewish customs and institutions. (1942)

ST. LUKE'S GOSPEL

THE REV. JOHN E. STEINMUELLER

THE Third Gospel and the Acts of the Apostles form two halves of what is really a single literary work. . . . The unity of authorship of both Books is clear. . . . Since the Acts was written at Rome in the year 63 or 64 A.D., the Third Gospel must have been written before that date.

Catholic tradition from the second century on is unanimous in attributing this work to St. Luke, the disciple and companion of St. Paul. . . . Its author shows himself to be a Gentile Christian of no mean literary ability and a disciple of St. Paul, whose teaching on the universality of salvation is here presented in a manner that shows unmistakable signs of Pauline influence. . . .

From Col. 4, 14 and Philem. 24 we know that Luke was with Paul during the latter's first imprisonment in Rome (61-63 A.D.). In the first of these passages he is called by St. Paul "our most dear physician," while in the other passage he is numbered among the "fellow-workers" of the Apostles. From Tim. 4, 11 we know that Luke was Paul's only companion in Rome during a part of his second Roman imprisonment. . . .

According to a fourth century tradition (Eusebius, St. Augustine) St. Luke was a native of Antioch and a member of the Christian community in that city as early as 43 A.D. . . . .

Although we know so little of the life of this Evangelist, we are justified in concluding from his writings that he was a peaceful and gentle man with a fine aesthetic temperament. For one of the outstanding characteristics of this Gospel is the special stress that is laid upon the operation of God's mercy and Christ's compassion for sinners. Likewise notable in this Gospel is the reverence shown toward womanhood. Many types of admirable women are presented to the reader: The Blessed Virgin Mary, Elizabeth, Anna the prophetess, the widow of Naim, the penitent woman, Mary and Martha, the ministering woman, Mary Magdalene.

Luke often emphasizes the social aspects of Christ's teaching: contrast, for example, the Beatitudes and Woes as recorded in his Gospel with the Beatitudes as recorded by Matthew. Greater prominence is given in this Gospel than in the others to Christ's love for the poor and to His teaching concerning earthly wealth.

This Gospel may also be termed the Gospel of prayer, since the subject of prayer is mentioned so frequently. St. Luke carefully notes the example of Christ Himself in this matter, and on several occasions is the only Evangelist to record that Christ then prayed. Similarly we find Christ's instruction on prayer recorded here at greater length. The Third Gospel alone has preserved the three hymns that the Church uses in her daily liturgy: the *Magnificat,* the *Benedictus* and the *Nunc Dimittis.*

This whole Gospel breathes a spirit of holy joy, the gift, no doubt, of that Holy Spirit of whom St. Luke speaks so often in the Acts. In fact, "the great joy to all the people" that overflows the hearts of the faithful every Christmastide, owes more than is usually realized to Luke's simple yet marvelously touching story of the birth of the Savior.

Even though the rather late tradition which makes St. Luke a painter may be very doubtful, still this Evangelist certainly shows that he was an artist in the more general sense of the word. With a few skillful strokes he delineates his brief biographical sketches and makes his portraits stand out as living beings. He is able to make the story that he is telling grip the very soul of his readers. He proves himself a master in portraying tenderness and sympathy for man's afflictions. . . .

Luke is more of a "literary" man than are the other Evangelists. . . . When the occasion allows, Luke shows that he can write as pure and faultless a literary Greek as any profane author of his time. In him genuine spirituality is not incompatible with secular learning. He alone of all the Evangelists links his Gospel account with the history of Syria and the Roman Empire. He is conscious of his responsibility as an historian and, even though he wrote under the inspiration of the Holy Spirit, he employs all human diligence "to follow up all things carefully from the very first," so that his readers "may understand the certainty" of the Gospel (I, 3 f.). . . .

Luke's primary source of information is the oral tradition handed down by the Apostles. By the *eyewitnesses and ministers* of the word the Evangelist means above all the Apostles. From Acts 21, 17 f.; 27, 1 f. it seems fairly certain that Luke remained with Paul during the latter's two years' imprisonment in Palestine. Probably it was especially during this time that Luke followed up this oral tradition to its original sources. (1942)

"OUR LADY'S GOSPEL"

MOST REV. ALBAN GOODIER, S.J.

IT IS commonly accepted by students of the Gospels that the first two chapters of the Gospel according to St. Luke come from, and have been virtually dictated by Our Lady herself. The Evangelist expressly tells us, as if to account for some events which the others do not record, that he has taken his narrative "from those who from the beginning were eye-witnesses." He says that he gives it, not on his own authority, nor scarcely in his own words, but "as it has been delivered unto" him. He says that he has been very careful to get at the exact truth, that he has "diligently attained to all things from the beginning," and that he writes in order that others may know that truth from its first sources. When, then, he plunges almost at once into the account of the Annunciation, we ask ourselves what other "eye-witness" was there of that scene but Our Lady, and from whom else could he have received the story? And this all the more since we know from St. Matthew that she concealed it even from St. Joseph. When, immediately after, he relates the story of the Visitation, who but Our Lady could have told him the exact words of the *Magnificat?* When he tells of the Nativity, who but a mother would have thought of recording that little detail, almost the only one we know of that event, that "she wrapped him up in swaddling-clothes, and laid him in a manger," because it was the best thing she could do under the conditions? Then there follow the other scenes, the Loss and Finding of the Child in the Temple, with the concluding statement: "And he went down with them, and came to Nazareth, and was subject to them. And his mother kept all these words in her heart. And Jesus advanced in wisdom, and age, and grace with God and men." These, and these only, are told us by St. Luke and by no one else; and are they not just those things which a mother would be likely to remember of the early years of her child? And are they not told in just a mother's language, especially the summary at the end?

Another fact in these two chapters confirms the impression that they have come direct from Our Lady herself; it is that through them both she is the prominent character. We are told things concerning her which no one but herself could have known, much less would have troubled to record, how she "was frightened," not at the apparition of the angel but at his message, and how she "argued with herself what on earth it might mean"; how on other occasions she "kept all these things, pondering them in her heart"; how she "wondered at the things that were said." Last of all, surely no one but Our Lady herself would have said of her that "she understood not"; she knew so much more than anyone else ever knew or could know, yet, because of her knowledge, knew also how much she did not know.

With good reason, then, many call these two chapters the Gospel according to Our Lady. And if it is her Gospel, her own "good tidings," one asks oneself whether her message is in any way new; whether in any way it differs from, adds to, what has gone before. Now if we study her own words, if, for instance, we compare the *Magnificat* with other like canticles, there is one thing which strikes us at once. When we look back on the Old Testament, Moses, the Psalms, the Prophets, we find that their words are addressed, first of all, to the children of Israel. They are the Chosen People, they are the heirs of the Redemption, in them the rest of the world is to be saved. Even when we come to Zachary, the father of John the Baptist, it is still the children of Israel that are chiefly considered. . . .

There is one striking exception: it is in the Canticle of Anna (I Samuel ii, 1–10) upon which Our Lady's *Magnificat* is built. In the Canticle, though spoken on the eve of the period of the kings of Israel, no mention is made of the Israelites apart from anyone else. The Lord, in this Canticle, is not only the God of Israel; He is God of all the world:

> "For the poles of the earth are the Lord's
> And upon them he hath set the world."

Whence the mother of Samuel concludes her Canticle:

> "The Lord shall judge the ends of the earth
> And he shall give empire to his kind
> And shall exalt the horn of his Christ."

Still, even with Anna, and some of the prophets whose vision also ranges throughout the world, the perspective is measured, as it were, with the eyes of one whose point of sight is the Temple of the God of Israel. When we come to the Canticle of Our Lady it is almost reversed. It is no longer "the children of Israel" that occupy the center of the picture, but the whole of the human race. She glorifies God for what He is, and for what He has done. She thanks Him for the great honor He has bestowed on her, His hand-maiden; and the reason is, not that, like Judith and Esther, she may become another national heroine, but

> "Because from this moment
> All generations shall call me blessed;"

that is, all the race of men shall benefit from the honor that has been done to her. In other words, in Our Lady's "good tidings," for the first time it would seem, the fruits of the Redemption are announced to all the world, the "children of Israel" are made to include the whole of mankind; and she confirms her message by the further announcement that

> "His mercy
> Is from generation unto generations
> To all them that revere Him."

Only at the end does she speak of her own people. This, she seems to conclude, is the meaning of the prophecies, and the promises of the Lord God. Infinite in power, infinite in mercy, He is the God of all the world, in all place and for all time, and the opening of the floodgates is the special glory of the children of Israel.   (1938)

John, perceiving that the external facts had been made plain in the Gospels, being urged by his friends and inspired by the Spirit, composed a *spiritual* Gospel.

ST. CLEMENT OF ALEXANDRIA (ca. 200)

ST. JOHN'S GOSPEL

THE REV. RICHARD KEHOE, O.P.

ST. JOHN'S Gospel is at once a work of history and a work of theology. But both the history and the theology are given a higher value than could belong to them simply as such, by being transfigured by the mystical mind of the author. Transfigured—not destroyed, nor in any way impaired. . . .

St. John was a mystic inasmuch as the truth that is contained in the theology of his Gospel—fundamentally, the doctrine of the enfolding of men through union with Christ into the embrace of the Blessed Trinity—is not a truth simply held by him as a proposition, but seen, or intuited as expressed in and really embodied and comprised in the person of Jesus Christ, Son of God and Son of Man. For him, to regard the person of Christ, to consider Him quite simply, quietly—as He sits by the well, as He walks, as He talks, as He simply is Himself—is to be in touch with all reality, to be at the heart of things. There is nothing to be hoped for, nothing available having true life in it, *outside* of, apart from, what is there to be contemplated. All life, all goodness is centered there for us. There is the Blessed Trinity loving and being loved in the communion into which our whole hope is that we should be drawn.

The compositional style of the book (when all necessary account has been taken of what is explicable simply as Semitic) manifests the contemplative mind of the author. It is not an analytical style—even in the doctrinal passages; it does not proceed with logical movement to its conclusions. It is an intuitive style; there is a hovering over the subject, a wheeling round to view it one angle after another—"In the beginning was the Word, and the Word was with God, and the Word was God" etc.; until some view is reached that resolves the movement, and the famous eagle folds its wings—"And the Word was made flesh and dwelt amongst us."

The Christ of St. John's contemplating is the living Christ who is both God and man. His mind clings to this double truth in such a "simple" way that the one truth is never for a moment lost sight of while the other is being emphasized. Whereas in the Synoptics it can be said that the Divinity of Christ is often held in reserve. The difference, as Père Grandmaison represents it, is that of the explicit compared with the implicit. "John being like a constant light, disclosing permanently the lines of a monument," whereas in the Synoptics this light shines rather in flashes of illumination. . . .

The Action (the "Argumentum") of the book lies in the encounter of the Grace of the Incarnation with the faith, the doubt, the disbelief of men. On the one hand is represented the revealing of Himself by Christ as Son of God, as the Life and the Light of the World—the shining forth of these truths in the "witness" provided by His actions (especially by His miracles) and by His teaching; on the other hand, the behavior of those who were thus challenged and beset by the Divine. The drama of the action is centered in the souls of men, for that is where the essential encounter took place. But in the outward order, too, there is a highly dramatic plot: in the story of the unfurling of the challenge, and of the grouping of the Jews in response. The stages are apparent, almost like acts in a formal drama, of Jesus' more and more open manifestation of Himself, of the increasing urgency of His appeal; of the gradual forming of a band of disciples completely devoted to Him; of the hardening of a body of opinion against Him, under the influence of the priests and leaders; and of the progress of that inner murderous movement that reached its climax with the cry of "Away with him, crucify him!"

But it is the dramatic issue working out with the souls of these men

280

that is chiefly presented to us. John is no inventor here, or artistic creator. He is simply a recorder and a realistic interpreter. The divine light, which is also divine life, shines upon men; who either then "walk in that light," and enter into life, or like Judas walk out into the "night," choosing death. The reality is black and white enough. . . .

What makes the issue tremendous and dramatic is that the action of men in relation to the grace of the Incarnation is shown as being of *immediate* life-or-death significance. The Son of God does not come promising and threatening respectively heaven and hell in eventual recompense for virtue and wickedness. He comes shedding light upon men, offering life—as the sun shines upon the face of the earth, responsible of itself only for the light, not for the darkness. "For God sent not His Son in the world to judge the world, but that the world might be saved through Him." . . .

One of the principal characteristics of the Fourth Gospel is the persistent use it makes of symbolical representation. Facts as well as words are made to speak. The outward events of our Lord's life, especially the miracles, but also even minor turns and physical features in the narrative, are so exhibited as to appear as illustrations of the doctrine upon which the author is intent. For example, in the miracle of Cana the change of water into wine is taken as a sign of the change effected by the Incarnation from the old dispensation of the Law to the new order of Grace, or of the transformation of nature by the grace of Christ. Or again, the raising of Lazarus to life is clearly meant to be a sign pointing to Christ as the Life of the world. Similarly it is commonly recognized that the miracle of the granting of sight to the man born blind, in which a sort of sacramental use is made by our Lord of the water of the pool of Siloam, is intended to stand as a sign that it is by faith in Christ conjoined with the sacrament of baptism that the divine light of grace must reach to men's souls. And so of the miracles generally: in this Gospel they are pointedly described as "signs," not as "mighty works." . . .

The symbolical interpretation is never achieved at the expense of historical truth; it is based upon unadulterated fact. The alleged instances of far-fetched, violent, or trivial symbolizing are repudiated as the inventions of the Critics themselves. The matter of the Gospel is understood to be charged with symbolical meaning, as it is, not because the author has doctored facts, but because he has *chosen* them in accordance with his purpose—being free to select from the whole range of the life of Christ whatever material he pleased. That he should have had this interest in the hidden, symbolic meanings of the divine history does not need to be explained by the Alexandrian influences. The influence of Old Testament and of Rabbinic ways of thought will substantially account for this general tendency of his mind. . . .

The symbolism of the Fourth Gospel may therefore be regarded as an inspired unveiling of the super-realist meaning of our Lord's life.

(1938)

I can still indicate where the blessed Polycarp preached . . . the addresses which he delivered to the people, as he described his association with John and with the others who had seen the Lord, and how he quoted their words. Polycarp also reported all that he had heard from them about the Lord, about his miracles and his teaching, as one who had received it from those who had seen with their own eyes the Word of Life, and it was all in perfect agreement with the Holy Scriptures.

ST. IGNATIUS, BISHOP OF ANTIOCH (ca. 105)

THE ACTS OF THE APOSTLES

THE REV. BRENDAN LAWLER, S.J.

You have a bridge and a road open before you leading from one part of the New Testament to another: namely, the Acts of the Apostles. From the familiar Gospels, along the easy path of the Acts, into the lesser known land of the Epistles; this is the obvious route to take.

Let us begin, then, by renewing our acquaintance with the Acts of the Apostles, that splendid, stirring, thrilling chronicle of the early years of the Church. St. Luke, the enthusiast, not content with being an evangelist, became the first historian of the Church of Christ. He had duly recorded the little parable of Our Lord: "What is the kingdom of God like, and to what shall I liken it? It is like a grain of mustard seed, which a man took and cast into his own garden; and it grew and became a large tree, and the birds of the air dwelt in its branches." (Luke xiii, 18-19). And he was inspired to record the beginnings of its fulfillment; the slow growth of the Church in the Garden of Israel, followed by its rapid spread from Jerusalem as far as Rome. Let us re-read the book of the Acts, therefore, not only for its own interest but also as a preparation for the reading of the Epistles. . . .

It is amazing what a multitude, and what a variety, of characters— real persons, not fictional "characters"—enter into the brief narrative of the Acts. There is St. Paul's professor of Pharasaic theology, who saved the lives of the twelve apostles, and St. Paul's nephew, who saved his uncle's life and forced more than forty men to break their oath. There is the lady Lydia, whose insistent hospitality St. Luke insists on recording; and there is Rhoda, the maid in St. Mark's house, who ran off and left St. Peter knocking at the door. Besides two new Herods, there is mention of the Christian foster-brother of that Herod who mocked Our Lord. A soothsayer as well as two magicians; two successors of Pontius Pilate and an unending series of Roman officials and soldiers; several rulers of synagogues and some Jewish Christians who were expelled from Rome; all of these make their sudden entry into the story, and as quickly disappear again from view. From the wealthy Sadducees (the party of Annas and Caiaphas) and the pious Pharisees in the Sanhedrin to the Epicurean and Stoic philosophers on the Areopagus: St. Luke has taken note of them all.

The evangelist-historian, St. Paul's "dear physician," was careful about his sources. He must have collected quite a number of documents; and whenever he made a voyage he must have kept a logbook of his own, from which he quotes: "We went on board and set sail . . . we ran a straight course . . . we landed . . . we stayed there seven days." . . .

It is so easy to read through the interesting narrative of the Acts, that we must force ourselves to consider its author's purpose, if we are to attend to those features which will help us to understand and appreciate the Epistles. Let us keep these two points in mind. (1) St. Luke has not set himself the task of describing missionary journeys, the first, the second, etc. He is not primarily preoccupied with journeys or the exact recording of itineraries. He is thinking rather in terms of Roman provinces, and the evangelization of province after province, and especially the organization of Christian communities in the chief cities of all the provinces lying between Jerusalem and Rome. (2) He makes no attempt at including everything in his history. He records unique events of importance. And then he concentrates for the most part on describing typical cases at some length; say, a specimen of the apostolic preaching in certain circumstances, or a good example of the kind of difficulty that had to be overcome, or a problem that had to be solved. (1954)

HIGH-LIGHTS IN THE LIFE
OF ST. PAUL

THE REV. C. C. MARTINDALE, S.J.

St. Paul, that is, Saul, came from Tarsus in Cilicia, a region and a city into which Assyrian, Persian, Macedonian and Roman cultures and religions had streamed; it was a city of schools; its youth flocked to these as hardly did the young men of Athens or Alexandria to their own universities. The Emperor Augustus himself chose his tutor from Tarsus, and at his suggestion revised the conditions of citizenship there and made them stricter. By Saul's time, citizens might be chosen only from the wealthier classes: there was a double aristocracy—that of wealth, and, within this, the elect group of citizens. Saul was very conscious of his own citizenship, which he had not bought, but inherited.

After his earlier education in a strictly Jewish, indeed Pharasaic, home, he went for further education to Jerusalem and studied under Gamaliel, entering thus the more rigorous of the two dominant schools of thought, that of Hillel. He says of himself: "I am a Hebrew, son of Hebrews; a Pharisee, son of Pharisees: according to the most strict sect of our religion I lived a Pharisee: I was irreproachable according to the justice that consists in the Law." He returned home, but was back in Jerusalem at the time of St. Stephen's martyrdom. So far, his austere fierce adolescence had turned its severities back only on itself. Now he diverted its terrible and tumultuous energies against those, the Christians, who were rejecting that system which, while he clung to it, he was beginning to find too much for him. He developed a perfect frenzy of persecution. Many passages in his letters reveal how the memory of this haunted him for years.

Then the thunderbolt fell. Saul was converted on the road to Damascus. And so soon as possible he went into the deserts of Arabia to recover. . . . He had been shown that Jesus was the Messias, and that a future of apostolate lay before him. . . . An entire life was being rooted up; and his very future, to be spent among the heathen, was the exact opposite to that which this Jew of Jews could have imagined. . . .

Yet indeed the moment he returned from his retreat, it looked as though he never would do anything. Men were frightened of him— who could believe that the persecutor had turned Christian prophet?— he had to fly from Damascus; even in Jerusalem he met with but a chilly welcome from all save a few. As for the Jews there, even the Hellenized Jews—within a fortnight they were plotting to kill him. He had to be spirited away, and in fact returned to Tarsus and stayed there at least three years. He does not reappear till he is *fetched*. In the year 43, it was heard in Jerusalem that pagans were being preached to in Antioch. Barnabas was sent to see what was happening. He was struck by the enormous field that lay open to the apostolate. He remembered Saul, whom he had befriended long ago in the Holy City, went in person to Tarsus and fetched him back, and they stayed a year together working in Antioch. A famine was foretold for Palestine; the Christians in Antioch made a collection, and sent it by way of Barnabas and Saul to Jerusalem where no doubt they related all that they had been doing among the pagans too. It was soon after this that by divine revelation these two men were "separated" for the special work of apostolate in the world at large, and they sailed in fact from the port of Antioch, going first to Barnabas's home-island, Cyprus.

On their return—disillusionment! Christians came from Jerusalem who were horrified to hear that Paul and Barnabas had not imposed the full observance of the Jewish ritual, in particular the practice of circumcision, upon their converts. . . .

Paul went up, he says, "by revelation." He set forth both publicly and privately what he had been preaching and its results. . . . In theory, the Apostles had nothing to add to what Paul believed and taught, nor he to their doctrine or practice. But they "gave me and Barnabas the right hand of fellowship, that I might go to the pagans, as they to the Jews." . . .

While Paul did not, as he insists, introduce any new doctrine of his own, he found that the next years of his apostolate were always interfered with by Judaizing Christians, who made things as difficult for him as they possibly could and even followed after him, as for example to Galatia, and tried to undo the work he had done. . . .

Paul himself passionately loved his people and was steeped in the

Old Testament. It may be impossible for *us* to get thoroughly into the mind and mood of those early Jewish Christians who watched him, none the less, apparently discarding with contempt what they still held to be so incomparably precious. . . . Even if those Jewish Christians admitted notionally the equal vocation of the Gentiles, they found it almost impossible to alter their instincts; to purify their soul's blood, so to say; *really* to believe that the Jew was *not* essentially better than the Gentile. . . .

St. Paul, entering the Christian Church, brought to it no new doctrine but an amazing personality, a personality which was developed into being what it was, because it was caught up into Christ's. He is proof in himself that to be "in Christ"—"I live, no more just I"—annihilates nothing that is individual nor even submerges it. Who could confuse St. Paul with St. Peter or St. John? Not the earthly life of man—why, not the transcendant life of God—is the focus of his existence, is his center of spiritual gravity, but Christ is. Human men live —in a sense. But they are not properly alive, until they live through, and in, that very source of life which Christ is. There had been a time when only Jews had the chance of looking forward, in some sense, to that Anointed One. They did not take that chance; nay, they rejected their Rescuer when He came. Therefore Paul turns to the Gentiles; to men who were the ancestors of ourselves. To us he preached his doctrine of co-crucifixion with Christ, in view of that co-resurrection without which no death would have been any good. . . .

And in preaching he gave himself no respite. What though he be but a frail vessel to contain so great a treasure? That overflowing power of his is from God, not from himself. . . .

He persevered. In the year, we think, A.D. 67, he was again in Rome, a prisoner in the filthy promiscuity of the Mamertine. Thrown back upon himself, scarcely able to be so much as visited in that reeking pit, he could not but contemplate his life, now narrowed to a vanishing-point, yet about to expand into the very circumference of Heaven. He—the baby that had been carried about in the hot orchards of the town Tarsus; the studious little boy; the fanatic young man who—could he ever forget it?—had done his best to re-crucify Christ in His Saints. Yet there came a moment when, on the road to Damascus, "Christ revealed Himself in me," a vision that not only shot forward its rays into the hard years that followed it, but drew all years alike unto itself, and was a universal moment, a fire exhaling, and absorbing, and redistributing itself, simply being Christ, beginning and end together, for what was Christ save Plenitude? In the dark prison, visions of those many cities may have flickered before him: gay Corinth; glistening Athens; flamboyant Ephesus; north up to Philippi and the Thessalonians—east into the healthy stony uplands of the Asiatics— Jerusalem, doomed within three years to be destroyed. All this crowded life was now so simplified, and all that remained to Paul was to die, to die worthily of his Lord. I don't suppose that anything save Christ occupied the mind of the very tired old man who was marched out of the Mamertine to the place where he should be executed. He was taken through noisy squalid docks and suburbs full of acrobats, ragpickers and collectors of broken crockery, run after at first by street-boys who found that he was being taken too far for them to trouble to follow him; then there were open spaces as the houses thinned; then, the Ostian street, and then the small road to the left. His back to the Tiber, to the Vatican circus where Peter had been killed, to the theatres and to the palaces with their waving violet curtains and the rose-petals falling from golden ceilings between marble walls, and to the enormous pagan temples, and to the God-Emperor. The absolute defeat. That world would triumph. Work everywhere unfinished—you might say, unfinishable. After all those people, now nobody. After all those places, now just the little wood where he was to have his head cut off—for after all, he was a Roman citizen, and couldn't be made an exhibition of. So, after three miles, he was swerved off into that by-road and taken into the pinewood where the health-giving springs gushed up, and, in the wood, they stripped him, for the last time (perfunctorily, we may trust), they scourged him, tied him to a pine tree, covered his eyes, and beheaded him.

Humble hands removed the Saint's remains and buried them in a little cemetery half-way back to Rome. Over that very place, not three hundred years later, a Roman Emperor built over those relics a vast basilica, and we still possess Constantine's laconic epitaph: PAUL APOSTLE MARTYR. You can still kneel in that place, with the dishevelled eucalyptus-leaves whispering around you, and the mysterious imprisoned sources talkative beneath your feet. But by now you will prefer to say nothing. You can never add anything to St. Paul.

(1938)

THE STRANGE POWER OF
ST. PAUL'S WRITINGS

THE REV. FERNAND PRAT, S.J.

IN GENERAL the Fathers of the Church agree with the Apostle when he refuses to use fine language. St. Irenaeus reproaches him for his inversion of the natural order of words; Origen for his obscure phrases; St. Epiphanius, for his involved sentences; St. Gregory of Nyssa, for using words which are obsolete or distorted from their usual meaning; St. Chrysostom, for carelessness in style; St. Jerome, for unsuitable words, idioms peculiar to Cilicia, and even for grammatical errors. Bossuet sums them up well when he writes in his celebrated *Panégyrique*: "This man, ignorant of the art of fine writing, with his rude forms of speech, with a phraseology which betrays the foreigner, will go to polished Greece, the mother of philosophers and orators, and, in spite of the opposition of the world, will there found more churches than Plato ever gained disciples by that eloquence of his which was thought divine. He will preach Jesus in Athens, and the most learned of its senators will pass from the Areopagus into the school of this barbarian." But here is the other side of the picture. St. Jerome praises Paul's force, energy and overwhelming power; St. Augustine, his passionate eloquence; St. Chrysostom, his charm and powers of persuasion; even the pagan Longinus, his oratorical fire and the vigor of his reasoning.

Into style, broadly speaking, there enter three elements: vocabulary, grammar and composition. It is recognized that Paul's vocabulary is, above all, biblical. The words foreign to the language of the Septuagint are most often of popular origin. St. Jerome calls them *Cilicisms*, because, not having met them in the authors with whom he was familiar, he erroneously thought them peculiar to the soil of Cilicia. A certain number of these have been recently found in the papyri or inscriptions of that epoch; and the further this kind of research is pursued, the more will be shortened the list of terms, the peculiar form of which had previously been attributed to the sacred writers. These writers did not endeavor to create new words which no one would have understood; they turned to all possible advantage the words in common use by giving them, in case of need, new shades of meaning. When addressing the people, they used the popular language, which was rich, picturesque, and pleasing.

Paul has been reproached with "a singular poverty of expression," which is too summary a judgment and one contradicted by the facts. No other writer of the New Testament has at his command so extensive a vocabulary. We know that he is fond of heaping up words which are almost synonymous, the various shades of which he wishes to expose. He likes also to use words similar in sound, as well as puns and antitheses, all of which presupposes an author's complete mastery of his language. The frequent repetitions of words are not a proof of linguistic indigence; it is rather a dialectical or oratorical procedure, intended and well considered, in order to fix the attention of the reader and better to imprint the thought upon his mind.

His syntax is certainly not classical syntax. If the solecisms, which can be rightly called so, are wholly exceptional, Hebrew expressions, although less numerous than has been claimed, are not rare. But his letters swarm with anacolutha—*i.e.,* unfinished sentences or such as end in a changed construction. . . . Many of these cases of carelessness can be explained by improvisation. Paul did not write his letters himself. The habit of dictation was then so common that to "dictate" meant in general to "compose." Certain allusions of the ancients would lead us to believe that the manual labor of the scribe was considered incompatible with the work of thought. The Apostle conformed to this usage, which the weakness of his eyes rendered more imperative for him. Hence his uncompleted phrases, changes of construction, incidents, parentheses, sudden passages from one thought to another, and frequent recurrences of the same idea. But while the stylists kept on carefully revising their first sketch, in order to cut down the faults in it and to efface its harshness, Paul packed it off just as it was, or with additions and new digressions. If he wishes—and perhaps without trying—he writes pages of flawless Greek; he handles in a masterly way the most delicate part of an idiom—the particles; and he clearly speaks Greek as his mother tongue and not as a foreign language, learned late in life and imperfectly acquired.

More intimate and more personal than anything pertaining to vocabulary and syntax is the order, the mode of expression, and the arrangement of the ideas in his letters. In a very true sense it has been said that the style is the man himself: "The language of Paul is his living image. As the body of the Apostle, a vessel of clay, bends under the weight of his ministry, so the words and forms of his language bend and break under the burden of his thought. But from this contrast spring forth the most wonderful effects. What power is in this weakness! What riches in this poverty! In this infirm body what a soul of fire! All the force, all the movement, all the beauty here come from his thought; it is not the style which carries the thought, it is the thought that carries the style. . . . Words and their ordinary signification are not sufficient to carry this overflowing plenitude of ideas and feelings. Each one of them has been obliged, so to speak, to carry a double or triple load. In a preposition or in a juxtaposition of two words Paul has placed an entire world of ideas. It is this which makes the exegesis of his Epistles so difficult, and their translation absolutely impossible." (A. Sabatier, L'apôtre Paul, 1896.)

The best way to understand them is to read them again and again. We must get used to this strange way of speaking, which at first repels and disconcerts us by its singularity. We meet with sentences whose sections somehow slide into one another, like the draws of a telescope; clauses running on and on without end and broken up into digressions and parentheses, the whole of which the eye seeeks vainly to combine. . . .

Paul is a vigorous reasoner, who moves at ease through the labyrinths of a long and abstruse movement. He never recoils before a useful digression, even though his work must thereby suffer from a literary point of view. Certain chapters of his present the appearance of geological conglomerates formed from sedimentary deposits and solidified lava; but the thought proceeds always, like an uninterrupted metallic vein, through these apparently heterogeneous masses. The incidental question having been settled, he returns to his subject by boldly emphasizing a word rather than by a definite transition. If he is not tormented by words, as he is accused of being, he is drawn on beyond all measure by the idea which he is pursuing, and it is true that his thought sometimes revolves about a word. He is fond of running through the whole gamut of the various meanings of a word in order to display his idea under all its aspects. Every occurrence of the slightest difference puts him on new ground, and he glides from one meaning to another with such ease that the transition is not always perceptible.

Moreover, he has a supreme indifference for his fame as an author. He laughs at the rules of rhetoric and sometimes also at the rules of grammar. If he frequently attains to the highest eloquence it is, St. Augustine says, without aiming at it. In him everything flows from the source, and from a mind overflowing with ideas and a heart able to impart emotion almost involuntarily. When Tertius or some other of his secretaries reads a letter of Paul's dictation over to him, do not think that the Apostle stops to polish an involved order of words, or a lack of sequence. On the contrary, he adds to them those exuberances with which his style is bristling, as if he feared by too much study and refinement to take away something from the virtue of the Gospel and by a display of human wisdom to cast a shadow on the brilliant triumph of the cross. (1926)

"THAT TRUMPET OF THE SPIRIT"

DANIEL-ROPS

IF SAINT PAUL is a great writer, it is because he is not a writer first of all, but a man. We know that each of his texts was bound up in its development with events and people; they are not the products of a mind securely sheltered in the refuge of a library, but the works of a conqueror, of a fighter, whose whole life was risk. His purpose, thus, was not to expound a doctrine, but to inform, reform, and affirm. All he thinks and writes, he thinks and writes in full flight, swept on by the violence of the struggle itself. And this spontaneous attitude of his is the same which is required of all who practice Christianity, for the Gospel is not a system of thought but a story, a drama; and what matters most is not to demonstrate it but to live it.

Thus, Saint Paul's personality was spontaneously incorporated in the message which was given him to bear, and as this personality was marvelously rich, varied, and complex, and as he also had realized the rare achievement of inner unity, it is his personality which, when all is said and done, smooths out all imperfections in his literary work and makes it what it is, a block of marble or of steel.

But is this the only explanation, the ultimate explanation? Certainly not. In a picturesque and stirring passage, Saint John Chrysostom, the most pertinent perhaps of the early Fathers up to the time of St. Augustine, has recalled the emotion he experienced when he read the Epistles of Saint Paul: "I recognize the voice of a friend; I have almost the impression of seeing him and hearing him in person." And he adds: "Then I exult joyously and arise from my sleep; the sound of that trumpet of the Spirit exalts me and overwhelms me with happiness." These last words tell all there is to tell.

If Saint Paul is the great writer whom we see, it is not merely because of his forceful personality, the subtlety of his intellect, the power of his genius; rather it is because he was the "trumpet of the Spirit." . . . "Walking according to the Spirit, living according to the Spirit," he also spoke and wrote according to the Spirit. . . . We shall be totally deceived as to the meaning and scope of his texts, if we fail to see there, above all, the ineffable zeal. Far more than a writer, a dialectician, or theologian, Saint Paul is an inspired genius, and in the fullest and most exact sense of the term, he is at once a genius and a saint. His art is merely the expression, pouring from his lips, of the overwhelming presence which dwells within him. . . .

It is in his letters that we must find and hear Paul's message—in those imperishable letters. . . . It is to these we must resort, and the revelations enclosed there will emerge with their great shattering bursts of light. Is it not true that at Mass, when the reading of the Epistle brings us some brief passage, our impression is one of immediate shock, which reaches the depths of our souls and suddenly illuminates the anguished darkness of the world and of ourselves?

The centuries flow and events move on, but the message of Saint Paul remains; nothing shall ever invalidate it. For anyone who considers his example, for anyone who hears his words, there emerge lessons which are ever new.

To the helpless feeling of negation and absurdity which is, for all of us, the worst temptation of the conscience, Paul opposes the unshakable certainty that there is a supernatural explanation, an ultimate revelation, which definitively sets forth the meaning of life.

In the face of the great treason of man, that universal oblivion into which the world is plunging, he declares, with unique persuasive power, the reality of a presence which no philosophy can abolish and whose infinite mercy no treason can discourage.   (1952)

THE EPISTLES OF ST. PETER

THE REV. O.-R. VASSALL-PHILLIPS, C.SS.R.

WHAT can be more thrilling than to observe how Simon Peter, a man who had spent at any rate a great part of his life without books, or much opportunity of obtaining any knowledge of men or affairs, excepting the spiritual knowledge which had been bestowed upon him by Christ, wrote without hesitation or apology to men of the most varied degree of culture, many of them philosophers, soldiers, courtiers, who had but one thing in common—the possession of that religion which Peter taught?

If we examine these Epistles of St. Peter we shall find, as we should expect, the language to be of the simplest. Yet their tone is that of the most complete assurance and authority. For example, what authority can be more confident in its claim than that of one who wrote of his "most dear brother Paul who, according to the wisdom given him hath written to you, as also in all his Epistles, speaking in them of these things wherein are certain things hard to be understood, which the unlearned and the unstable wrest, as they do also the other Scriptures, to their own destruction"? (2 Peter 3:15.)

St. Peter was an unlearned fisherman. St. Paul was learned with all the learning of his time, nor was he afraid to withstand St. Peter to the face when, in a matter of conduct, he thought that he was to be blamed. Yet we do not find the great St. Paul writing of the Epistles of St. Peter as St. Peter did not hesitate to write of the Epistles of St. Paul—and many of us can hardly imagine him doing so. If, when fishing on the Lake of Galilee, Simon son of John had been told that one day he was to write, or even to be supposed to have written, such words as these concerning the Letters of a scholar of such high repute as Saul of Tarsus, who once had sat as a favorite pupil at Gamaliel's feet, how unthinkable it would have seemed! Yet, after his transformation under the Hand of Christ, the magisterial warning fell from his pen onto the papyrus as readily as of old the nets had fallen from those same hands into the waters of the sea. At the same time, with authority he placed St. Paul's Epistles among "the other Scriptures."

Solemn was the declaration of Simon Peter to the first Christians, many of whom, through his witness, had come to believe in the Christian religion, that it was not "by following cunningly devised fable" (the Douai version has "*artificial* fables") that he had made known to them the power and presence of our Lord Jesus Christ; for he and the other Apostles had been eye-witnesses of His Greatness (2 Peter i, 16, 17).

The reference is to the evidence to be derived from the scene of the Transfiguration which St. Peter had witnessed with his own eyes. . . .

It is evident that St. Peter claimed to teach not only orally, but also

293

in authoritative writings, concerning Jesus of Nazareth whose glory he had beheld "when we were with him on the holy mount." . . .

The fisherman of Galilee, in accordance with his Master's promise, has come before the world as an indefatigable fisher of men. This "more firm prophetical word" was delivered by St. Peter in these official Letters. . . .

When Simon the fisherman had first become acquainted with Jesus, the carpenter, he knew him as simply Jesus of Nazareth. Soon he recognized him as the promised Messiah—then—"flesh and blood hath not revealed it unto thee, but my Father in Heaven"—as the Son of the Living God—finally, as "our Lord Jesus Christ" or "our Lord and Saviour Jesus Christ."

When we read the documents we see the evolution of his faith taking place before our eyes. Belief in the Godhead of Jesus Christ, in the Incarnation, the Redemption, was the formulated teaching of the chief of Christ's Apostles when in the first years of the Christian era he wrote his Letters to the Faithful scattered throughout the Roman Empire. This is undeniable, for his words are susceptible of only one interpretation. . . .

From the Christian point of view there is a fragrance still hanging over all that St. Peter wrote which is from Heaven, and was also a completeness in the events of his life which fit flawlessly into the teaching and expectations of our Faith.   (1932)

ST. JOHN'S APOCALYPSE

THE REV. C. C. MARTINDALE, S.J.

St. John's Apocalypse seems to define itself. Its title is this: *John's Apocalypse,* or *Revelation*; its first word, The Revelation of Jesus Christ. And this word Apocalypse, or the Removal of the Veil or Covering, is not only frequent in the Greek Old Testament, but not rare on the lips of St. Paul. . . .

The habitual gaze of the prophet is focused on humanity, for the inspired lifting it up to God; that of the apocalyptist upon God, so as to descend thence upon humanity, and to interpret and direct it in terms of that ineffable contemplation. . . .

How is the symbolic language, in which apocalyptists expressed their doctrine, to be accounted for? God might, of course, reveal, dictate, the symbols as directly as He might the doctrine. And, of course, the whole message of the apocalyptist (in the case, say, of Daniel, or St. John, or any canonical work) is *inspired*. But it is clear that much of the symbolical language, and even the forms of the language, are traditional and "derived." This is a *literary* origin. Let me, before illustrating that, point out two *psychological* ways in which any writer might come to write under symbolic imagery, whether traditional or not.

Sometimes the spiritual intuition might be so pure and sublime that in no way, save by symbols, could it be suggested to one who had not shared it. The notion might be so tremendous, unaccustomed, impatient of formulae and phrases, that some other vehicle than definitions for the intellect must be sought. . . . Often the seer would himself feel his choice of symbol to be painfully, even ludicrously, inadequate. Perhaps St. John himself felt regretful when certain symbols seemed the traditionally correct material to use. . . . Again and again ecstatics, who constantly use the words "to see," "to hear," and describe forthwith sights and sounds, deny that eye or ear perceived anything whatsoever. The intuition has to clothe itself in thoughts, and these cannot emerge into the reflex consciousness without *some* robe of imagery, supplied by the imagination, and in the long run through the senses. . . .

Very likely, too, the nucleus of the image, the substantial point where the analogy holds good, may be quite small and simple. The poetic fancy may proceed to develop or decorate this after the revealing light has passed, or at least in its after-glow. . . .

Such then, is the psychological process when a man *first* experiences, whether by natural flash of intuition or by divine revelation, some abstract spiritual fact, and then seeks to express it in terms of the imagination and then in words. . . .

St. John . . . left nothing of the apocalyptic imagery just as he found it, and almost everything he used he immeasurably improved. Yet even a genius is not all the time at the crest of his inspiration-wave; the impulse may flag; and then, even as he writes, he does so laboriously and will cease so communicatively to express all that he has within him; it may, indeed, in its full significance, be latent to himself. Even a poet scarcely realizes all his meaning; and a prophet need not know, either, the full bearing of his words.

There are here principles that make it much safer for us to study the symbolism of St. John. We need scarcely ever find ourselves left to *mere* conjecture. Sometimes we cannot tell what he means; we may seldom feel sure we know all that he means; but we can always have good reason for relying that we are on the right track and not yielding to arbitrary, subjective fancy.

We see first that he could use much traditional symbolism that was meaningful to a Jew, or to a Judaic convert, of his period, but that need not appeal to us, alien in blood and distant in time and space. We need not feel half impious if imagery dear to their minds cannot be of value to ours. Even the meaning of details may be quite lost to us, and for ever, having never been anything save locally applicable, and understood not even by men of the ensuing generation, or non-Asiatics. . . .

Further, we are made alert to distinguish the substance of the symbol from its decoration or elaboration, to discern only the vital point of contact, and not to waste time trying to evolve an interpretation for each detail of a picture, seeing that they are there only to make it vivid and to "carry it across.". . .

Again, we are invited to expect that in some cases the sight of a material object will have come first—for example, a volcano, a meteor, a waterfall—and then the material event or fact may be half deserted for the sake of the spiritual thing suggested by it. In other cases, some overwhelming spiritual concept will have come first—for example, the Holy Trinity or the presence of Christ in the Church—and then the image may be offered almost under protest, as the poor, yet best, algebraic formula, almost, of what it seeks to convey.

And we should add that these two sorts of symbols unite at least, in this—they are there to reveal, each in its measure, the Hidden. But another kind exists, not to reveal, but to conceal. It is chosen, not by poetic preference, nor in helpless ecstasy, but because it would have been dangerous to speak plainly. Much, if not most, apocalypse was written to encourage the Faithful during, or on the eve of, persecution. Thus the latter part of Daniel clearly envisages the period of Antiochus Epiphanes; and John's Apocalypse alludes to the reigns of Domitian and Nero, and to the Asiatic troubles generally. The Christian community would have been worse endangered should its literature be seen to attack the Government or to preach "disloyalty." Thus certain parts of such apocalypse would be written, quite deliberately, "in cipher." And other things were too holy to be alluded to save under veils, as, for example, the Eucharist.

We shall, then, remember that some of an apocalypse will probably deal directly and primarily with historical facts, some with spiritual truth. So it were futile to try to interpret such a document as, in all its parts equally, history disguised; or, again, to refuse to look for any interest in historical facts on the part of its writer. No one key will open all its locks. A reader will, then, be wise to start, when possible, from ascertainable elements, such as the conditions of the apocalyptist's times and environment; the necessary, or probable, contents of his memory; the normally probable or possible limits of his self-expression, and then only go on to seek for transscendental meanings. Yet he should also be careful to remember that the seer is never dealing with human happenings merely for their own sake. . . .

Enough to have formulated some principles for scanning evidence, some hints towards the formation of a judgment; to provide some hope at least of seeing through John's eyes, of hearing with the ears of those to whom his book was for the first time read. The rest we must leave to the guidance of God's Spirit and to the permissions of the Church. For, once more, we shall never forget that whether we be right or wrong in our views on the human coefficient, the human psychological machinery, we are certain about the divine coefficient, the guaranteed inspiration. However wholly an inspired book is its human author's book, it is wholly that of its divine Author. In a line—*John's* words have *God* for Author. . . .

Apart from the apocalyptic passages in the Gospels, and those in St. Jude's and St. Peter's Epistles, there is no canonical New Testament apocalypse save St. John's. . . .

John's work, though unique in inspirational dignity and spiritual character, and, indeed, in sheer literary value, was not, in its literary character, an isolated phenomenon; it takes its place in a stream of literature flowing across whole centuries. Notice, however, that John's book was the first to bear, explicitly, the name *apocalypse*. Other documents either imitated this or have been so named by critics who saw they were of the same literary *genre* as St. John's. . . . He was absolutely at home in the apocalyptic atmosphere, and was so familiar with its special phraseology and favorite symbolism that he uses these naturally and by preference, and could count on being understood, temperamentally and in the mass, if not in each detail, by his immediate readers. . . . The other apocalypses as sheer literature come nowhere near John's—his tremendous personality would anyhow recast what he borrowed; he scarcely ever quotes, save where the ancient phrasing was so perfect that any substantial alteration would have seemed sacrilege, or when (apparently) he introduces, as St. Paul does, fragments of Christian hymns already dear to Christian feeling. Even so, he rather explicitly alludes to what his readers knew so well than reproduces it. At the outset he stamps his personality on the work by prefixing to it his own name and whereabouts, and speaks clearly to men who knew and had had dealings with him, unlike the other apocalyptists, who took the names of ancient seers and saints—Enoch, Baruch—and threw their compositions back into a half-mythical past. Besides, the contents and inspiration of St. John's Apocalypse are sundered from those of all the rest by the gulf which, when all is said, separated Christianity from the purest, even, of prophetic Judaism; he puts the ancient words to the service of a quite new doctrine, and to my feeling it is almost an offense to compare his glorious book to anything else whatsoever. . . .

This lesson, if none other, is cried aloud by the Apocalypse—that the world does not offer us nonchalantly a choice between good and the less good, even between good and evil, but that there is a conflict, an appalling battle for our souls; that the armies of heaven and hell are clashing over us and for us; that Dragon and Wild Beast are ravening for us; that Satan has no will but to brand us forever with his mark; that if we do not worship God, and find Him everywhere and re-worship Him there again, the whole world turns into an idol, into a thousand idols; and what should be for us an image and a likeness of God, without interspace becomes the image of the Beast. John is maddened, one might almost dare to say, by the sight of men involved in these tremendous things, and knowing it not.

(1922)

THE TWELVE APOSTLES

ABBE CONSTANT FOUARD

BARTHOLOMEW is the least known of all. It has been agreed upon that he is the Nathanael whom Philip found meditating under a fig-tree, and led to his divine Master. Truthfulness and godliness were the keynotes of his character; undoubtedly with these he combined modesty, for from that hour in which he obeyed the call of God we never see or hear anything more of the son of Tolmai. There is a tradition which tells of his having evangelized the Indies; that he was burned alive, and crucified with his head downwards.

His friend Philip was among the first of the Galileans who were moved to seek John the Baptist, hoping to find in him the longed-for Messiah. The Gospel speaks of his gentle spirit, readily responding to Jesus' appeals, sympathizing with the distress of the throngs that followed the Master into the desert, but slow to believe that a few loaves would be enough to satisfy them; slower still to fathom the Mysteries of faith, for even at the Last Supper he begs the Saviour to let him see the Father, of whom He is always speaking. Polycratus, Bishop of Ephesus, informs us that Philip had been married; his daughters were numbered among the first Virgins; and he himself slept in the Lord at Hierapolis, in Phrygia.

As to Simon, we merely know that he was called the Cananean, a name which Saint Luke translates as the Zealot; and this term was also used to distinguish him from Simon Peter. Can it be that this Apostle belonged to that famous Sect which revenged every transgression of the Law, not simply with burning reproaches, like the Prophets of old, but like Phineas, with unsheathed sword? We know what part these Zealots played in the last days of Jerusalem; how they became the terror and scourge of the whole countryside, making it reek with blood, spreading ruin and death on every hand. Would Jesus have called one of these fanatics to Him; would He have thought it wise to admit into equal fellowship this Jew, Simon, who rebelled against every tribute extorted by the hated foreigners, and Levi, collector of the Roman taxes? Yet in this there would be nothing repugnant to the plans of the Master, for He made little account of human prudence in His works, and "chose that which is foolishness in the world's eyes to confound the wise, so that no man should glorify himself before Him" (I Cor. i, 27).

Matthew has left behind him more than a name,—a divine Book, his Gospel. In it he speaks in one single instance of himself, and that is only to tell us that he was a Publican, a butt for the contempt and hatred of Israel, but that nevertheless Jesus chose him.

Thomas's character may be more clearly deciphered. With a frank, practical spirit, which was easily bewildered by the Mysteries of faith, he declared with perfect simplicity, even in the midst of the Last Supper, that he could not understand the words of the Lord.

"Master," said he, "we do not know where you are going, nor which way the road lies."

After all Jesus' Ministry was finished, after all His miracles, Thomas had not yet become grounded in the firm faith that He was God; after the Resurrection we see him still unable to put trust in this new wonder—dejected, despairing, demanding that the Master permit him to touch His wounds with his hands before he would believe. And notwithstanding, he had a generous heart; for when Jesus braved the wrath of the Jews face to face, that He might raise Lazarus up from the dead, it was Thomas who incited the Apostles with those words which all our Martyrs have repeated after him:

"Come, let us go and die with Him!" (John, xi. 16)

James and Jude were the two sons of Alpheus and Mary. According to a tradition mentioned by Eusebius, a sister of the Holy Virgin, like her called Mary, had married a brother of Joseph, named Alpheus or Cleophas. He too must have died during Jesus' sojourn in Nazareth, for the Gospel observes the same silence concerning him that it does as to Joseph. But for the two sisters, it would seem that they kept together; and the numerous children of Mary, wife of Cleophas, are those brothers and sisters of Jesus of whom the townspeople spoke in these terms: "Are not His brethren named James, Joseph, Simon and Jude? and are not His sisters all here amongst us?" (Mark vi. 3) It is the usage in Sacred Scriptures, and is, in fact, a general custom in the Greek language, to call even distant kinsfolk brethren. That term therefore only refers to these four cousins of Jesus. Throughout the whole ministry James and Jude continued to be just what they were then—hard-working mechanics, whose minds were filled with longings for earthly goods. It needed the descent of the Holy Ghost upon the day of Pentecost to transform these kinsmen of the Lord into Apostles, to inspire Jude with that mighty Epistle of his, and to make of James the Less one of the most illustrious Bishops of the new-born Church.

As Pastor of Jerusalem during nearly thirty years, the latter fostered and strengthened the perfect good-will which bound the Pagan and Jewish converts together; at the first Council he suggested the wisest resolutions, and it was he who protected Saint Paul against the unreasoning and fanatic partisans of Judaism. All Jews who became Christians held this servant of God in veneration as their leader, and cherished with deep respect his Epistles, addressed "to the twelve tribes dispersed throughout the world," in which the

Apostle scourges the vices of his fellow-countrymen, their strifes, their haughty and grasping character. The later years of James were passed in prayer. . . . His death was worthy of such a life. At the Festival of the Pasch, the High Priest Ananias and the Council of the Sanhedrin commanded him to exhort the Jews to give up their faith in Jesus. The holy man allowed them to lead him out upon one of the galleries of the Temple, and promised them he would speak to the people, but it was only that he might seize one last chance to glorify his Master.

"Wherefore would you question me concerning Jesus?" he cried out. "He is seated at the right hand of the Almighty, and will appear again upon the clouds of Heaven."

His furious persecutors fell upon him and threw him down upon the pavement below, and there they stoned him. As he was dying, the aged Apostle drew himself up, and remained kneeling long enough to beseech God to forgive his executioners; whereupon a man who had armed himself with a fuller's mallet strode up and put an end to his sufferings. His people buried him close by the Temple. Eight years later Jerusalem was only a charred heap of ashes.

And now we have to speak of the most illustrious of the Apostles, —Simon and Andrew, sons of Jonas; James and John, the sons of Zebedee. These four fishermen of Bethsaida form a group by themselves, and at their head we always find the Prince of the Apostles, Simon Peter. The least known among them is Andrew, whose personality is, as it were, overshadowed by his brother's brilliant renown. After having brought Simon to Jesus, he disappears in the background. But if his life was hidden, his death shed such radiance about it, that the priests and deacons of Achaia sent tidings of the glorious event to the whole Church. Their narrative enables us to follow step by step, every act of the Martyr,—the examination, the replies of Andrew, and his protracted tortures. He died upon the cross, uttering such cries of love for Jesus as thrilled the hearts of those through whose soul the sound reechoed, while they wept in silence.

Beside Andrew, there are Peter, James, and John, who are always the chosen ones among the chosen few, the intimate companions whom the Master admitted to His confidence and familiar friendship. We see them, the only ones present at the raising of Jairus's daughter; the only ones at the Transfiguration; the only ones at the Agony of the Saviour. Jesus has told us what made Him so particularly attached to the two sons of Zebedee; it was because their great hearts burned in fierce flashes, like the lightning; whence it was that He gave them that beautiful name—"Sons of the Thunderbolt." They had something of its resistless rush, and sometimes, too, its destructive wrath. Witness the day when they called down the fire of heaven upon a Samaritan village which refused to harbor them. They had inherited this unbounded zeal from Salome, their mother. Having devoted herself to the Saviour's cause, faithfully following Him even to His Cross, the wife of Zebedee the fisherman dared to dream of a place for her sons at the side of the Christ, and upon His Throne. Jesus tried to curb this ambition by reminding them that His glory was to be bought at the price of suffering.

"Can you drink of My Chalice?" He asked.

"That we can," instantly replied the sons of Salome.

This confidence touched the Lord; and it was then He granted to James that, before all others, he should not only drink this cup of sorrow, but that he should drain it in a single draught. His zeal marked him out for a victim to the sword of Herod Agrippa, and he in fact was the first of the Apostles to meet the Martyr's death.

The other son of Salome was to survive them all. Soaring above the earth, to the inaccessible heights of his heavenly home, he led a hidden life so long as Peter and Paul held the Christian world in the bonds of faith. But at the end of the first century, when the Witnesses of the holy Word had vanished one by one, and when heresy threatened the youthful Church, the voice of John pierced the cloud. His Gospel, the Epistle which announced it, and the Apocalypse, were like so many sheets of lightning, now dazzling our sight, now thrilling us with peals of thunder. . . . Undoubtedly "the disciple whom Jesus loved" had great tenderness of heart, but it was a heart which throbbed in unison with a soul of fire. . . . John's rightful emblem is not the Dove, but the Eagle. . . .

The character of Simon, son of Jonas, presents no such opposite traits. It is all summed up in the name which Jesus bestowed on him: "Thou art Peter, and upon this Rock I will build My Church." The great Apostle, therefore, was to serve as the Foundation of the Church—was to be for his brethren as a Guide and infallible Head. And after the election of the Twelve, the Lord made known these prerogatives of Peter so publicly and so emphatically, in order that all might bow before him. Ever after this day we find him speaking and acting in their name. At Capharnaum, when the Master demanded sadly, "And you—will you too go away?" (John vi, 68-70), it was he who responded, in the name of all the rest—

"Lord, to whom should we go? You have the words of eternal life!"

It was he who, at Caesarea, in the land of Philip, once again proclaimed the faith of the Apostles—

"Thou art the Christ, the Son of the living God."

This lofty dignity conferred upon him became the occasion of his fall; it puffed him up with vain-glory, turned his energy into presumption, his firmness into blind obstinacy; it went so far as to make him openly contradict his Master, and drew down upon him that severe reply—

"Get thee gone, Satan: thou art a scandal unto Me, for thy thoughts are not of God, but of man." (Matt. xvi. 23.)

At the close of the ministry of Jesus, Simon, son of Jonas, is not any longer the immovable rock, but like a loose stone on the road, which a woman's hand may fling aside into the ditch. Yet even then it was not all over with Peter, since after his overthrow he but made for himself a surer abiding place, and in his sorrow found firmer foundations. Overwhelmed with his humiliation, he nevertheless rose up in "the greatness of the power of God" (Cor. iv. 7). Henceforth neither his faith nor his mighty courage were ever to fail him; we encounter him everywhere at the head of his brethren, the first to grope his way within the tomb of Jesus, and to gaze upon his Risen Lord; the first to get into the little ship at that last miraculous draught of fishes; the first to cast himself into the sea, to go to meet the Saviour; first, too, to drag up on the shore the net, which had not broken beneath the weight of its one hundred and fifty-three fishes.

Before He went away from their sight into the skies Jesus laid upon Peter the charge of pasturing the flock, to feed His sheep, as well as His lambs. The Apostle fulfilled the command of the Lord, stood at their head, ordered their manner of teaching and the form of their government, and by stamping the new-born Faith with his seal, gave it the character which it was to bear unto all future ages, making the first acts of the infant Church the Acts of Peter.

In the Apostolic College there is still one gloomy figure left which each of the Evangelists thrusts down to the lowermost rank,—Judas, son of Simon, the man from Kerioth. . . . All that we know of him, apart from the tale of his treachery, is that his skill in the management of money won him his position of trust as Treasurer of the Apostles. Hence he must have gained their confidence from the outset; and indeed he retained it up to that last Passover, for it was at his instigation that they murmured against the Magdalene, as she poured out her perfumes upon the head of Jesus. Though he grew ever more depraved and desperate, the man from Kerioth had always succeeded in blinding their eyes; so that on the night of the Last Supper, when the Lord foretold the crime in whose shadow they sat, no one dreamed of charging Judas with it; only the calm glance of Jesus could read the heart of the thief. How many were the words spoken by the Saviour to the multitude which in the ears of this faithless follower must have resounded in tones of appeal or reproach! Now He is urging them to true charity: "Do not heap up treasures upon the earth. . . . There, where your heart is, there is your treasure also. . . . You cannot serve God and Mammon." Now He gives utterances to His feeling of horror: "Have I not chosen you Twelve? And there is one among you who is a devil!" The divine Master could not resolve to abandon "this son of perdition." At Gethsemani, once more, He kissed him, and called him His friend.   (1879)

THE GOSPEL AND THE SECULAR
CONSCIENCE

JACQUES MARITAIN

BY VIRTUE of the hidden work of evangelical inspiration the secular conscience has understood that the political realm and the flesh and blood paraphernalia of the things that are Caesar's must nevertheless be subject to God and to justice. It has understood that the entire art of domination and all the crimes which the princes and the heads of nations carry out to conquer and consolidate their power can certainly give them power but inevitably turn out for the misfortune of the people. Christianity cast the net of the Gospel upon the Pagan Empire and the Pagan Empire died of it, for there is no quarter given between the evangelical law of the Son of God and the law of the Empire which sets itself above God. . . .

Under the often misunderstood or disfigured but active inspiration of the Gospel, the secular conscience has awakened not only to the dignity of the human person, but also to the aspirations and the *élan* which are at work in his depths. . . .

In the very realm of spiritual life the message of the Gospel has revealed that the person is called to the perfect freedom of those who have become a single spirit and love with God; but in the realm of temporal life the repercussions of the Gospel's message were to stimulate the natural aspirations of the person to liberation from misery, servitude, and exploitation of man by man. When you know that we are all made for blessedness, death no longer holds any terror; but you cannot become resigned to the oppression and enslavement of your brothers, and you aspire for the earthly life of humanity, to a state of emancipation consonant with the dignity of this life.

What has been gained for the secular conscience, if it does not veer to barbarism, is the sense of freedom, and the conviction that the forward march of human societies is a march toward the conquest of a freedom consonant with the vocation of our nature.

Finally, under the inspiration of the Gospel at work in history, the secular conscience has understood that in the misfortunes and suffering of our existence, crushed by the iron laws of biological necessity and by the weight of pride, injustice, and wickedness of men, a single principle of liberation, a single principle of hope, a single principle of peace, can stir up the mass of servitude and iniquity and triumph over it, because this principle comes down to us from the creative source of the world, stronger than the world; that brotherly love whose law was promulgated by the Gospel to the scandal of the mighty, and which is, as the Christian well knows, God's own charity diffused into the hearts of men.   (1944)

If there is anything in this life which sustains a wise man and induces him to maintain his serenity amidst the tribulations and adversities of the world, it is in the first place, I consider, the meditation and knowledge of the Scriptures.

ST. JEROME (ca. 400)

Forget not the words that thy eyes have seen: and let them not go out of thy heart all the days of thy life.

DEUTERONOMY 4:9

INDEX OF AUTHORS

With Sources

309

Baunard, Louis (1826–1919)
The Evening of Life, trans. J. L. Stoddard, *218*
Benedict XV, Pope (Giacomo della Chiesa), (1854–1922)
Spiritus Paraclitus, 47, 57
Boniface, St. (680–750)
Letter to Bishop of Winchester, trans. Hugh Pope, O.P., *163*
Bossuet, Jacques Bénigne (1627–1704)
Discourse on Universal History, trans. Msgr. Victor Day, *155*
Chesterton, Gilbert Keith (1874–1936)
The Everlasting Man, 213
Chrysostom, St. John (ca. 347–407)
Hom. xii, 4, trans. E. C. Messenger in *Evolution and Theology, 138*
Clement of Alexandria, St. (ca. 150-ca. 215)
Quoted by Eusebius, *279*
Quoted in Knights of Columbus pamphlet from *Stromata, 1. vi. 106.*
Council of Trent, *Diaria, v. 91* (Denzinger, *Enchiridion,* 785), *60*
Daniélou, Jean (1905–   )
Advent, trans. Rosemary Sheed, *146, 179*
Daniel-Rops (Henry Jules Petiot), (1901–   )
Sacred History, trans. K. Madge, *128, 151, 156*
St. Paul, Apostle of Nations, trans. J. Martins, *291*
Devivier, Walter (1833–1924)
Christian Apologetics, trans. Ella McMahon, *109*
Dirksen, Aloys Herman (1901–   )
A Commentary on the New Testament, prepared by Catholic Biblical Assn.,
271
Dubarle, A. M. (contemporary)
Introduction to Theology, vol. 1 of "Theology Library," by a Group of
Theologians under editorship of A. M. Henry, O.P., trans. William
Storey, *57*
Dyson, Robert A. (contemporary)
The Kingdom of Promise, 164
Faulhaber, Michael von (1869–1952)
Judaism, Christianity and Germany, trans. George D. Smith, *170*
Felder, Hilarin (1867–1951)
Christ and the Critics, 2 vols., vol. 1, trans. J. L. Stoddard, *223*
Fillion, Louis Claude (1843–1927)
The Life of Christ, 2 vols., vol. 1, trans. Newton Thompson, *234*
The Study of the Bible, trans. John C. Reville, *76*
Fouard, Constant (1837–1904)
The Christ, the Son of God, trans. Geo. F. X. Griffith, *298*
Francis de Sales, St. (1567–1622)
Les Controverses, quoted in *Introduction to Theology,* trans. William Storey,
62
Gibbons, James (1834–1921)
The Faith of Our Fathers, 103
Gigot, Francis Ernest Charles (1859–1920)
General Introduction to the Study of Holy Scripture, 63
Outlines of New Testament History, 185
Goodier, Alban (1869–1939)
The New Testament: Papers Read at Summer School of Catholic Studies,
Cambridge, England, ed. by Lattey, *248*
Witnesses to Christ, 276
Graham, Henry Grey (1874–   )
Where We Got the Bible, 73

310

Grandmaison, Léonce Loizeau de (1868–1927)
Jesus Christ, 2 vols., vol. 1, trans. Basil Whelan, *204, 267*
Gregory of Nazianzen (ca. 325-ca. 389)
Fifth Theological Discourse, in de Lubac's *Catholicism,* trans. L. C. Sheppard, *29*
Gregory the Great, Pope St. (544–604)
Quoted by Chateaubriand in *The Genius of Christianity,* trans. C. I. White, *45*
Griffiths, Bede (1906–   )
The Golden String, 123
The Life of the Spirit, vol. 8, Nos. 1-2, "Lectio Divina," *36*
Heinisch, Paul (1878–   )
The Theology of the Old Testament, trans. W. G. Heidt, *132*
Huby, Joseph (1878–1948)
The Church and the Gospels, trans. Fenton Moran, *239*
Hugh of St. Victor (1096–1141)
De Scripturis, trans. Beryl Smalley in *The Study of the Bible in the Middle Ages, 96*
Ignatius of Antioch, St. (?-ca. 107)
Quoted by Irenaeus in *Ad Florinum, 282*
Irenaeus, St. (?125-ca. 200)
Against the Heresies, trans. W. W. Harvey, *109*
Jarrett, Bede (1881–1931)
Meditations for Layfolk, 23
Jerome, St. (ca. 340–420)
Epistle, liii, 7, quoted by Benedict XV in *Spiritus Paraclitus, 49*
Epistle, xxii, trans. Hugh Pope, O.P., *96*
Epistle liii ad Paulinum, 102
In Ephesios, prologus (*P.L.* xxvi), quoted by W. F. Barry in *The Tradition of Scripture, 305*
In Ezech, quoted by Benedict XV in *Spiritus Paraclitus, 222*
Tractate in Marcum, quoted by Benedict XV in *Spiritus Paraclitus, 40*
Johnson, Humphrey John Thewlis (1890–   )
The Bible and Early Man, 136, 137
Jones, Alexander (1906–   )
The Kingdom of Promise, 164
Unless Some Man Show Me, 107, 141
Justin Martyr, St. (ca. 100-ca. 165)
Hortatory Address to the Greeks, quoted by Gigot in *General Introduction to Study of Holy Scripture, 54*
Kehoe, Richard (contemporary)
The New Testament: Papers Read at Summer School of Catholic Studies, Cambridge, England, ed. by Lattey, *279*
Kempis, Thomas á (1380–1471)
The Imitation of Christ, trans. Richard Whitford, *30*
Knox, Ronald Arbuthnot (1888–   )
Miracles, 261
Trials of a Translator, 83
La Grange, Marie Joseph (1855–1938)
The Gospel of Jesus Christ, 2 vols., vol. 2, trans. Members of English Dominican Province, *206*
Lattey, Cuthbert Charles (1877–1954)
The Religion of the Scriptures: Papers from the Catholic Bible Congress, Cambridge, England, *160*

311